D0611920

beyond the campus

beyond the
campus

How Colleges and Universities
Form Partnerships with
Their Communities

David J. Maurrasse

Routledge | *New York   London*

Published in 2001 by

Routledge
29 West 35th Street
New York, NY 10001

Published in Great Britain by
Routledge
11 New Fetter Lane
London EC4P 4EE

Routledge is an imprint of the Taylor & Francis Group.

Transferred to Digital Printing 2003

Copyright © 2001 by Routledge

All rights reserved. No part of this book may be reprinted or reproduced or utilized in any form or by any electronic, mechanical, or other means, now known or here-after invented, including photocopying and recording or in any information stor-age or retrieval system, without permission in writing from the publishers.

Library of Congress Cataloging-in-Publication Data

Maurrasse, David J., 1968–
     Beyond the campus : how colleges and universities form partnerships with their communities / David J. Maurrasse
          p.   cm.
     Includes bibliographical references and index.
     ISBN 0-415-92621-1 — ISBN 0-415-92622-X (pbk.)
     1. Community and college—United States. 2. Urban universities and col-leges—United States. 3. Universities and colleges—United States—Public services. 4. Education, Higher—Social aspects—United States. I. Title.

LC238.M375 2001
378.1'03'0973—dc21

                                                                00-055328

Contents

Foreword

Angela Glover Blackwell
Founder and President of PolicyLink

As the nation searches for innovative leaders and answers to the continuing question of how to achieve social and economic equity, the community building movement has emerged as a promising approach for securing lasting results and systems change. The community building approach has the following characteristics. It involves community residents and professionals working together to take collective action aimed at solving problems and enriching lives. Additionally, the approach relies on strengthening existing organizations and networks and creating new partnerships to bring about change. It assures that the capacity is built to tackle tomorrow's challenges. All of these efforts result in improved lives, greater social equity, and new standards for life in community.

Community building cannot occur unless all stakeholders are involved through collaboration and partnership. In that regard, institutions of higher education are key community assets. David Maurrasse, a scholar of community building and university-community partnerships, recognizes the incredible power of linking universities and communities. In this book, he adroitly identifies the challenges associated with effective community engagement and offers solutions. Ultimately, he provides an important analysis of the role of "community" in these local collaborations. Instead of promoting institutions of higher education as the leaders and the sole generators of solutions, the book regards low-income communities and their residents as equal partners, bringing great wisdom and experience. Firmly grounded himself in the principles of community building, Maurrasse offers refreshing insight for authentically connecting institutions of higher education to low-income communities.

This book could not be more timely as low-income communities across the country have refocused our attention on strategies that work in revitalizing their neighborhoods. Through creativity and imagination, they have taken over the driver's seat in the search for solutions and are implementing innovative strategies targeted at quality-of-life issues, such as improving education and health outcomes for children, linking residents to jobs, and reversing the decades old dynamic of urban disinvestment that has left deep pockets of poverty behind.

Through their efforts, low-income communities are reawakening the civic life of the country and redefining for a new millennium the meaning of participation.

Appropriately, university-community partnerships have acquired national recognition as the two have worked together to improve the quality of life in America. University-community partnerships tend to engage stakeholders who have not previously worked together. In fact, in some cases, these stakeholders have taken opposite sides on solving community problems. By focusing on the community building opportunities, Maurrasse uses an associational approach that emphasizes relationships and the connections among the participants involved in the partnerships. This analysis reveals innovative decision making mechanisms and new venues where all partners can have an equal voice. In each of the four case studies, examples are provided of how low-income communities can drive social change and lead conversations about their social, cultural, and economic futures. As low-income communities across the country continue to join similar conversations, especially in the case of partnering with institutions of higher education, the nation may witness new and innovative strategies for success.

In many low-income communities, institutions of higher education are important and powerful untapped assets. Many of these institutions are located in cities with deteriorated infrastructures and little economic opportunity. Moreover, these local universities, colleges, or community colleges are the only remaining large employment base. Unlike large corporations that have relocated, these institutions cannot just pick up and go. This situation offers an excellent starting point for building partnership. Therefore, appropriately, many institutions are turning their attention toward the surrounding neighborhoods and becoming the very best partners that they can be.

These partnerships will not work, however, unless there is leadership from the top. A sympathetic faculty member or even an entire department is not enough. As noted in Maurrasse's research, it takes a commitment on behalf of the chancellor or president to institutionalize these partnerships within the university.

To achieve lasting solutions to the long-standing problems of inequity, communities need the academy. To be grounded, of service, and a part of the future, the academy needs to reconnect to community. Maurrasse's timely book offers useful strategies for building these essential partnerships.

Acknowledgments

To acknowledge everyone who had a hand in this book by name would be daunting. Undoubtedly, this book is the product of a massive group effort. If I must start somewhere, it has to be with the Rockefeller Foundation, which enabled me to conduct the research for this book while on staff. For all intents and purposes, they funded this effort. Immediate extra special thanks should go to Chet Hewitt of Rockefeller, who brought me there and gave me the flexibility to bring my own ideas into Rockefeller's existing work. Aida Rodriguez and Julia Lopez of Rockefeller's Working Communities Division were also critical supporters. My assistant at Rockefeller, Byron Karabatsos was essential to arranging meetings and taking on many of the, often unnoticed, tasks.

Everyone who I interviewed at the institutions of higher education and surrounding neighborhoods indicated in this book also deserve special notice. As you read this book, you will see that the interviews are the bedrock, foundation, and essence of this study. The unique and rich information provided by them is not easily obtained. People like Ira Harkavy, Lucy Kerman, Diane Bordenave, Sybil Morial, John Pecoul, Nedra Jasper Alcorn, Joe Givens, Brian Murphy, Susan Alunan, David Hadaller, and Carlos Acevedo were not only interviewed, they arranged all of the other interviews for this book. I very much appreciate that all of these people took time out of hectic schedules to meet with me. The Rockefeller Foundation enabled me to make grants to further the work at each of these universities or colleges, which was the least that I could do.

All of those important figures in the field of higher educational/community partnerships, such as Victor Rubin and the Department of Housing and Urban Development's (HUD) Office of University Partnerships, Earnie Osborne and Seedco, Smita Singh and LINK, Liz Hollander and Campus Compact, David Cox, Nancy Thomas, Zelda Gamson, Ron Mason, Cynthia Farrar, and others deserve thanks for expanding my thinking on various issues confronting the field. As a Rockefeller staff person, I worked with a number of higher education/community partnerships not featured in this book. Conversations with representatives of those institutions and neighborhoods also influenced my thinking on these issues. Some examples include the cast of the Bayview/Hunter's Point Neighborhood Jobs Initiative in San Francisco; the University of California at San Francisco; the Department of Health and Human Services in San Diego; the Consensus Organizing Center at San Diego State; San Diego Dialogue at the University of California at San Diego; the Consensus Organizing Institute; the Egan Center at Depaul University; the Center for the Study of Race, Inequality, and Politics at Yale University; and the Office of New Haven Affairs, also at Yale. My time in California led to a May 2000 conference on higher education/community partnerships hosted by the University of California at Santa Barbara. A lot of rich perspectives came from the diverse crowd at the conference, and I should extend thanks to all of them for contributing to my thinking on these issues.

The Institute for Social and Policy Studies at Yale University provided critical research funding to support the development of the many transcriptions that are essential to any qualitative endeavor. Ann Fitzpatrick of Yale and family masterfully wrote up pages upon pages of transcriptions. Aldon Morris of Northwestern University, who always has been a valuable advisor to my work, and Josh Gamson of Yale University provided important initial commentary on the concept for this book. Hazel Carby and Cathy Cohen of Yale University also were important initial commentators. Yale's Program on Nonprofit Organizations provided me the opportunity to get feedback from a diverse audience much later in the process. While Ira Harkavy is heavily featured in the book, he was also a critical reader of an earlier draft.

The community-building field also provided valuable insight on the role of institutions of higher education in comprehensive community revitalization efforts. Organizations such as the National Community Building Network, PolicyLink, the National Neighborhood Indicators Project, the Urban Strategies Council, DC Agenda, the Neighborhood Improvement Association of Savannah, Georgia, the Aspen Institute, and the Empowerment Zones and Enterprise Communities (EZEC) Funding Consortium all helped me think about both the community and higher education sides of partnerships. Of course, special thanks to Angela Blackwell, founding director of PolicyLink, for writing the foreword. I also cannot ignore PolicyLink staff members, Josh Kirschenbaum and Heather Tamir, who provided valuable commentary.

Finally, thanks to the Routledge press, and Ilene Kalish in particular, for really pushing me to move this book along in a timely fashion without compromising quality.

Introduction

On a seventy-five-degree humid February morning in New Orleans, I peer out of a car window at rows of decaying brick buildings. Windows on some of the two- and three-story houses are boarded up. Occasional graffiti adorns the walls. Numerous African-American men and women are milling about, some in discussion, while others sit or stand alone, possibly dreaming of better days. This is the C. J. Peete Housing Development. Most of these residents will be relocated, as the development soon will be demolished.

As the car begins to slow down, one small building stands out. Apparently a hub of activity, people are conversing on the porch and stairs. Some are African American, some white. This fact is striking, as there don't appear to be any other white people for blocks. In big green letters, the acronym "CAP" is displayed prominently on the building's front facade. This is an office for the Campus Affiliates Program—a partnership program between Xavier and Tulane Universities. This is what I am here to see.

The two universities jointly manage the C. J. Peete Housing Development and work closely with the community, crafting a comprehensive community development plan to address the multiple needs of Peete's residents. This expanded role is part of what the two universities call the Center for the Urban Community. Professors, students, and staff frequent this neighborhood and develop close working relationships with residents, especially the local activists. Permanent staff members manage the office.

What is striking is that C. J. Peete is not located in the neighborhood of either Tulane or Xavier, and yet both university presidents embrace this effort. One might ask whether this is the role of a university. What business does Xavier or Tulane have getting involved with a public housing complex? How is such involvement an educational or academic enterprise? Is this a charitable exercise? Is this where colleges and universities should be investing their energies?

Actually, community partnerships[1] such as this are happening at colleges and universities nationwide. A movement is emerging. University presidents are placing community partnerships higher on their agendas. Offices for community outreach are increasing their internal standing at colleges and universities, receiving bigger budgets and more exposure.

These partnerships are relevant to a variety of issues confronting higher education. They extend far beyond local relationships; they force us to think about the overall purpose of higher education. There are many hotly contested issues in higher education in the United States and internationally, ranging from affirmative action[2] to the significance of tenure[3] to the exploitation of employees and the increasingly corporate nature of higher education[4] to the content of curriculum.[5] The study of higher education/community partnerships[6] adds an important dimension to the debates around these topics. The issues impacting affirmative action, tenure, and curriculum are tied to the broader relationship between academia and society—higher education's relative accessibility and relevance to the majority of Americans. For example, labor demands at universities throughout the country have hit the headlines. If the employees of these universities or colleges live in the local area, and they often do, then labor issues affect community relations. In terms of affirmative action, if the number of students of color decreases on campuses due to shifting policies around the issue, then greater ties between institutions of higher education and local public schools are central to maintaining access for students of color.

The organizations and people that give funding to colleges and universities are taking note of this movement, and are either providing grants for these efforts or assessing the possibilities of doing so. In fact, I was appointed a foundation officer with the responsibility of assessing the potential of higher education/community partnerships to improve conditions in communities. In 1998, I took a leave of absence from my position in the departments of sociology and African-American studies at Yale University. I ended up at the Rockefeller Foundation immersed in these issues not only as an observer, but as a potential catalyst for future directions in the field. What I quickly realized, for reasons that I will elaborate at greater length later, is that these partnerships between communities and universities or colleges are taking place largely in urban areas. The rural agenda was the driving force behind the development of the land grant institutions back in the 1860s. Now the innovations in higher education/community partnerships are surfacing primarily in large cities. This was appropriate for my work at the Rockefeller Foundation, where I managed a program entitled "Building Community," which focused on comprehensive community-based efforts to revitalize urban neighborhoods. My charge was to see if these community-driven efforts could benefit from building a pipeline to academia—creatively drawing upon the resources at institutions of higher education to solve local problems.

I traveled around the country, visiting interesting and diverse programs at universities and colleges. Some institutions focused on economic development, others on technology. From the arts to the social sciences to engineering to the law, institutions were partnering with communities in many ways. At some institutions, the primary community partnership activity was funneled through teaching,[7] while others focused on the research aspects of higher education.[8] Some of the partnerships did not engage the academic aspects of higher education at all, connecting more closely to administration.[9]

After having seen the lay of the land, I created a small grants program to further learning about the field. "Innovation Grants," I called them, with the goal of improving the scope of partnerships and building the capacity of community organizations to access resources in academia. Through the Rockefeller Foundation, I funded both institutions of higher education and community-based organizations. Four of these university or college grantees are featured in these pages: the University of Pennsylvania, Xavier University of New Orleans, San Francisco State University, and Hostos Community College of the South Bronx.[10] This book is a comparative analysis of these four institutions of higher education and their community partnership initiatives. Referrals from people inside and outside of the field led me to these places. They are diverse types of institutions in different geographic regions with diverse demographics. They are all within urban centers, some of which are located in very close proximity to poor neighborhoods.

Hostos Community College in the South Bronx of New York City is a "bilingual" institution serving a largely Latino population. Hostos is the result of the community's demand during the late 1960s for a higher educational institution in this very poor neighborhood. In many ways, Hostos *is* the local community with its locally representative student body. The development of this community-based population always has been its goal. San Francisco State University, a public urban university, is clear about its role as a critical participant throughout the city of San Francisco. Although not directly situated within a poor area, San Francisco State's outreach through its Urban Institute and other initiatives extends into some of the more distressed areas in the city. Historically black, Xavier University sends more African-American students to medical school than any institution of higher education in the country. But it has become known for working throughout the city of New Orleans on a number of other issues. The semiautonomous Xavier Triangle is a community development corporation on campus, which is designed to address the needs of local residents. The Center for the Urban Community is the Xavier-Tulane University partnership discussed at the beginning of this chapter. Finally, the University of Pennsylvania, the largest employer in the city of Philadelphia, is connecting with local organizations, the school system, and industry in order to revitalize the neighborhoods surrounding the campus. Penn is a major research university— the type of institution one might suspect is least able to find consistency between core mission and genuine partnership with the local community. Nevertheless, major research universities shape what many perceive to be the role of higher education. A relatively successful model of community partnership at a place such as Penn could open the doors to a more applied, useful, and relevant approach to higher education nationwide.

The Fate of Communities Is the Fate of Higher Education

Poor communities in all of these cities have been hit hard by broader socioeconomic circumstances that continually shape the urban landscape. Taking a glance at some of the poorest urban areas in the United States, one can see that several industries have vacated the premises,[11] seeking to lower operating costs either through cheaper land and labor or through technological advances. Communities persist and survive in areas that have lost much of their infrastructure. Economic development initiatives could improve abandoned and dilapidated property in these neighborhoods, but one hopes not at the expense of the existing population. Gentrification looms in many urban areas as the booming economy has driven up property values in cities nationwide.

But whether or not the housing stock is dilapidated, the streets are dirty, the crime is high, the businesses have skipped town—local colleges and universities remain. It is difficult to imagine institutions of higher education packing up and leaving their neighborhoods given their vast acreage and local investments.[12] They are sticky capital. Not only are they sticking around, they are significant sources of employment and generally essential to local economies. In over one third of the urban areas in the United States, a university and/or university-affiliated hospital is the most significant local employer.[13]

Universities and colleges are equipped to contribute effectively to their local neighborhoods in many ways, academically, economically, and beyond. For the most part, however, they are underutilized local assets. Recent partnerships are seeking to change that. But is this movement a fad? These partnerships are a product of history. While the idea is not new, urbanization altered the environment for many colleges and universities. From New Haven to New York to Chicago to Los Angeles, we increasingly began to see colleges situated in very close proximity to poor urban neighborhoods over the past few decades. Although these institutions were among few remaining local assets, the initial higher educational response to distressed urban areas was separation. Many colleges and universities put up walls and expanded police forces to heighten the distinction between themselves and their immediate surroundings. The tensions between poor and working-class urban residents and some institutions of higher education festered, often symbolized in instances such as crimes committed against university personnel and students or the displacement of local residents by college or university buildings. Because of such incidents, higher education began to take greater note of its permanency in these neighborhoods. Even those institutions not directly situated in deteriorating areas began to recognize the interdependency between, for example, the conditions of urban neighborhoods and student recruitment. Their increasingly diverse student populations brought a different set of priorities to the classroom. We can say now that the fate of communities is the fate of higher education.

On another front, with the devolution of responsibility for a variety of social services moving from the federal government to local public institutions, and from those entities to any variety of organizations, expectations have shifted. Services once considered the government's business now are being taken on by nonprofit organizations, private vendors, and institutions of higher education. External entities such as federal and local governments and some foundations have been looking to colleges and universities to fill this void.

It is also important to note that these communities hardly have been passive recipients of the good graces of academia. The community-building and community development movements have been gaining steam. These efforts have convened people from all walks of life in solving many of the challenges facing urban areas. Add to the mix the knowledge, facilities, person power, and influence of academia, and we have great possibilities for effective partnerships.

Despite the growth in these partnerships, effective implementation is still in need of improvement. Academia must travel a long way from its traditional relations with poor urban communities. Not only does academia have to work itself out of the *punitive* approach of primarily policing urban communities, it has to guard against some other tendencies that have sparked tension with local communities. Community partnerships are beginning to progress beyond the *paternalistic* approach of deciding what is best for communities without seeking local input. Partnerships also have been challenging the *lab* approach, where communities are treated solely as subjects of study and never benefit from the results of research projects conducted on them. A lot of bitterness remains in local communities after decades of mistreatment from some universities or colleges. One of my goals in writing this book is to point out these problems and offer productive solutions to improve the relationship between institutions of higher education and their communities.

The involvement of universities and colleges in community partnerships is making a difference in communities, as the case studies in these pages suggest. But the necessary ingredients for the sustenance and enhancement of these efforts rest considerably within the academy.[14] In other words, the long-term preparedness of higher education to develop a lasting commitment is partly dependent upon its ability to change institutionally. Concurrently, community-based organizations also will require some degree of enhanced infrastructural capacity and political savvy in order to get the most out of partnerships with major institutions. The irony of partnerships of this sort is that each side of the equation must effectively prepare and collaborate *internally* in order to do so externally.[15]

The Importance of Mission

All universities and colleges have something akin to a mission, that is, a statement of purpose. This institutional mission addresses the overall reason for their existence. As a written document, a mission statement articulates the aims of an institution, but it hardly captures the full scope of operations and culture. Regardless of the rhetoric within a mission statement, implementation remains the critical component that brings any vision to a reality. For the purposes of this work, I am thinking of *mission* more in terms of a "way of doing business," in addition to a "reason for being." In some cases, institutions of higher education may be suited to partnering with local communities rhetorically, but various aspects of their structure and culture may hinder healthy community partnerships. Although a number of institutions of higher education are beginning to promote community partnerships, greater institutional change may be required before they are prepared to be useful to surrounding neighborhoods over sustained periods. In other words, sometimes talk is just talk.

Institutional commitment to community partnerships cannot be assessed through rhetoric alone. Commitment is more than a handful of students and professors working with community-based organizations. We can assess commitment through indicators of institutional priority. Do community outreach efforts transcend one person or a tiny handful of people? Are faculty who are engaged in community partnerships rewarded for their work? Is the central administration placing high priority on community outreach? Is service incorporated into both the core academic mission and the economic mission of the institution?

Mission statements also leave ample room for interpretation. Complex organizations can function successfully with numerous uncoordinated activities.[16] Some general interest in community affairs exists at most institutions of higher education, but it coexists with several competing ones. Although this varies by size and type, institutions of higher education tend to operate successfully with numerous departments, offices, institutes, and centers that essentially pursue their own missions. While central administrations govern universities and colleges, they do not control or micromanage the environment. Different groups within the academy may all justify the same activity differently. For example, administrators may see the economic advantages to community partnerships, while faculty may stress the educational opportunity, while students may stress the obligation of the institution as a local neighbor. Collective agreement is not a prerequisite for efficiency in complex organizations; however, the most effective organizations tend to have as much collective buy-in and input into an organizational mission as possible.[17]

The lack of cohesion within institutions of higher education may be generally understood by those within academia; however, when partnering externally, this lack of cohesion can create confusion. It is not uncommon for two programs from different departments to be put into action in the same neighborhood without consulting or communicating with one another. Higher education/community partnerships historically have often been inconsistent and uncoordinated, leaving neighborhood residents wary of even the most well-intentioned outreach efforts. It would be unrealistic to expect all units in the academy to be in sync around community partnerships. But, partnerships can benefit from a deeper institutional commitment. Community residents are more likely to buy into partnerships with higher education when they can see such commitment. This includes greater internal coordination, multiple departmental involvement, and the support of the central administration. Some of this also boils down to money. A number of colleges and universities are beginning to designate existing funds in support of community partnerships, but too many still rely on new external funds. A discontinued program is a common reality in the academy, but a discontinued community partnership could prove disruptive or even devastating to local residents.

While a true common interest sometimes is difficult to decipher in academia, those in the leadership of complex organizations have more flexibility in shaping institutional decisions around their interests.[18] For this reason, college or university presidents are essential to the continuation, expansion, and enhancement of community partnerships. Community partnerships at all of the featured institutions in this book have significant presidential support. However, this has not always been the case. Their past experiences stress the difference that presidential support can provide.[19]

Outline of the Book

Whether or not an institution of higher education can justify and sustain community partnerships is a complicated proposition. The nature of these partnerships depends on a broad range of factors:

- The type of institution of higher education
- The historical relationship between the partners
- Power relationships between the institution and the community
- The availability of external funding
- The relative support of the public sector
- The capacity of community-based institutions and governing structures
- The institutional culture of the college or university
- The historical development of the mission of the college or university

- The institutional commitment of the college or university
- The backgrounds of the higher educational representatives, and the demographics of both community and institution

Similar factors affect partnerships involving other institutions and industries. If social responsibility to surrounding communities is not seen as essential in these institutions, it is marginalized. Other types of major institutions are critical to addressing the challenges facing poor and disenfranchised urban communities.

The first chapter of this book provides the current and historical context shaping the recognition of the need for higher education/community partnerships. It also analyzes the relative significance of research, teaching, and service in the context of today's urban economy. In this chapter, I analyze the characteristics of the current higher education/community partnership movement.

The second section is the bulk of this book. Here I analyze the various case studies, guided by the major questions of this work: Are community partnerships compatible with the missions and organizational cultures of these four diverse colleges and universities? Have these institutions developed an institutional commitment to the sustainability of these partnerships? How do various factors influence the ability of these institutions to justify and commit to the partnerships? Unless otherwise noted, the sources for all quotations in this and the final section are the interviews listed at the back of the book.

Chapter 2 focuses on the University of Pennsylvania's outreach effort and the capacity of a major research university genuinely to incorporate community partnerships into its mission and culture. Like all chapters in this section of the book, it addresses the evolution of current incarnations of community partnership. The actual partnership activities are analyzed within the context of the critical factors influencing the university's role in the community. Chapter 3 addresses San Francisco State and the mission driving a public urban university in relation to local civic engagement. Chapter 4 considers the particular context of Xavier University, its outreach efforts in New Orleans, and various related dynamics. Chapter 5 focuses on Hostos Community College and the nature of an institution that was built to serve its local community.

The third and final section of the book is largely analytical, comparing and contrasting the case studies and providing recommendations for future research as well as policy. Chapter 6 addresses the varying missions of these institutions of higher education in relation to their partnership initiatives. I analyze the commonalities across the different types of institutions but also the degree to which various factors shape the nature of the relationship between these institutions and their surrounding communities. I extract the best practices that transcend the type of university and geographical area but also grapple with the distinctions. I discuss the practical future applications of these types of relationships, recommending topics for future research and policy. I also discuss gaps in the field of higher education/community partnerships. I address opportunities to improve uses of higher educational resources for societal gain but also analyze obstacles within higher education and elsewhere. This chapter may be a guide not only for university and community stakeholders, but also for foundation officers, policymakers, and anyone who stands to benefit from efforts toward social responsibility by higher education.

Community partnerships often are compatible with the general stated missions of colleges and universities. But are colleges and universities willing to extend their commitment beyond rhetoric? Are they prepared to develop the necessary institutional commitment to be valuable assets to poor and disenfranchised communities? These four institutions have spent decades grappling with their relationship to the urban communities that surround them. How have they progressed? How have they failed? What can higher education, communities, and anyone with a stake in leveraging resources to make the world a better place do to improve these partnerships?

Chapter 1

The Mission of Higher Education

What is the purpose of higher education? What goals should colleges and universities attempt to pursue? What obligations do colleges and universities have to society? Academic missions are not static; they can shift with societal needs and historical contexts. Core academic missions of institutions of higher education have changed over time from serving an elite, to teaching the liberal arts, to producing scientific research, to teaching vocation, to providing service. Most of today's colleges and universities adopt comprehensive missions spanning an array of elements, but often including some combination of teaching and research, liberal arts and sciences. Service often has been a third element alongside teaching and research, but its security can be tenuous depending on the institution.

Historically, changes in the broader environment spawned appropriate amendments in the missions of colleges and universities.[1] This has been true for most major institutions and industries. The rate at which institutions can adapt to societal change rests on multiple factors. Given the many different types of institutions of higher education, adaptation to the burgeoning expectation that colleges and universities will be involved in community partnerships will vary significantly.

As much as higher education appears to be moving toward involvement in local communities, the institutions also are becoming increasingly corporate in nature. The outsourcing[2] of labor is a good example. While corporations meet some particular societal demands, they primarily are driven by the bottom line — profits. Institutions of higher education ideally are driven by the fulfillment of a social mission. Developing minds, leaders — social uplift is the charge of higher education. These concepts, according to many involved in higher education/community partnerships, can be extended into community development — the development of people inside and outside of the institution. Higher education, the community partnerships movement suggests, must as a part of its mission take ownership of its broader environment; the institution must see itself as a citizen with a responsibility to its neighbors.

Scholars have increasingly been analyzing the inherent responsibilities of citizenship. Groups interests, some argue, are not naturally distinct from self interests.[3] The communitarian movement, popularized by Amitai Etzioni, for example, promotes individual responsibility to fellow citizens, rooted in collective interests.[4] These concepts can be extended to institutional citizenry; the high education/community partnership movement is rooted in such ideas.

While postsecondary education was once the bastion of the elite, higher education has become increasingly accessible to the masses.[5] The United Nations Educational, Scientific and Cultural Organization's (UNESCO) 1998 World Conference on Higher Education highlighted the global "massification" of higher education, in which institutions once accessible to less than one percent of the population in some countries are now flanked by other colleges and universities that have expanded the field of citizens with postsecondary degrees. Today, the perception of the stuffy ivory tower institution teeming with sweatered prep-school offspring of the captains of industry is no longer an accurate reflection of the state of higher education. Most institutions of higher education now have diverse student bodies, including many working-class people with a host of real-world life challenges.[6] Working-class people of color in student bodies and even faculty and administration can influence the priorities of higher education, including the degree of participation in surrounding communities.

The relationship between higher education and community varies by institution, and the mission of higher education varies by the type of university or college. However, while few in number, major research universities dominate societal conceptions of the role of higher education. A comparative analysis of different types of institutions of higher education highlights some of the critical distinctions in the contextual circumstances of many colleges and universities. Nevertheless, the influence of major research universities may in fact dwarf that of other institutions of higher education. Robert Rosenzweig said of the approximately one hundred such institutions:

> Although that may seem small in number—indeed, is a small number, in comparison with the total of thirty-five hundred post secondary institutions—it is a group whose influence and importance far exceed its percentage of the total. Not only do these universities conduct most of the nation's basic research; they also educate the vast majority of future college teachers and research scientists of all types as well as leaders of the learned professions. They are the most visible of all educational institutions, and, for better or for worse, they are the models that many others in this country and abroad strive to emulate. What happens in them and to them matters.[7]

As one begins to imagine policy changes specifically designed to enhance the civic engagement of institutions of higher education, major research universities would have to play a critical role in order to shape the entire academy's approach to local communities. However, major research universities, with their rise to prominence during the twentieth century, have not been in the forefront of constructing models of community partnerships. Many residents of communities in close proximity to these universities would argue that their powerful neighbors have done more harm than good.

For any college or university the broader idea of taking on greater social responsibility boils down to fulfilling that mission without infringing upon the rights or interests of others. Institutions of higher education are in the precarious position of satisfying multiple interests in the fulfillment of a mission. The core academic mission holds one set of priorities; economic aspects of the mission drive another set of priorities. The two are intertwined, but not always in sync. Further engagement in communities only expands the number of constituents with a stake in the institution. To take account of perspectives of faculty, administrators, students, trustees, staff, and donors, not to mention government, the private sector, and local communities is daunting. It's an imposing management challenge. Nevertheless, each of those constituency groups holds a stake in the institution. Understanding their priorities only improves how the institution interacts with them. Openness to their questions, concerns, and interests only strengthens the institution.

During the twentieth century, for example, student protest was one of the more salient examples of an interest group bringing to the table strong disagreements with the priorities of central administrations. Despite administrators' resistance to such protest, the missions and operations of higher education certainly have been enhanced by student demands. Student protest has made universities more diverse, more sensitive in their investments, broader in their curriculum, and increasingly more responsible to their surrounding communities. Student movements continue to hold academia accountable and drive the enhancement of various aspects of higher education. Stronger relationships with community will pave avenues for local input. If higher education/community partnerships continue to grow at a similar rate, colleges and universities will be forced to take account of community voices in more significant ways. This effectively would strengthen the service aspect of the higher educational mission and enhance the institutional civic responsibility of colleges and universities.

Evolution of the Role of Higher Education

It is difficult to discuss historical debates on the role of higher education without addressing nineteenth-century British scholar and preacher John Henry Newman's seminal work, *The Idea of a University*, originally published in 1873. Newman defines a university as "a place for teaching universal knowledge in order to mandate the presence of theology as a science of sciences."[8] According to Newman, a university education is not professional or vocational, rather it expands one's outlook and capacity for social and civic interaction.

And this is the reason why it is more correct to speak of a university as a place of education, than of instruction, though, when knowledge is concerned, instruction would at first sight have seemed the more appropriate word. We are instructed, for instance, in manual exercises, in the fine and useful arts, in trades, and in ways of business; for these are methods which have little or no effect on the mind itself.... When we speak of the communication of knowledge as being education, we thereby really imply that that knowledge is a state or condition of mind; and since cultivation of mind is surely worth seeking for its own sake...." (85)

A university produces, according to Newman, a "gentleman," who is polished and worldly, yet not above laypersons. Influenced by the Catholic church, Newman stressed that students should pursue excellence yet remain loyal to higher religious pursuits of contributing to society. These ideas, although rooted specifically within Catholic ideology, stress a higher educational mission that promotes contribution to society. The training of contributors to society, Newman argued, was a function of building their intellects. "If then a practical end must be assigned to a University course, I say it is that of training good members of society. Its art is the art of social life, and its end is fitness for the world. It neither confines its views of particular professions on the one hand, nor creates heroes or inspires genius on the other. Works indeed of genius fall under no art; heroic minds come under no rule" (125). Referring to the characteristics of a universally educated person, Newman maintains, "He is at home in any society, he has common ground with every class; he knows when to speak and when to be silent; he is able to converse, he is able to listen; he can ask a question pertinently, and gain a lesson seasonably" (126).

The holistic nature of universities does indeed have utility as Newman argues; however, it does not seem certain that great contributions to society naturally flow from a well-rounded "universal" education. Current community partnerships are rooted in the idea of societal contribution, but they demonstrate a conscious commitment to extending higher educational resources outside of the institution. A college or university has to demonstrate the will to take responsibility for the external environment.

While Newman and others laid the foundation for liberal arts, scientific research would eventually coexist with and in some cases dominate the higher educational landscape. George Washington was among the first to call for some federal role in advancing scientific research. In 1796, he called for a Board of Agriculture, which would encourage experimentation.[9] Such thinking ultimately led to sweeping legislation like the Morrill Act of 1862, and the Hatch Act of 1887, which established experiment stations at the land grant universities created through the Morrill Act. Eventually, scientific research became incorporated into several institutions of higher education, leading to gradations among research universities. Major research universities, often known as "research 1" institutions, have come to control a significant percentage of the resources designated for higher education.

In the United States, the dominance of major research universities is heavily supported by powerful external interests. "For government, business, and the major foundation, the best criterion for research investment is the proven performance of blue chip institutions."[10] It was not until after World War II that a large cluster of American research universities rose to positions of global preeminence, as the federal government began to rely heavily on these institutions for scientific expertise. This allowed new research universities to significantly enhance their international profiles.[11] The war highlighted the role of science and technology in modern military strategies, leading Vannevar Bush, director of the wartime Office of Scientific Research and Development, to advocate for harnessing the existing resources of universities for scientific ends. This direction only facilitated the application of scientific research to other areas.[12] Research universities fulfilled demand stemming not only from government, but from foreign students.

Prior to the war, $31 million was available for scientific research. "A quarter of a century later, that figure had multiplied twenty-five times in constant dollars. Virtually all of the increase was the consequence of the federal government that stressed the importance of research as a central university function, a sharp departure from earlier years" (Rosenzweig, 1998, p. 2). While the research mission thrives in the most prominent universities and is often aspired to by the vast field of other institutions of higher education, the top-secret, militarily-driven research came under heavy criticism by some internal university constituents, especially students. The anti–Vietnam War movement played a critical role in limiting secret research on campuses nationwide (4). Prior to that era, research and development expenditures more than tripled between 1957 and 1968.

> Academic research personnel in public universities grew from 13,000 to 23,000 and in private universities from 12,000 to 23,000. The federal share of research funds grew from 53 percent to 75 percent in public universities and from 66 percent to 82 percent in private universities. Total higher educational enrollment grew from three million to more than seven million. Enrollment in public doctoral universities grew from 800,000 to 1.9 million. Private doctoral university enrollment went from 440,000 to 650,000. The number of doctorates awarded in science and engineering grew from 5,800 to 14,300. (5–6)

Politicians' dissatisfaction with "violent disruptions" on campuses during the late 1960s and early 1970s led to lower federal appropriations to universities and more stringent conditions of financial support. Moreover, a general public suspicion of science emerged (9–10). Ironically, liberal arts remained a centerpiece of undergraduate education in the United States throughout the rise of scientific research. But as we head into the twenty-first century, scientific research still drives the majority of funding into universities.

Today, Newman's "idea of a university" survives, but universities have taken advantage of their scientific capacities. The fulfillment of government demands for research and the promotion of knowledge for its own sake coexist. But, what does this mean for community partnerships? How much of the research produced in higher education ever reaches communities?

I would argue that making a societal contribution has to be a more active process, in which communities present their priorities to the academy, and research is conducted accordingly.[13] While on the surface this may fly in the face of academic freedom, it would not be very much different than accepting government support for research. Government may be the messenger of societal needs, but do policy makers really know better than residents at the neighborhood level? In fact, many public officials often rely on academics to articulate societal needs. If academics do not have a direct pipeline to the voices of communities, then how can they really know the issues? Community partnerships have the potential to create a smarter higher educational system—one that is truly in tune with the critical issues facing the cities, the farms, and all in between. The academic mission can be more than fulfilled through higher education/community partnerships.

Higher Education and Meeting Societal Needs

Throughout the colonization of America, new immigrants attempted to cultivate the country's vast natural resources, from oil to forests to land suitable for growing numerous food crops. Particularly as colonizers began to move westward, improved agriculture became an increasing priority. With societal demand moving in this direction during the late eighteenth century, higher education eventually followed suit. The concept of "land grant" was based on the need to provide practical education, which would enhance the skills and capacity of farmers.[14] This thinking initially facilitated the establishment of elementary schools on land provided by the federal government—an extension of the Northwest Ordinances of 1785 and 1787, which "laid the foundation for a national system of free education"—and ultimately expanded the availability of higher education as well to a broader cross-section of the population, particularly working farmers (7). Scientific education had, by this time, increased in its significance within higher education, particularly because the public began to see the potential practical uses of science in solving the challenges of daily life.

The United States Agricultural Society was established in 1852 in response to the demand for experiments, essays, and reports on improvements in farming practices (6). With its headquarters in Washington, it boasted a membership of three hundred societies in thirty-one states and five territories. This coalition pushed for congressional support for higher educational programming in agriculture and the mechanical arts. Prior to the passing of the legendary Morrill Act of 1862, which effectively established the higher educational land grant system, the University of Michigan in 1837 and the University of Wisconsin in 1848 were established based on an 1836 authorization of two "townships." These were the first colleges of agriculture — direct responses to the conditions of the time. Higher education was compelled to adapt to demand, spawning universities with the mission of enhancing the agricultural economy. Prior to the establishment of these new institutions, higher education was not suited to take on these challenges. Someone had to take action to support the interests of farmers.

It was Jonathon Baldwin Turner of Illinois who spearheaded the push for federal land grants to establish colleges of agriculture and the mechanical arts (8).

> Turner's plan was influenced and guided by Jeffersonian ideals. He sought to develop young people's reasoning faculties, enlarge their minds, and cultivate their morals so that commerce, agriculture, and manufacturing could prosper to the benefit of every American. Education was truly in the public interest. The plan included three basic goals: (1) to establish colleges that would be open at minimum cost, to laborers in agriculture, commerce, and the arts who needed educational assistance; (2) to develop curricula that would include instruction in practical and vocational subjects for the benefit of the working class; and (3) to endow these colleges by grants of land from the enormous holdings of the federal government. (9–10)

The issue of access to higher education during this period was inextricable from public service or civic engagement. The student bodies of the institutions envisioned by Turner were the target community, and it was through enhancing their capacity that societal needs ultimately would be served. When Justin Smith Morrill introduced the land grant bill, it passed through both the House and the Senate and was signed into law by President Abraham Lincoln on July 2, 1862. Among Morrill's justifications for the act were both the demand for scientific instruction in colleges as well as the need to make some of the vast public lands that the federal government had been giving away to corporations and railroads available for the good of the masses. Morrill also noted the "monopoly on education" perpetuated by those families that had been highly educated over several generations (16–17). Prior to the act, only 2 percent of Americans were educated beyond the twelfth grade.

Due to the overwhelming external demand for increased access, institutions of higher education were put in the position of opening up and responding to community desires or risking the loss of their constituencies. Some of the already established institutions altered their operations. Others were slow to change, but eventually "became more open and populist in response to new competition" (Rosenzweig 1998, 2).

While these new institutions of higher education were not explicitly exclusive to whites, African Americans and Native Americans effectively were denied access. Not only were 90 percent of African Americans enslaved at the time the act passed, but "free blacks" were barred from admissions. In 1890, Morrill passed another act, which became synonymous with the concept of "separate but equal" and called for equal distribution of resources between black and white colleges. The act was presented twelve times before becoming law.[15] While rhetorically noble, this act did not bring about equality between black and white universities.[16] It was not until 1978 when the Tribally Controlled Community College Act was passed to stimulate the development of different types of institutions of higher education near Native American reservations that major legislation took steps toward meeting the particular needs of disenfranchised Native American communities.[17]

The Smith-Lever Act of 1914 was critical to the development of explicit outreach components within institutions of higher education that resemble today's community partnerships. The act was designed to assist institutions of higher education in disseminating practical information about agriculture and home economics for applied purposes. It specifically mentioned the need for agricultural "extensions" to provide "instruction and practical demonstrations in agriculture and home economics to persons not attending or residents in said colleges in several communities."[18] The federal government provided 50 percent of the resources associated with this act. The remaining half was to be provided by a combination of state, county, and local authorities. This joint funding strategy led to the term "cooperative extension."

Despite the successes of the land grant system, higher education is still generally perceived as distant from the needs of society, particularly those of the poor and disenfranchised. In their reflections on the land grant institutions of higher education, scholars and other stakeholders began to revisit the purpose of these universities. The land grant model significantly increased the capacity for food production in the United States, in fact becoming a model to the rest of the world. In recent decades, however, many have suggested that the land grants have not changed with the times.[19] Although a significant portion of the United States remains rural, fewer people are employed in agriculture, and with increasing urbanization, fewer people are even acquainted with agricultural methods and food production. Numerous attempts at rekindling the impact of land grants continue.[20]

Particular scholars as well as student activists historically have encouraged higher education to be relevant and responsive to its surrounding communities. Beyond the land grants, a number of other variations of higher education/

community partnerships have surfaced since the nineteenth century. John Dewey, during the late nineteenth and early twentieth century, for example, promoted the concepts of "participatory democracy" and "participatory action research."[21] Francis Bacon promoted similar ideas during the seventeenth century. While at the University of Chicago, Dewey and the university's president, William Rainey Harper, argued that universities were the "prophets of democracy" (Bensen et al. 2000, 9).

Like land grants for rural areas, urban universities began to reflect on meeting the needs surfacing through the expansion of cities. Urban universities, like the University of Chicago in particular, were designed to meet the particular needs of city residents. While urban universities have never reached their full potential to serve their neighborhoods, the topic remains on the table, providing the foundations for today's partnerships.

According to Lee Bensen and Ira Harkavy, "Democracy . . . should be the soul of the American schooling system, particularly its most strategic component, the research university" (1999, 2). They maintain that three revolutions have occurred in higher education over the last two centuries:

> The first revolution, of course, occurred in the late nineteenth century. Beginning at Johns Hopkins in 1876, the accelerating adoption and uniquely American adaptation of the German model revolutionized American higher education. By the turn of the century, the uniquely American research university had essentially been created. The second revolution began in 1945 with Vannevar Bush's "endless [research] frontier" Manifesto and rapidly produced the Big Science, Cold War, Entrepreneurial University. The third revolution, we (optimistically) believe, began in 1989. The fall of the Berlin Wall and the end of the Cold War provided the necessary condition for the "revolutionary" emergence of the Cosmopolitan Civic University—a new type of university engaged in the advancement of democratic schooling and practical realization of the democratic promise of America *for all Americans*. (2)

It may be optimistic to suggest that the general thrust of higher education will be characterized by the "Cosmopolitan Civic University" over the next few decades. However, just such a university would be well-suited to meeting society's current challenges. Bensen and Harkavy suggest that "after 1989, the combination of external pressure and enlightened self-interest spurred American research universities to recognize that they could, indeed must, function simultaneously as *universal* and as *local* institutions of higher education—cosmopolitan civic institutions not only *in* but *of* their local communities" (3). Indeed, they focus squarely on the research university—those institutions most closely associated with ivory tower distance from local concerns. It is more difficult to imagine a "revolution" in this field than in the community college system, for example, since it has been the historical mission of such institutions to serve a local community. Potentially, then, community colleges could play a critical role in assisting research universities in the construction of a sincerely locally driven mission. To varying degrees, historically black colleges, public urban universities, and land grant institutions also have a history of responsiveness to local concerns prior to current trends in higher education/community partnerships.

The Changing Urban Landscape

Institutional support for community partnerships at major research universities appears to be the most distinctive aspect of this current movement. As stated in the introduction, it also appears that the urban context has been a critical impetus in fostering higher education/community partnerships. The "enlightened self-interest" of which Bensen and Harkavy speak is often urban in character.

Given the flight of capital from urban areas in recent years, residents in poor neighborhoods are left with limited opportunities and are facing greater social isolation.[22] In this increasingly global economy, the corporate world exercises its flexibility and mobility through downsizing and merging (facilitated by advances in technology) on the one hand and by moving to suburban areas or "developing" countries (which provide a wealth of inexpensive labor and land) on the other. These conditions increase unemployment and threaten job security for the working poor. In recent decades, it has become increasingly clear that colleges and universities are among the few significant institutions that remain in close proximity to poor urban neighborhoods. Unlike corporations, academic institutions do not have the option of moving, given the vast acreage of university campuses. Institutions of higher education have a particular geographical interest vested in their surrounding communities.

All of the cities discussed in this book have been significantly impacted by changes in the economy. Philadelphia and New Orleans have experienced significant declines in manufacturing. San Francisco and New York have experienced expansion in downtown areas, but a decline in surrounding neighborhoods. Economic booms in the latter cities have driven real estate and other costs far beyond the means of the majority of residents, exacerbating already vulnerable circumstances for the poor and disenfranchised. Poor residents on the periphery of downtown areas in these cities may fall victim to increasing gentrification.

With universities playing an increasingly significant role in the overall economic health of urban communities, the need for greater engagement among colleges and universities in their surrounding communities is taking center stage. A university or a university-affiliated hospital is currently the biggest employer in approximately one third of all urban areas in this country, effectively blurring the lines between institutions of higher education and the local residents whom they employ. But despite this growing connection in recent years, relationships between institutions of higher education and their neighbors are not automatically harmonious. As has the corporate world, some universities have attempted to wither the job security of existing employees, seeking to limit permanent new hires and replace them with temporary labor. The decrease in employment opportunities has contributed to an increased labor supply for certain types of low-skilled jobs. This has given universities the option of providing lower paying and less stable jobs to urban residents, often through outsourcing agencies, which may provide limited benefits and job security.

These circumstances reduce the overall buying power of residents, contributing to the closing of small businesses and deteriorated housing, in other words, declining property value. Some universities have seized upon these opportunities and bought significant properties. Such property acquisitions in poor urban areas can have a variety of effects, including redeveloped housing and new businesses; however, such purchases do not always benefit residents. Many would argue that they rarely do. Gentrification fueled by universities has tended to displace neighborhood residents and make it increasingly clear to these communities that they are unwanted in their own backyards. Universities have poured funding into private police forces, seeking to protect students from the criminal behavior of urban residents. Such dynamics lead to tension between universities and their surrounding communities manifested in crime, protest, and overall resentment.

Many major research universities such as Yale, Columbia, the University of Southern California, the University of Chicago, and the University of Pennsylvania, among others, sit in close proximity to poor urban neighborhoods. This is common as well for public urban universities, historically black colleges and universities, and community colleges. The contrast, however, is greater at the major research universities, where the student bodies are significantly distinct from the local residents and the university resources far outstrip local ones. The previously popular defensive strategy taken by the academy in relation to their surrounding neighborhoods only fanned flames of resentment among the locals. A recent article by Gurwitt offers a similar analysis to Bensen and Harkavy's, suggesting that universities and colleges in such situations are motivated by an "altruistic self-interest," that if they do not act to improve local conditions, then they could go down with the neighborhood.[23] If a neighborhood is deemed "unsafe" or "deteriorated," a university or college might lose students and especially faculty who are concerned about setting up roots, buying homes, and sending their children to school. Current urban conditions consequently have influenced the recent efforts at community partnerships in higher education. While the concept of community outreach among institutions of higher education is not new, recent socioeconomic circumstances have spawned a new angle—and interest—in approaches to partnerships.

The Necessity for Change in Higher Education

Bensen and Harkavy suggest that higher education's search for relevance in society is critical to its survival. As previously stated, responsiveness to societal needs always has impacted the institutional health of higher education. Academic institutions would probably persist without significant change, but they might thrive by grounding their approach in meeting demand—demand not just by a few, but by the broader society and the local one. This is particularly true in the case of poor and disenfranchised populations, where needs are most severe.

Former director of the Center for the Urban Community in New Orleans and current president of Jackson State University, Ron Mason, suggests that the academy's move toward community partnerships is a matter of "self-preservation." He said in an interview in 1999, "I think if you look closely enough, you're going to see that a lot of the activity is in and around the neighborhood that the school exists in." He continued, "And almost every major city has a major university that started out in a neighborhood and ended up not being in the kind of neighborhood they thought they wanted to live in." His comments once again speak to self-interest rooted in a changing urban landscape. However, Mason argues that the other major motivating factor for institutions of higher education to enter into community partnerships is "that the industry itself is changing":

> I think that employers, parents, and students are looking for more relevant experiences when they go to an institution of higher education. I think that they want to have the experientially enhanced type of activity that makes it a full educational experience. The industry is being required to become more connected to the everyday problems that people face. And it's hard for institutions with these kinds of resources to do just basic research when there's so much need out there to start to apply our work to actual problems and actual suffering that people experience on a daily basis.

Mason speaks to a growing reality in higher education, but, again, this is more the case at some institutions than others and is primarily true of the major research university.

Mason ultimately argues that all of higher education was originally based on a paradigm that was quite inclusive of the kind of work found in today's higher education/community partnerships: "Higher education is built on a theory. Let's say higher education is a stool, and the stool has three legs: research, teaching, and service. There's a reason that it has three legs. The service is there because it keeps the teaching and research honest. It keeps them connected to everyday problems that people have to address. And that is part of what the role of an institution of higher education ought to be." Mason suggests that higher education had never truly evolved into this original "three-legged" conception and is, in fact, "coming into its own." He defines service within higher education as "experiential learning opportunities that enhance the educational process." Such a definition, according to Mason, "works from a university perspective."

Indeed, from the vantage point of a university or college, such a definition probably would be appropriate across the full range of types of institutions of higher education. It is compatible with an overarching higher educational mission because it "enhances the educational process." However, "experiential learning opportunities" may or may not actually benefit communities. How can we find a universally agreed upon approach that can satisfy the needs of both higher education and communities? It is in models of mutual benefit that we will find long-term, healthy partnerships. If experiential learning opportunities are not effectively serving community needs, then communities will not trust institutions of higher education. It could be the case that such learning opportunities do benefit communities, but unless the interests of communities are built into the community partnership, the potential for failure always looms.

Nevertheless, Mason's central point—that higher education is returning to its roots by adopting an integrated approach of teaching, research, and service—is important. Self-interest in the context of a changing urban landscape, linked to the historical conception of service, teaching, and research, is critical in the emergence of the current higher education/community partnerships movement.

External Supporters

One can conclude that the concept of a more engaged and responsible system of higher education, particularly in urban settings, is, as Bensen and Harkavy suggest, a part of a burgeoning social movement.[24] In my travels over the last couple of years, I have witnessed an increasing desire among faculty and administrators to find the best possible ways to partner with local communities. Those internal to higher education are beginning to demonstrate a visible commitment to community partnerships. Concurrently, a number of people and institutions external to academia are promoting the overall expansion and enhancement of such partnerships. As the federal government had been a major force in past changes in higher education, some current initiatives suggest that federal support may further advance today's higher education/community partnerships. State and local governments, foundations, and national policy organizations are also critical players in building this movement. What remains to be seen is whether or not current commitments to community partnerships will lead to long-term changes in how colleges and universities do business.

One of the leading external financial supporters of higher education/community partnership initiatives is the federal government's Community Outreach Partnership Center (COPC) program through the department of Housing and Urban Development (HUD). This effort provides approximately four consecutive years of financial support to community partnerships at institutions of higher education nationwide.

The current director of the COPC program, Victor Rubin,[25] suggests that significant improvement has been made in the field over recent years, as more of the funded institutions are willing to take on numerous interrelated issues in specific neighborhoods and build the capacity of local organizations to address local needs. Strategies aimed at lasting relationships, in which communities can continually count on higher educational resources, are on the rise. In fact, the COPC program is at a point where it discourages proposals focusing on short-term projects. COPC is encouraging the field of higher education/community partnerships to take a long-term approach to establishing trusting working relationships with neighborhood-based stakeholders. As Rubin put it, the program encourages "universities to take things on, take things over, not just find other sources of support, but put things in the core mission and core budget." Important to COPC as well as this book is a two-way analysis of such partnerships. Success in partnership requires internal change for academic institutions and communities. Community-based organizations do not necessarily understand all of the internal dynamics driving institutions of higher education and vice versa. But each party, particularly on the higher education side, should adapt to the respective internal patterns to make the partnerships work. COPC explicitly impacts these dynamics through encouraging central administrative financial support at various institutions of higher education, and "engaging a multiplicity of disciplines and professions rather than just one or two."

Ultimately, COPC is a critical external driving force asking higher education to ensure the long-term security of community partnerships. This level of commitment would require the sustained involvement of more than a handful of individual researchers or departments. COPC is cultivating the development of good examples of partnerships in order to help the field build upon the lessons emerging from these partnerships.

It is important to keep the progress in the field of higher education/community partnerships in perspective. Only so much can change in a decade. The COPC program has been in existence since 1992. According to Rubin,

> It's still true that a lot of these partnerships are motivated in part by the university's need to improve and control its surrounding environment. That's always been the case for a lot of urban universities. But they are, as far as I can tell, much more sensitive—much less arrogant; much less pushing their own agenda by sheer political force or chicanery; and much more actually digging in and doing community development work. So those things are all important. Another thing—I don't know if it's new or not—but in urban public universities there's a close connection between the agenda for inclusiveness in the student body and the need to do constructive community partnerships in the neighborhoods where the students came from.

As previously discussed, the increasing diversity of the student body in some sectors of higher education is another means by which colleges and universities become connected to poor and working-class neighborhoods. Location is not the only motivating factor for a college or university's entry into community partnership. Institutions of higher education are finding multiple justifications for entering this field of work.

The simple question of how to enter communities is one with which many of these institutions grapple. However, as Rubin suggests, the COPC initiative has helped institutions of higher education navigate various questions through practice. There is no reason to believe that your typical university professor automatically will be comfortable sitting in a community center in a poor neighborhood trying to collectively solve problems facing the area. But now that some of this work has begun to evolve, more are beginning to grapple with the question of how to maintain and institutionalize these partnerships and how to do them well. Getting a complex organization, such as a university or college, to find avenues for continued support of new initiatives is challenging. In fact, it has often been the case that what appears to be a university-wide commitment to community actually rests in the hands of a few particularly committed people. Victor Rubin speaks from his experience of having seen such situations:

> There's this sort of "great man" or "charismatic leader" advantage and problem where a lot of these are really dependent on one or two staff or faculty. And an institution that is in that situation has to be able to pass it along—has to be able to train other people to take on this kind of work.

Institutions of higher education often are not designed to support community outreach initiatives for the long term, especially when faculty members are doing the work. Although many institutions refer to tripartite missions of teaching, research, and service, actual institutional mechanisms are not designed to reward "service." The service dimension, especially in major research universities, often is treated as supplemental. The predominance of research as the most legitimate form of scholarly activity even has caused institutions that have historically rewarded community service to shift their agendas. In order for community partnerships to become a true extension of the missions of institutions of higher education, the idea of service on the part of faculty should be legitimated. Many colleges and universities have written mission statements alluding to some notion of service and/or responsibility to societal well being; however, in practice, one begins to see the marginality of outreach activities in the overall institutional agendas. As Rubin says, part of the question of the longevity of higher education/community partnerships "lies within the university rather than the community." He continues:

In other words, if the work becomes central to the academic mission of the university, it's more secure even though it's work in the community. And that's an interesting conversation to have with community members. They're saying, "Can you get me another student to work for me?" And I'd say, "If you can help me show why this is critical to the graduate program, I can probably get you more students and more money than if I just send you one person now and that person helps you write your grant proposal." Planning for the long term and making the case jointly helps. So being in the academic mission in the university, recognizing that this is valuable, is probably the only way, except in cases where the university's very survival depends on having a viable neighborhood. Then they have a very strong business and institutional incentive to stay involved for other reasons. So there's sort of two ways here. One is if there is some kind of economic incentive for the university, they'll stay involved. It is out of self-interest, but hopefully provides something useful for the community. But the other is really changing, particularly graduate education in professional schools.

Rubin's experience as the former coordinator of one of the COPCs for many years at the University of California at Berkeley and his current work at HUD tell him of the necessity to find compatibility between higher educational mission and community needs. As Mason and Bensen and Harkavy also suggest, self-interest from the higher educational perspective is paramount. But while self-interest is important motivation for the university, the work may lead down different paths, not all of which would prove beneficial to the community. Self-interest could lead a university to fully gentrify a neighborhood and displace many of its existing residents; it could improve its public image absent of meeting community needs. However, if community partnerships or, more broadly, social responsibility becomes inextricable from the academic mission of the institution, then the longevity of partnership initiatives is most likely. The academic mission of institutions of higher education is essentially the driving force. Economic and administrative pursuits support the academic mission; they don't drive it. The more that teaching and research intersect with service, the more likely partnerships will survive.

According to Rubin, among the good examples of higher education/community partnerships are those that began with a specific self-interest and later expanded beyond their immediate neighborhood into other areas of community work as a result of their experience. A number of institutions, which neither have an immediate self-interest due to the condition of their surrounding neighborhood nor have a student body that is representative of poor or working-class local neighborhoods, also appear interested in some aspect of community partnerships. Whether readily apparent or not, all institutions of higher education have something to gain from community partnership. Historically, this has been the case given the interconnectedness between teaching, research, and service.

Today, it seems that social circumstances have illuminated the need for a more engaged higher education. Something is in the air, as I have experienced in my travels. Maybe the existence of external funding sources such as COPC is the primary factor for some institutions. However, it seems that higher education is searching for its role in the face of criticism. Maybe it is realizing its potential to create knowledge and improve society beyond teaching and research.

One major effort, Campus Compact, is galvanizing college and university presidents around the "civic responsibility of higher education." Since the effort involves senior administrators in higher education, it is increasingly influential in shaping higher education's search for significance in the twenty-first century. Compact's Presidential Leadership Colloquium has developed a Declaration on the Civic Responsibility of Higher Education, which calls for a "recommitment of higher education to its civic purpose."[26] The declaration sees the education of students in democratic principles as central to the higher educational mission. Through education of this nature, graduates of colleges and universities will exhibit a greater interest in society and their participation in the democratic process. As stated in the declation: "We must ask if we are doing enough for our students, or if higher education, too, is disengaged from the democratic purposes of society. If students are to use their knowledge and skills to make their nation and its communities better places to live and work, we must ask whether the colleges and universities that educate them are, in fact, using their store of knowledge and skills for democratic engagement" (3). The infusion of democratic principles into curriculum is critical to community partnerships. The partnerships are the means by which colleges and universities demonstrate institutional citizenship: "Higher education cannot create good citizens if we in higher education do not practice the democratic principles we espouse" (4).

If the mission of higher education includes community service as a demonstration of democratic principles, then the community partnerships discussed in this book are compatible with mission. However, this burgeoning movement has to recognize the magnitude of the institutional commitment necessary to engage in community partnerships for the long term. Compact's declaration indicates as much, "A successful national movement to reinvigorate the public purposes of higher education will be reflected in the behaviors on each of our campuses, and also in change in the processes by which our campuses are assessed, accredited, and ranked, so that civic responsibility efforts are recognized and encouraged."

It continues, "We also urge you to join in seeking recognition of civic responsibility in accreditation procedures, Carnegie classifications, and national rankings (such as *U.S. News and World Report*)" (4–5). This is where the declaration is most astute in recognizing the comprehensive nature of the task at hand. Rhetorical commitments to community partnerships or, more broadly, "civic responsibility" only begin the journey. As previously stated, research is paramount. It is the primary means by which colleges and universities achieve national recognition. Consequently, many colleges and universities channel their energies toward traditional research even in cases where research historically has not been the primary focus of the mission. Like Mason and Bensen and Harkavy, Compact grounds the current movement in higher educational principles established a long time ago, but if the institutional systems to sustain these efforts are not in place, community partnerships will not be effective. Colleges and universities can reiterate, enhance, and reinforce rhetorical commitments. However, true compatibility between the higher educational mission and community partnerships requires some change in the *functions* of institutions of higher education, accrediting institutions, academic journals, and the many other policy-setting entities in the academy.

For some institutions, these bold visions for deepening higher education's connection to and responsibility for society are a stretch. For others, we may be discussing only a mild reconfiguration in mission and operations. Despite the noble efforts of Campus Compact, is it possible to make a general statement about civic responsibility in higher education given the vast diversity among colleges and universities? The declaration also focuses heavily on the higher educational side of community partnerships, indicating goals to foster greater involvement in service among students and faculty.[27] Of course, as a higher educational policy institute, its emphasis is appropriate. But how important is the impact of these service efforts on communities? It is one thing to be involved in service, it is another actually to be helpful. Being helpful, as borne out in the following chapters, is to hold the needs of the communities as high as those of the institutions or individual faculty, students, or administrators involved. It is to be patient and build trusting relationships. It is to be around for the long haul. This all goes back to the institution's commitment. A course lasts three or four months. Students are on campus for a few years. Faculty research projects last for a few years. Foundation grants always come to an end. Communities, however, are permanent. How can higher education ensure that its commitment is genuine?

Chapter 2

Have Ivory Tower, Will Travel

The University of Pennsylvania and West Philadelphia

If excellence in research breeds prestige, why would a top-flight research university invest in community service? The mission of most major research universities is to produce quality publications written by well-respected professors. These professors should be highly regarded by their peers, who review their work. Yes, teaching is also important. The production of knowledge through research is presented to students in the classroom. But research is the primary aim of these big-name universities, whether public or private. Objectively observe! Talk about what's going on; don't get too involved. This is the image of the major research university attitude—the veritable "ivory tower," removed from the realities of the world. As discussed in the last chapter, service was an important aspect of earlier conceptions of the role of higher education. However, service is unquestionably lowest on the totem pole at the vast majority of contemporary major research universities, even though knowledge production can emanate from community service.[1] At least at this point in history, service does not drive the reputations of major research universities. On the immediate surface, the incentives to be involved in service are not readily apparent at major research universities. The missions of major research universities and community service do not appear to be compatible at first glance. Then why does the University of Pennsylvania, a reputable Ivy League research university, invest so much time and money in its neighboring community? And what do these efforts have to do with Penn's mission?

In a city teeming with universities, the University of Pennsylvania stands out as a major research institution with Ivy League status and substantial resources. Not only is it the most prestigious university in the city, it also happens to be the most significant local employer. The socioeconomic relevance of the University of Pennsylvania has increased over recent years as Philadelphia has lost a healthy amount of its industry.

Founded by Benjamin Franklin in 1740 as the Charity School of Philadelphia, "Penn" had the explicit purpose of serving the city. It was chartered as the first nonsectarian college in 1755, and in 1791 it became "America's first university" with a multidisciplinary curriculum. Penn's mission has always included the merging of theory and practice into teaching and research.[2] Over the years, the university has evolved into one of this nation's premier institutions of higher education, particularly known for its Wharton School of Business. The current written mission of Penn, as stated in its 1997 strategic plan, is "to generate knowledge that is unconstrained by traditional disciplinary boundaries and spans the continuum from fundamental to applied. Through this new knowledge, the university enhances its teaching of both theory and practice, as well as linkages between them" (s-3). Penn's mission statement continues:

> Penn excels in instruction and research in the arts and sciences and in a wide range of professional disciplines. Penn produces future leaders through excellent programs at the undergraduate, graduate, and professional levels. Penn inspires, demands and thrives on excellence and will measure itself against the best in every field of endeavor in which it participates. Penn is proudly entrepreneurial, dynamically forging new connections and inspiring learning through problem-solving, discovery-oriented approaches. Penn research and teaching encourage lifelong learning relevant to a changing, global society. Penn is a major urban university that is committed to strength and vitality in each of its communities. In this connection, Penn will:
>
> - Encourage, sustain, and reward its faculty; nurture, inspire, and challenge its students; and support and value its staff;
> - Strengthen and appreciate the diversity of its communities;
> - Support free expression, reasoned discourse, and diversity in ideas;
> - Pursue positive connections with the city, state, and region and a mission of service to its neighbors in West Philadelphia;
> - Develop and support its connections to alumni and friends; and
> - Foster the growth of humane values. (s-3)

In writing, Penn is committed to working with the local community. It is rooted in the university's history. But how does the commitment play out in practice? Commitment to excellence as a research university is at the core of Penn's "strategic goals." Do community partnerships contribute to excellence in research? Penn aspires to being among the "top ten in undergraduate education" and "moving into the top tier" (s-3). Research universities primarily achieve their prominence through scientific research driven by government funding, not by engaging with local communities. Another dimension of Penn's mission is producing professionals. Professor Lee Bensen says, "Penn's mission is still to produce graduates for industry and business—professional school. That's what the college is doing; they're producing people from the point of view of the student who wants to get a good job." What do community partnerships have to do with students' job prospects? Penn's ongoing challenge is to justify its community partnerships in relation to its mission whether it is related to students' future prospects, faculty research, or the university's economic standing. A number of interrelated factors impact Penn's ability to make community partnerships a central part of its mission over the long haul, such as:

- Penn's public image
- The presence of committed university faculty, administrators, and students
- Multiple departmental involvement in community partnerships
- The commitment of the central administration to community partnerships
- The adaptability of the institutional structure and culture to a supportive environment for community partnerships
- The presence of a central unit to encourage and coordinate outreach activities
- An externally supportive environment among government and funders
- Avenues for residents to influence the direction of Penn's outreach initiatives
- Demographics in the community and the university
- Penn's historical tradition of public service.

All of these factors will help constitute Penn's institutional commitment. These are the factors that ultimately will determine whether Penn's community partnerships go beyond the efforts of a few committed individuals or rhetorical references to social responsibility.

Evolution of Current Outreach Initiatives

For over a century, the West Philadelphia community has lived in the shadow of Penn. Penn relocated to West Philadelphia in the 1870s. Throughout the earlier part of the twentieth century, tensions were high between the University of Pennsylvania and the community, despite Benjamin Franklin's original service-inclusive vision for the institution.[3] In the last decade, circumstances in the socioeconomic conditions of Philadelphia gave rise to a renewed commitment to civic engagement at Penn. Currently, Judith Rodin, the university's president, is supporting an extensive effort to revitalize and build relationships with the local community. The areas of housing, schools, retail, economic development, and safety all are being addressed alongside community-based stakeholders who play the roles of partners as well as advisors. This "urban agenda" is one of six priorities discussed in the institution's overall strategic plan.

Rodin suggests that Penn is experiencing a renaissance of sorts, returning to the original vision of Benjamin Franklin, what longtime scholar of education Ernest Boyer called the "New American College," which connects "thought to action, theory to practice."[4] The concurrent deterioration of urban neighborhoods and the lingering presence of institutions of higher education in close proximity to those areas heightens the university's expected role and responsibility. Rodin said, "America may be experiencing its strongest economy in 25 years, but too many city neighborhoods lack jobs, adequate housing, and decent schools. For Americans living in these urban neighborhoods—and for those institutions located in their midst—this is a recipe for future disaster. Increasingly aware of the scale of this crisis, a number of those institutions are taking action."[5]

An important part of Penn's current community partnership is to admit to previous mistakes. One of Penn's current initiatives explicitly points to the historical mistakes of the institution. For example, during the 1950s, Penn effectively demolished a local neighborhood called "Black Bottom" in order to build what it calls University City. Instead of running from that past, Penn has sponsored a local play to be performed on the incident.

Perspectives on the evolution of current community partnerships vary. While the conditions in the local community pushed Penn to reflect on its responsibility, longtime resident Larry Bell places more emphasis on the killing of a professor in 1995 as the central impetus. He said, "There were some departments of the university that have always been doing outreach, but it wasn't university-wide until a couple of years ago when a professor got killed in the community." He comments that such a response has historical precedent; his organization, the West Philadelphia Partnership, was created after a student was killed in 1959. Another resident, Della Clark, elaborated on the origins of Penn's current community partnerships: "And then they had a couple of students that got killed and shot also in the past two or three years, which prompted them to recognize that they can't build some wall around this university. It's got to connect to the community. And if you connect to the community, the community understands your value, then it will have to protect you and you will have less violence."

A part of the idea of higher education/community partnerships is that institutions of higher education need not set only external examples, but internal ones as well in order to be truly effective at this kind of work. Ira Harkavy, the director of Penn's Center for Community Partnerships, speaks of the democratic responsibility of higher education in its broadest sense, stating, "Well, there were periods when the universities were more democratic here, and they still weren't doing good stuff. They were ripping down homes. Because part of [the assumption you hear on] this side is, 'If we all can converse and have democracy here, then we're fine out there.' I don't believe that. I think you've got to do both."

Penn is dependent upon its immediate neighborhood for survival. It is situated in an urban area with a recent history of poverty and crime. As a result, Penn has an explicit interest in revitalizing the community in order to make itself more attractive to students and faculty. As Harkavy puts it, "If I were to categorize it, I'd indicate that there's a kind of very focused media self-interest that relates to physical location. And I think that that is crucial to Penn and any other large urban research university in the midst of poverty."

Penn did not simply come to a realization of its need to partner more effectively with the community on its own. Outside consultation played a major role. Carol Scheman, Penn's Vice President of Government and Community Affairs, recalled the origins of the current community partnerships agenda: "There are people here who think that they thought them up. They didn't make it up. I didn't think it up. It came from long-term consultation with the community. It actually came from the work of faculty and graduate students—a number of Ph.D. dissertations in which a group of students—particularly from community planning and the Graduate School of Fine Arts—spent their entire dissertation work working with the community on coming up with what was necessary to be done. It was literally years of listening, years of working, years of study, years of surveying."

Academically, Penn's incentive for engaging in community partnerships is knowledge production. Economically, its incentive is based on physical location. As will be discussed later in this chapter, Penn is engaged in numerous economic development initiatives explicitly designed to revitalize the local neighborhood. Jack Shannon, Penn's Managing Director of Economic Development, said of the centrality of physical locale, "If you really are going to support the mission of the university, you have to have that type of vibrant city life that goes along with an institution such as Penn in a city such as Philadelphia. If you don't have that then you have the whole host of problems that starts with attracting the best possible students for your institution all the way down the line to keeping the best possible faculty members, and others here, in." Shannon's remarks demonstrate the interdependent relationship between the university and its neighborhood and the way in which the academic and economic dimensions of Penn's mission intersect. The quality of faculty and students is dependent upon the conditions of the surrounding neighborhood.

Since the university cannot pick up all of its vast landholdings and find another location, Penn must make serious choices about how it wishes to relate to the community. From Shannon's administrative post, he sees the business side of the equation. In other words, revitalizing the local community is good business. It boils down to competition. "So unless you're in what's perceived to be a vibrant and vital community, you're at a distinct competitive disadvantage to others— quite frankly, with the Columbias, Harvards, Yales, and Princetons." Shannon refers to the vibrancy of the community, which does not necessarily attack poverty and other inequalities. An institution can be in a fully gentrified local area, which has displaced poor people of color. It seems that Penn must determine how to meet its self-interest as an institution and concurrently make ethical decisions about assisting the more impoverished residents in the neighborhood.

Harkavy advocated what many at Penn call "enlightened self-interest"—an understanding of decision making based on self-gain, but with a moral and ethical dimension. He explained, "There's a number of faculty and students all motivated by that moral mission. Universities teach far, far more by what they do than by what they say." Apparently, the symbolic aspect of a university's actions affects not only public perception of the institution, but sets examples by which to live.

Vision for Community Outreach

Penn sees itself engaged in a protracted effort to improve the quality of life in local neighborhoods, particularly those west of the campus. Those involved are attempting to design a comprehensive strategy, focusing simultaneously on a number of issues, including schools, housing, retail, economic development, security, and safety. Their approach coordinates interrelated issues because they have seen the shortcomings of piecemeal strategies. Rodin wrote, "Decades of experience and the wisdom of community partners and advisors have convinced us that a piecemeal response to today's urban realities is no response at all. Our approach must be multi-faceted, our resolve stronger than ever."[6] From the perspective of senior administration, therefore, Penn's involvement in the community is not a strategy separate and apart from the socioeconomic direction of the local community. The comprehensive approach to community revitalization is reflected in Penn's stated strategies:

> The University's outreach focuses on five different fronts:
> • Safe, clean, and attractive streets and neighborhoods;
> • Excellent school options;
> • High quality, diverse housing choices;
> • Reinvigorated retail options;
> • Increased job opportunities through economic development.[7]

Penn's community partnerships are the fourth of five goals for the university, indicated in its strategic plan:

> The University will plan, direct, and integrate its government and community relations to enhance its missions of teaching, research, and service. The University also will clarify and strengthen the links between its academic programs and the public service performed by its faculty, students, administration, and staff.

Strategic Initiatives

To achieve this goal, the University, working with the schools, will take the following steps, among others.

> • Strengthen relationships with the executive branch, Congress, and federal research agencies and work aggressively with them to influence program

development and policies that support the scholarly and teaching activities of private research universities.

- Continue to build and maintain effective relationships with the governor and state legislators.
- Build partnerships with corporations, educational institutions, medical institutions, and others that have financially invested in Philadelphia, to share resources and services that strengthen the community.
- Consistent with the University's basic missions of teaching and research, work with the community to promote economic development and increase the quality of life in West Philadelphia.

  Continue efforts to increase University purchases from local businesses.

  Promote business partnerships, public safety, and transportation initiatives.

  Continue efforts to improve local elementary and secondary schools.

  Encourage the development of service-learning programs at the University, in furtherance of Penn's long-standing commitment to the integration of theory and practice.

  Encourage innovative opportunities for voluntary participation by Penn students, faculty, administrators, and staff in appropriate public service activities.[8]

This strategic goal reflects both internal and external dimensions to Penn's commitment to the local community. Not only is Penn focusing on strengthening relationships with local institutions, it is stressing the need for external engagement to enhance its institutional mission. The goal explicitly refers to potential harmony between community partnerships and academic programs. Scheman said, "I think it's important that all of what we do is related to the institution's core mission. I think there are a lot of institutions that have done community service that starts and then fails, and creates expectations and then fails. We've tried to be extremely mindful in doing nothing that is not something in our core interests." Scheman firmly believes that the university should not be engaged in any community partnership activities that "won't last" and are not "solid business decisions."

Rodin has demonstrated a great deal of leadership with respect to Penn's relationship to the community. She grew up in the area, and has now returned as president of the university. Upon taking the position, she convened deans, Ira Harkavy and others to develop rules for research in the community to ensure that Penn's research would not be exploitative of local residents. The presence of community partnerships among the priorities of the strategic plan is, therefore, not out of character for Rodin.

The implementation of Penn's current strategic plan builds upon preexisting initiatives, heavily spearheaded by Ira Harkavy and the university's Center for Community Partnerships. For example, the university established a University City Special Services District (UCD) to coordinate related services, such as sanitation and security, as well as advocate for capital improvements and better services. Another Penn initiative, UC Brite, was a $1 million program to install residential lighting on 123 square blocks. Penn's approach to local schools includes a k-8 school assisted by Penn, which will integrate Penn's resources into the school. Such an initiative is not only a new public school, but a potential model for successful primary education in urban areas facilitated by university involvement. Penn also works closely with the Board of Education in order to enhance the quality of existing local public schools.

The myriad Penn-sponsored community partnerships span numerous aspects of the university. The case for the compatibility of these activities with the economic and academic aspects of the mission is compelling. Not only is the person designing and implementing community partnerships, Harkavy, a strong advocate, but President Rodin is as well. Their commitment is essential to these partnerships. But to what degree are these partnerships truly integrated into the university? How can one really tell when the commitment transcends strategic plans? Rodin's support is probably a good start. The support of presidents and other administrators opens the doors to financial support and provides a protective voice internally. A closer look at the various dimensions of Penn's community partnerships will illuminate some of the other factors that influence the university's level of institutional commitment.

The Various Dimensions of Penn's Community Partnerships

Economic Development—The Major Research University as an Economic Engine

The University of Pennsylvania's economic development strategies to revitalize West Philadelphia include expanded income-generating opportunities for residents, the development of new businesses, and improved housing. Penn has committed approximately $200 million toward these efforts, which are managed primarily by the Office of the Executive Vice President.

Included among Penn's current economic development efforts is an extensive $120 million complex called Sansom Common, which includes residential, retail, and public spaces between Thirty-fourth and Thirty-eighth streets and along Walnut and Sansom streets, directly on the campus. A hotel currently under construction will join new townhouses, a Barnes and Noble bookstore, a café, and a number of other shops. This effort has created activity in the center of campus well into the night in a well-lit setting. Previously, the area had been rather dim and barren at night, sometimes troubled by criminal activity.

One hundred forty new jobs for residents from West Philadelphia are a byproduct of this effort. Penn is making a special effort to hire local contractors and employ a vast majority of locals in the new businesses. Minority business enterprises and women's business enterprises have received 40 percent of the contracts.[9] Since the hospitality industry is becoming the central focus of the city's development, Penn is working with a job-training program to prepare residents to work in a variety of local hotels.

Penn's development strategy built upon the history of other joint ventures between "large nationwide suppliers and local minority-owned businesses," according to Shannon. He described the university's current procedure in developing these opportunities:

> So under the new contract what we're doing is we're taking a whole entire commodity area and saying, "If you're the successful bidder, you get the entire area." You're not going to have, you know, others nipping at your heels and because somebody over in X department has a favorite preferred vendor, they still get the ability to keep them on board." But in order to get that contract you've got to provide us top notch quality services. You have to provide a great price and you also have to be actively involved in as many aspects of the business as possible . . . and show how you're going to take that relationship and build the business, not only for yourself, but for the minority venture partner. And that allowed us to think and create a much better environment so that it did not appear to be touted or perceived as, "You're setting aside business for a minority client or this is all smoke and mirrors for a minority client." Instead, we actually are getting higher quality services because now when a copier breaks down, you know that there's only one copier company on campus.

Access for a local minority-owned business on the one hand and improved services from vendors on the other is the mutual gain. This sort of win/win strategy runs through the various elements of Penn's partnerships. Mutual gain is an important aspect of partnerships, but it is clear that Penn calls the shots. They have the jobs and the contracts. Shannon identifies prospective vendors by scanning a "database of minority businesses, women-owned businesses, and locally owned businesses and [doing] a cross match of business opportunities that we think offers growth potential." Penn also searches for the businesses themselves. These efforts are important for the local community, with good results, but a commitment to community partnerships would suggest a greater role for local residents and businesses in the design of such strategies.

Other economic development initiatives have extended to Fortieth Street on the outskirts of campus, often thought to be a line of demarcation between the campus and community worlds. The centerpiece of the project is a movie theater that showcases independent films. The university enlisted actor Robert Redford and the Sundance Cinemas project to create an "art house" of sorts. The structure also will house a child care center, an art gallery, a bar, a café, a video library, a jazz club, a newsstand, and various informal gathering places.[10] Redford said of the project, "Our Penn site is a great model for integrating ourselves into local communities in a way that will enhance both Sundance Cinemas and the cultural life of the cities in which we will be located."[11] Penn is sharing the cost of developing the site along with General Cinema, which partners with Redford in managing Sundance Cinemas. A parking area and a fresh foods market also will be developed nearby. According to Shannon, for these related economic development activities, Penn is "taking the lessons we learned on Samson Common when 45 percent of the contracts in construction went to minority firms or women-owned firms." Potentially, then, this particular project will serve the community through enhancing services and culture that can be consumed by students and residents.

Penn has paid special attention to jobs for people of color in these efforts. Since it outsources significant amounts of work, hiring strategies for low- and semi-skilled jobs must go through contractors. As a major research university and a significant local employer, Penn is uniquely positioned to demand its own terms. It brokers deals with contractors to ensure that they hire locally and from underrepresented populations, and when it uses its power to the advantage of community residents, partnerships can have a significant impact. Shannon said, "Can I get out of the operating engineers union sufficient minority and female labor to do environmental or mediation contracts, which I just did for the Civic Center, and have 80-plus percent of hours worked by those individuals? Absolutely. Because, you know, base line I can do that 40 percent without even thinking. If I get a good contractor like Turner and really push the unions, I can get 80 percent because their benches are comprised predominantly, at this point in time, of minorities." Along with hiring comes training if Penn pursues a long-term vision for the economic self-sufficiency of its employees and those of its contractors. They sponsor apprentice programs in various trades, which provide a combination of training and employment, enabling residents to develop specialized skills on the job.

Activities of this sort remind us that universities like Penn are businesses—economic engines. When we wonder about how a major research university might be useful to a local neighborhood, it is clear that academics are only one piece of the puzzle. Jobs, contracts for local businesses, and training opportunities are among the most essential needs in many urban areas today. On the surface, this may appear divergent from the higher educational mission, but as stated earlier, the economic development of a surrounding neighborhood assists the academic goals of colleges and universities. As the next chapter will demonstrate, the interdependency between a university and a city's neighborhoods can extend far beyond the immediate surrounding area.

Housing is another critical area of economic development prioritized by Penn. Housing strategies focus on acquiring and rehabilitating property in partnership with city and community groups and providing mortgage assistance for Penn staff and affiliates to remain in the neighborhood. One aspect of this housing strategy is to acquire unsuccessful or incompatible retail establishments to be converted into more useful institutions for the local area.

As previously mentioned, University City was created to geographically distinguish Penn from the remainder of West Philadelphia. It is a triangular stretch of land from Thirtieth to Forty-ninth street. As of April 1998, only about 1,100 of Penn's 16,335 employees lived in University City.[12] As a result Penn is seeking to encourage greater numbers of faculty and staff to live in the local neighborhood without displacing existing residents. This approach is modeled after a Yale University program that started in 1994 and led to the purchase of 280 homes within three years. Penn is providing cash grants of $3,000 per year for seven years or $15,000 up front to any Penn staff member who purchases a home in University City with the intention of staying for seven years. Existing Penn homeowners in the area, through the Home Improvement Loan Program, can receive up to $7,500 in matching funds for external renovations of their houses. Through Penn's Guaranteed Mortgage Program, mortgages are guaranteed at 120 percent of the purchasing price, enabling home sales with no money down. A *Philadelphia Inquirer* editorial stated, "Fact is, the university's future depends on succeeding in this endeavor. That's where Penn is going to be for a long time. The University is already funding 60 percent of the budget for the University City District."[13]

The University Takes Responsibility for Public Education

Penn's housing strategy calls attention to the interrelationship between multiple issues affecting neighborhoods. In order for staff members to live in the neighborhood, they must feel comfortable raising children locally. The school system in particular should be of high quality. Therefore, Penn is partnering with Philadelphia's school district in order to establish a university-assisted pre-K-to-eight public school. Not only would this approach ease the minds of those who would otherwise send their children to private school, it would ease overcrowding in the existing public schools. Penn also is providing the site for another local school. Both are scheduled to open in 2001. While the schools will be public, they will be designed to become models for advancements in teaching and learning. According to a *Philadelphia Inquirer* editorial, "This is notable because most elite universities' participation in k-12 education involves running private academies, not bolstering public schools."[14] The same editorial continues, "This project is a good example of enlightened self interest. Penn needs West

Philadelphia to thrive, to preserve the university's appeal to students and scholars, and good schools make neighborhoods thrive. And it's using patient partnering, not bulldozing ahead on its own, to cultivate its garden."

The Philadelphia Federation of Teachers supports the effort, which has Penn selling two parcels of land to the school district "at nominal cost."[15] The university is making use of their vast landholdings in the provision of a site, while the school district's capital budget is funding the construction of the school. The first school, which will be housed in a renovated building at Forty-second and Spruce streets, will span pre-kindergarten to the eighth grade. This elementary school is not a magnet program. Penn spokesperson, Kenneth Wildes, Jr. said it is important that the school "should be a neighborhood school and not a magnet, and that it be a catalyst for the community."[16] The other school will be the new home for the George Washington Carver High School for Engineering, a magnet school that is currently housed in a former elementary school building with limited space. The new site for Carver High School will be on Thirty-eighth and Market streets. In addition to providing the land for the schools, Penn will provide up to $700,000 per year ($1,000 per student) for the elementary school for ten years after it is built. Although the school district will continue covering the cost for Carver, Penn will make teachers and students available to the high school.

Teachers and tutors through the Graduate School of Education will offer significant academic support at the elementary school. Through this model, graduate students will be exposed to the realities of inner-city education while students in the school will receive better preparation and increased attention. Penn is treating this effort as not only an opportunity to enhance the livelihood of the local neighborhood, but one to improve the training of future teachers in public schools. The long-term potential of this approach could influence approaches to teacher training throughout higher education. Penn faculty and students also will assist in constructing the curriculum at the school. They will keep school teachers abreast of the latest teaching methods, aiding school teachers in the classroom, and enabling teachers from other Philadelphia schools to observe and learn.[17] The elementary school also will house a series of year-round, seven-day-per-week social services, including health care, day care, and adult education.

According to the *Philadelphia Inquirer*, "Penn officials vowed to help in fundraising efforts for every public school in the neighborhood surrounding West Philadelphia and University City High Schools." [18] The elementary school is projected to cost $14 million, serving up to 700 students. Penn staff have begun to represent the university in heading up two of the city's "cluster resource boards."[19]. Susan Furman, Dean of the Graduate School of Education, is the chair of the West Philadelphia Board, while Ira Harkavy is the chair of the University City Board. Each cluster includes a high school and ten to twelve feeder schools. This essentially splits the school district into smaller, more manageable working groups. Josephine Robles, the Center for Community Partnership's coordinator of the cluster resource boards said:

> So the thinking was that if you had this large business organization partnering with a particular cluster, that organization also would bring in additional members from the community, from the local business organizations, that would then work with the schools around whatever goals the particular cluster felt were important and necessary for their schools to achieve. Or for their schools to succeed—their children to succeed. And our mission is to, and I have it right here, is just to coordinate, leverage, advocate through these resources what the children need in order to succeed, not just while they are in school but also once they graduate.

Through Penn representatives Harkavy and Furman, the university builds a pipeline to local schools. The coordinator at the center brings the various resources together, brokering between the schools and the partners. As Robles explains, "So, the school identifies a need in this particular area among our goals and then I go to the partners to say where we can help."

Penn has been able to leverage relationships with various institutions, such as Aramark, a large food service corporation. Aramark owns schools, nurseries, and day care centers, but it has only recently developed relationships with particular local public schools. Robles said, "So we've gotten them to make some major commitments in that sort of career. They have hired some of our kids for the summer and will probably continue in the fall and hopefully expand that. They're also working with us on nutrition curriculums and also food management."

Mellon Bank has also been working with Penn, providing career internships with fourteen slots for local children during the summer. Another burgeoning partnership is with Pierce College, which focuses on business and professional curriculum and is building a Pierce satellite school within West Philadelphia High School. The coordinator said, "What we have been doing really is just identifying the strengths and interests of the particular organizations, then working with our schools to find out what they would like and need from our partners, and then bringing everybody together." She gave the example of the Philadelphia Museum of Art: "We have a place like the Philadelphia Museum of Art which is working with one of our local elementary schools, and they built a mural. They taught the children how to make murals and how to make the tiles—art classes, and the kids will see their work displayed on the side of a building, you know, in their own neighborhood. So they'll get the sense of community and seeing their artwork up someplace."

Robles reflected on the unique role of Penn on the boards: "When you look at the membership of the organizations that they partner with, we are the only university that has taken on a cluster resource board." Penn has broadened the scope of the goals of the boards, which originally focused on school, career, and mentoring. Eventually, Penn met with all of the partners and stressed that they were not looking for short-term gains. They stressed that Penn is more interested in developing long-term relationships and that the partners should take ownership of the work. For example, they did not want places like Mellon Bank and Aramark simply to give donations absent of more direct forms of involvement. As a consequence, Robles says, the partners often come to Penn with ideas: "It's not just us asking them. And I think again because we brought them in, because we engaged them, because they've seen the importance of this, they've been extremely wonderful working with us, and that goes across the board with all of our organizations."

As an economic engine and as an advocate for improved public education, Penn has leveraged its financial and professional resources in partnership with the city. These efforts take advantage of the significance of Penn to Philadelphia. The city government and major businesses have been partnering with Penn in these efforts. The mutual gain goes across the board from improved local conditions for university staff and students to job opportunities and improved education for local residents.

Managing Community Partnerships

Center for Community Partnerships

Much of Penn's community partnership activities are managed by Ira Harkavy's Center for Community Partnerships, which was created in 1992. The Center emerged out of the Penn Program for Public Service, created in 1989. This program replaced the Office of Community-Oriented Policy Studies, once housed in the School of Arts and Sciences. Thus, the main academic vehicle for community partnerships gradually moved closer to the central administration. The current center is tied to the Office of the Vice President for Government, Community, and Public Affairs. Funding for the center comes partly from the university's endowment along with other resources from external sources.

The historical positioning of the center within the university demonstrates the evolution of an institutional commitment to community partnerships. The function of building relationships with local communities gradually has moved closer to the president. Now Penn even is committing some of its greater than three-billion-dollar endowment directly to these efforts.

The stated goals of the Center for Community Partnerships are to:

- Improve the internal coordination and collaboration of all university-wide community service programs

- Create new and effective partnerships between the university and the community

- Encourage new and creative initiatives linking Penn and the community
- Strengthen local and national networks of institutions of higher education committed to engagement with their local communities.[20]

The three stated types of activities in which the center engages are "academically based community service, direct traditional service, and community development."[21] Academically based community service is the direct link between community partnerships and the core mission of the university, as it emphasizes applied "problem-oriented" teaching and research. Penn's approximately one hundred service learning courses are included in this category. Unlike the previously discussed economic development activities, a number of the center's initiatives touch the academic side of the university. The mutual gain between the university and community has been established in terms of economics, but what about the academics? How do community partnerships advance the arts and sciences? The center's work extends far beyond academics, but its coordinating function enables the lessons from community partnerships to feed back into academic departments.

The center promotes community partnerships, but it also teaches the university how to be successful in these efforts. Navigating a local community can be complex. Where does an institution like Penn begin? Churches, schools, local public agencies, local nonprofits, and businesses all are potential players in community partnerships. Understanding the vast array of services and organizations in a community can be as daunting for residents as it is for Penn. The center currently is mapping the community. Mark Barnes of the center said that the map will "allow us to better identify what's out there and better communicate what's out there to community groups so that they can utilize that information to access those types of services."

Penn cooperates with a number of local institutions, but it appears that the university has chosen to treat the public school system as the central neighborhood-based institution. In addition to the School of Education's role in the emerging public school, many of Penn's service learning programs from other disciplines are structured as partnerships with various other schools. The center helped to develop "university-assisted community schools" which bring students, parents, and community members within a particular geographic area together around education and a variety of other activities. The center sees schools as central meeting places with the ability to convene residents of all walks of life. Given the focus on public schools, Penn is forging a direct avenue to the residents most in need of some assistance.

The center boasts an extensive array of programs outside of its central work. One program is called Penn VIPS (Volunteers in Public Service), which is designed to coordinate as well as stimulate the volunteer activities of students, faculty, and alumni. The pamphlet for the program states, "Benjamin Franklin, founder of the University of Pennsylvania, thought that the true purpose of education was to promote service to the larger society. Penn's ongoing work with the community is a true expression of that purpose. The Penn Volunteers in Public Service (Penn VIPS) has been established to provide a vehicle for staff, faculty, alumni, and the West Philadelphia community to work together through community service activities and events." Isabel Sampson, the director of Penn VIPS said, "It is my job to get Penn faculty, staff, and alumni to volunteer to do things in the community. We want to make sure that it's understood that not only do we want our students volunteering, but we also want to set the example by volunteering ourselves."

"Saturday Schools" is one aspect of Penn VIPS's work. Sampson said, "We work in some of the community schools like Salzburger, Turner, Shaw, and we just ask people [we are connected with] to volunteer to teach at these schools [on Saturdays], and they do a variety of things—lots of computer, lots of GED help. Most recently we had a job academy where two of my volunteers developed a program where they help people in the community find jobs." Sampson suggests that Penn VIPS allow the center to take on a number of miscellaneous requests, which might not fall within the parameters of other existing projects. She said, "We're not limited. We don't have to tell people, 'Oh no, we can't accept that request.' We can accept all the requests, and then we can put it out there, and we've been very lucky in that somebody always responds." Although a number of needs in fact can be met effectively, it is also the case that the magnitude of the interrelated issues impacting the lives of local residents cannot be fully addressed by volunteers. Sampson noted that residents often want more, and want more time spent with them. The Penn VIPS program is also working toward an institutional commitment as an extension of the explicit coordinating function of the Center for Community Partnerships. Thus, not only is the center forging ahead, generating its own partnerships, it is providing some cohesion to the vast array of individual volunteer efforts on campus.

Penn's creation of a specific volunteer program helps to consolidate what often has been a challenge for universities. In many ways, major research universities are a collection of independent actors. Faculty especially are encouraged to be entrepreneurial, but not necessarily a part of an overall organizational strategy. Departments often don't communicate with one another. In the face of these limitations, the center prepares the campus to be useful to local communities by tweaking and coordinating the skills and resources of various members of the university community. The underlying suggestion is that change goes both ways. If the goal of community partnerships is to improve local conditions, then what must the university do internally in order to be more effective in those endeavors? The center approaches the university's preparation not only through coordination across the campus, but through training as well.

The center's Public Service Internship program, for example, trains undergraduates during a twelve-week summer program in a problem-solving curricular model to enhance their capacity to engage in local activities. It almost goes without saying that students or faculty are not automatically knowledgeable about the dynamics of working in poor and working-class urban neighborhoods. Training is necessary to familiarize members of the university with the community. By the same token, community-based stakeholders are more empowered when collaborating with an institution of higher education if they are educated about the inner workings of universities. No specific initiative, however, trains residents to navigate the university. From what I have seen in my travels, this appears to be a major need in the field.

Nevertheless, the center does have an initiative to build the capacity of local community-based organizations. While the resources of the university, through community partnerships, might prove beneficial to many local residents, dependency on the university probably would not be helpful in the long run. The Program in Nonprofits, Universities, Communities, and Schools (PNUCS) improves the nonprofit field by way of community-asset mapping and technical assistance from volunteers. A certificate program in nonprofit management and a masters program in community-based nonprofit administration in the School of Social Work also are included in this program. These initiatives put skills in the hands of local organizations to help them effectively address the challenges facing them. The content of this program was community-driven. The center originally convened about twenty-five local nonprofit organizations in focus groups, which asked, "What do you need and what do you want to see?" Mark Barnes, who works with this project recalled, "And after reading their responses, folks were really concerned about whether or not Penn as an institution was just providing lip service and they were going to take their ideas, run with them and create something that will take them over." Once everyone got beyond these rightful suspicions, various areas were identified. The organizations wanted direct technical assistance (especially in fundraising, accounting, and technology), assistance with staff recruitment, and seminars. The organizations also wanted to network with each other. The ideas of these organizations became the basis for the approach of PNUCS. They eventually led to the development of a certificate program.

This example demonstrates the necessary negotiation process inherent in these partnerships. First of all, listening to what local people identify as their needs only enhances the long-term possibilities for productive relationships. One cannot underestimate the significance of building trust among partners in the relative success of community partnerships. Secondly, Penn's public image due to its historical tensions with the community continually will surface. Penn continually must be aware of both its image in the community and its power. In this example, Penn had to yield some power to the local organizations. Rather than deciding on an approach with community input, PNUCS both solicited what the organizations perceived as the priorities and incorporated those perspectives into the work.

The center receives funding from the Department of Housing and Urban Development's Office of University Partnerships, which administers COPC (Community Outreach Partnership Center) grants, discussed in the last chapter. Penn's COPC brings together faculty, students, and staff from the School of Arts and Sciences, the Graduate School of Education, the Graduate School of Fine Arts, the School of Social Work, the Wharton School of Business, and the Morris Arboretum. Getting various departments to work together around a common concern is not an easy task; however, the process of identifying the specific areas around which each of these divisions can be useful has stimulated greater cohesion. The COPC program requires grantees to work with a community advisory board. Penn's advisory board identified the issues around which they think Penn can be of assistance, including entrepreneurship, brownfields and urban flooding, education and job training, information about West Philadelphia, technology, and capacity building for nonprofits and community development corporations.

Overall, the center is the primary coordinating unit for community partnerships. Its work has spun off a number of different activities. Harkavy has played a critical role in not only coordinating existing activities, but stimulating new ones. He and his colleagues directly contact faculty in various departments who have little history working in communities. But, someone like Harkavy demonstrates for faculty precisely how their expertise can be of assistance to the community. The expertise and knowledge are already there, especially in major research universities; the challenge is to leverage such abilities for a greater good. Faculty are forced to ask themselves, "What is the practical application of my research?"

Faculty, Applied Research and Service Learning

Professor Ann Spirn in the Fine Arts Department is one example of a faculty member who has posed this question to herself. She has been teaching service learning courses for several years. Her work in the Mill Creek neighborhood has been an opportunity both to directly engage students in solving real world problems and to implement some of her research. The Mill Creek neighborhood in West Philadelphia developed largely during the late 1800s and early 1900s. Underground flood plains in the neighborhood have been causing cave-ins[22] over the last seventy years. Many areas where these have taken place are now vacant lots. Not only does the situation destroy property, it brings numerous health hazards. The population of the area, which is located mostly in the West Philadelphia Empowerment Zone, ranges from the very poor to middle class, and is almost entirely African American.

Spirn began working on the flood-plains issue in Mill Creek in 1987. She had been doing similar work in the Boston neighborhoods of Dorchester and Roxbury while on faculty at Harvard University. When she came to Penn in 1986, she was looking for a neighborhood where she could address the correlation between flood plains and vacant land. Originally, she and her students were helping to build and design community gardens in the area. They gathered a database and computerized the information. It was through this work that Spirn learned of the Mill Creek watershed. The Center for Community Partnerships subsequently recruited Spirn to work in schools in the neighborhood, and she has been working closely with students and teachers out of the Sulzberger Middle School in developing curriculum. Sulzberger is also a community school, which provides courses for adults on Tuesdays and Saturdays.

Much of the planning for Spirn's work and the application of her expertise is conducted in collaboration with the Mill Creek Coalition (MCC), a neighborhood-based organization addressing various environmental issues, including flood plains. Current initiatives build upon a history of relationships between Spirn and the community over the last twelve years. She recounts,

> That four-year grant [made in 1987] made all the ground work for everything that came since. Basically, we've been working off that database ever since. And working off those relationships that I formed back then with community gardeners. So, for example, Frances Walker lives across the street from Aspen Farms community garden, And most of her neighbors are members of that garden. There are fifty gardeners. We worked to help redesign that garden in 1987 to 1988, and I'm still involved with them, and I've brought them into contact with the schools. So everything sort of came out of those—the intellectual base, the data, and the social contacts all came out of that early work. And then I moved my base into the school; Ira Harkavy recruited me as a faculty member to start doing some community school work. And I started doing that in 1994.

This example demonstrates the value of consistent relationships between university-based stakeholders and community-based constituents. The relationship may begin addressing one particular issue, but the continuous collective discussion about the state of the neighborhood leads to other ideas and other strategies. Once the relationships are solidified, numerous avenues can be taken. All of the previous work in Mill Creek is now being incorporated into a "comprehensive community plan for the neighborhood, cosponsored by the Mill Creek Coalition."

Since Spirn has resided in close proximity to these residents, she feels her relationships are stronger and interdependent. She said,

> Because I'm a neighbor it makes it, I think, easier. I automatically know who to talk to. I already know who the formal leadership is. And the people you'd better talk to or else you're not going to get anything done because this is a strong

community base.... Neighborhoods are the thing here. And neighborhood groups, if you don't work with them, you're stuck. So we all have the informal method and the formal method. I work with all of the community groups in the immediate area. And I'm going to be on the Board of the West Philadelphia Partnership.

By living in the area, Spirn has a stake in the well-being of this locality. Her example relates back to the housing issue. If Penn's housing efforts are successful in the long run, mixed economic communities will be created, where faculty and administrators will have even more compelling reasons to ensure the continuous improvement of the neighborhood. One way in which Spirn is able to maintain a consistent presence in the neighborhood is by incorporating neighborhood involvement into her courses. Spirn is both a faculty member within the Graduate School of Fine Arts and the codirector of the Urban Studies Program. She leverages this joint appointment to teach one course per semester in the neighborhood. She teaches a graduate course through Fine Arts and an undergraduate course through Urban Studies. She said of the situation, "It's very important for continuity to always be here and not disappear one semester and then suddenly you're back a whole year later."

This comment stresses the significance of consistency to successful community partnerships. Institutionally, course schedules are not designed for year-long relationships with local communities. Spirn creatively finds ways to remain working with the community through her courses for consecutive terms. The students come and go, but Spirn is the consistent force. This enables her to forge trusting relationships with the residents in the neighborhood, facilitating the entry of future groups of students into the area. Overall, Spirn is a good example of how both teaching and research needs can be met through community partnerships. Although major research universities have high expectations of faculty in research and publication, creative efforts can allow service and research to be complementary. The broader mission of knowledge-production is being served through teaching, research, and service in the work of Spirn and others like her.

Spirn's service learning courses are only a few among many. These courses tend to transcend disciplines. They are heavily concentrated in the School of Arts and Sciences, but they branch into the professional schools. Joann Weeks of the center made particular mention of the involvement of the departments of anthropology, history, and English. The role of the School of Education, as previously mentioned, has also been significant. Weeks said, "We are beginning to crack into biology and some of the other sciences, and the School of Engineering has come a long way in working with us." Engaging the various departments is a continuous challenge. "Ira has always wanted to get the medical side of the campus much more involved. It just makes sense, but it's a struggle."

She did mention that the dental school has been responsive. While one might wonder about a dental professor's interest in community partnerships, faculty in that department have been rather innovative. Dental and geology faculty have been working on projects that teach middle school students science. They ask the middle school kids to collect their siblings' baby teeth to analyze them for lead content. When high lead content is identified, the students have to trace the potential sources of lead.[23]

Bill Labov, a longtime linguistics professor at Penn, along with African-American students from the Dubois House on campus transformed the nature of tutoring to African-American youth in West Philadelphia. In the midst of the ebonics controversy,[24] Labov and the students focused on the need to tutor African Americans based on their cultural and linguistic patterns. They created the entirely student-led "hip hop center" to develop innovative tutoring styles targeted specifically to African-American youth. This is because, as Labov explained, they found that "hip hop has had a transforming effect," that it was "the most powerful motivating force for kids as young as the second grade." Labov's own research has been transformed due to these experiences. As a linguist, he has been able to identify various forms of practical application in teaching people how to read: "A lot of our work consists of taking the rhythms of ordinary speech and trying to transform it into things that the kids will recognize as being their own." Professor Lee Bensen sees literacy tutoring as one of the important roles that Penn can play. This is one area where he thinks Penn's community partnerships could improve. In his eyes, further attention to the issue would be an opportunity to engage numerous departments on campus. He said, "There is no set of faculty and students who are working on what is an enormously complex problem—and that is, How do you get inner city African American kids to learn how to read? That requires sociology, psychology, economics, linguistics, history, etcetera, etcetera."

The center's mission to coordinate has had many successes in expanding the reach of community partnership activities. Service learning has been a relatively easy way to get particular faculty members in various departments directly involved without disrupting the essence of their work. They already must teach; the center simply asks them to make the teaching relevant to the community and give students real-life learning experiences. But, as Bensen suggests, the challenge of coordinating multidisciplinary involvement is an uphill battle due to the historical structure and culture of universities. He said, "Universities are fragmented beyond belief. Every individual professor teaches his own course without any reference to whatever else goes on in higher education. There aren't two courses in the history department that ever have been given in any way that have any relation to each other except that they happen to be in the same chronological period, in the same country." He continued, "Universities have become conglomerates of individual entrepreneurs who are concerned only about their own specialized interests." Bensen emphasizes that higher education does not have to be stuck in this mode. The current culture in higher education, as discussed earlier, is a function of the development of the contemporary research university. Universities were not always operating in such a manner.

Taking the Show on the Road—Penn and Other Institutions of Higher Education: PHENND and WEPIC

Penn is becoming one of the better known universities for community partnerships. Its experiences could help a lot of other colleges or universities collaborate with their local communities. Being a major research university, it has the opportunity to bring significant credibility to higher education/community partnerships of all types. But, while major research universities have a lot to offer, other types of institutions of higher education bring a different set of skills and experiences to the table. In Philadelphia, Penn is one of a number of other colleges and universities. The PHENND Consortium (the Philadelphia Higher Educational Network for Neighborhood Development) allows Penn to partner with other local institutions of higher education around issues affecting Philadelphia. PHENND, now with thirty-six members, was formed in 1987 to encourage local institutions of higher education to involve their students and faculty in neighboring communities. The consortium is administered through Penn. PHENND's director, Karl Nass, describes their work, "So what we do with the thirty-six higher eds in the region is seek ways to support, to strengthen, and to build a higher ed community partnership. We do this through a variety of ways—providing various grants, sub-grants, faculty course development similar to those that are awarded through here, across the region."

PHENND's origins date back to 1988 when Ira Harkavy got together with representatives of Temple and other universities. Joann Weeks, also on staff at the center, said of PHENND, "We're really just trying to see what higher eds can do and how one higher ed could help goad others into doing more." The initiative is expanding rapidly. Its membership increased by eight institutions last year and expects to add four more next year. Indeed, many of these institutions do not have the extensive involvement of Penn in their local neighborhoods, but the discussions among the members creates a sense of best practices for the work, guiding some of the less experienced institutions with models and lessons. Recently, the consortium held a forum on civic responsibility, which assessed the field of higher education/community partnerships in the region. Teams of faculty, staff, administrators, and students from various local institutions of higher education discussion critical questions regarding the progress and gaps in the field.

The initiative provides small grants of between $3,000 and $4,000 to encourage specific institutions of higher education to develop particular community partnership projects. They received twenty-eight proposals, when only nine grants were available. Obviously, PHENND has helped to stimulate significant interest in community partnerships among other universities. Partnering with other institutions enables Penn to share its lessons with others and comparatively reflect on its own approach. The more Penn becomes recognized as a leader in the field of higher education/community partnerships, the more important is its relative institutional commitment to enhancing and expanding its current efforts. Its involvement with other universities may raise expectation of Penn's ability to deliver for communities.

Mediating between Penn's resources and the community is the West Philadelphia Improvement Corps (WEPIC), which addresses another aspect of Penn's relationships with public schools. WEPIC is a school and community revitalization program founded in 1985. Its goal is "to produce comprehensive university-assisted community schools that serve, educate, and activate all members of the community, revitalizing the curriculum through a community-oriented, real-world problem solving approach."[25] Through WEPIC, Penn works with thirteen public schools, but most intensively with six, including two high schools, one elementary school, and three middle schools. The West Philadelphia Partnership, a collaboration of neighborhood organizations, community leaders, institutions (including Penn), and the School District of Philadelphia, coordinates WEPIC.

Like PHENND, WEPIC is another means by which Penn influences the approaches of other institutions of higher education. As a major research institution, Penn has convening power. In other words, when Penn creates an initiative and invites other institutions to the table, the others actually attend. WEPIC is a replication project, which assesses the feasibility of the development of university partnerships with public schools and local communities around the country. This is a formal avenue through which Penn can share its lessons with other institutions of higher education nationwide, as well as gain from the lessons of those universities and colleges. According to the program's director, Joann Weeks, "We've used this as a vehicle to ratchet up the level of interest in university-community school partnerships in the sites that we've been working with."

Through WEPIC, Penn now works with nine sites. As Weeks describes the program, "The work all has to be school-based and interested in this k to 12 partnering, but each project has its own slight variation, and it really has let them grow." The collaboration examines various "extended school service" models that are being adapted around the country. They emphasize strategies for bringing the community resources to assist schools. They stress keeping school doors open throughout the day and evening, and bringing in new programs in the after-school hours. Weeks said of the various models,

Some of the other models are much more traditional youth development type models. And to bring in both social workers and youth workers—those type of people to run after school programs, and it's less connective and back to the school day. So we're really trying to help them make the marriage of the two. And much like PHENND, we run an annual national conference that has averaged about 150 people or so in the last couple of years.

Thirty universities attended the last conference. Similar to PHENND, WEPIC brings Penn in contact with other types of institutions of higher education. When asked about the significance of the type of institution of higher education in helping or hindering community partnerships, both Nass and Weeks spoke of the challenges of institutions with fewer resources. Weeks described one of her partners at a community college:

> From the college side, David's biggest challenge right now continues to be reaching out to faculty. He's only got at this point a really small cadre of faculty working with him. It's the non-traditional-age student. . . . And he's making [community partnership] a big part of his course and other faculty members', but it's a big issue. You've got people who don't live right on campus like us. They're twenty, thirty miles away.

One of the clear advantages of these intercollegiate partnerships is the ability to identify the factors that impact an institution's ability to engage in community partnerships. As will be discussed in chapter 5, the dynamics of partnerships are extremely different when the student body largely *is* the community, and when the campus is a set of buildings intermittently dispersed among other community-based institutions. The University of Pennsylvania not only enjoys the advantage of significant resources, but also has a relatively uniform student population with which to work. Most students live on campus and are in a particular age group. On the other hand, Penn does not have an overwhelming number of faculty and students of color who might bridge the gap between the university and local neighborhoods as is the case in all of the other colleges or universities featured in this book. Moreover, Penn is not an institution renowned for its activist tradition, and it does not attract an identifiable cadre of activists in the administration and faculty.

Two Sides of Change—How Penn and the Community Adapt to Community Partnerships

It is important to note that both institutions of higher education and communities can gain from community partnerships. None of the examples in this book should be seen as charitable activities; they are more like strategic alliances that advance institutional goals. The University of Pennsylvania gains immensely from its community partnerships, maybe more than the community. Mutual gain is the ideal end goal. Administratively, economically, and academically, institutions of higher education gain from community partnerships. In other words, these various examples of community partnerships are not marginal to the mission of Penn in all of its dimensions. In fact, they complete the higher educational mission. For communities, if they are effective they add valuable resources to help increase the self-sufficiency of local entities.

Because partnerships of this sort have not been perfected, the management of them is a work in progress both for institutions of higher education and for communities. While both Penn and the local community are realizing some gains from the partnerships, each must adjust in order to continue to enhance the partnerships. For the community, this could mean increasing the capacity of community-based organizations and improving collaboration among local actors. For this university, this means institutional change. Given the power of Penn in relation to the community, it is particularly incumbent upon the university to make the necessary institutional changes to adapt to community partnerships. In order for community partnerships to work over the long term, universities or colleges must be institutionally committed. They should provide an atmosphere that is conducive to the advancement of community partnerships. While Penn has found compatibility between community partnerships and its existing mission, the university must internally adapt if partnerships are going to grow and improve, especially if they are going to yield positive outcomes for local residents. Nevertheless, Penn is one of the more committed universities of its type.

Impact on Campus Life and the Community

Among major research universities, Penn is leading by example, taking the angle of mutual interest, explicitly maintaining that community partnerships create advantages for both the university and the community. Campus life has directly and indirectly benefited from community partnerships. For example, partnerships have stimulated greater internal communication and enhanced a common sense of mission among departments. There has been an increased interest in Penn because of community partnerships, particularly among students. Through Penn's extensive service learning courses, students have been exposed to experiential learning opportunities and have been in communication with populations they may not otherwise have approached. The nature of service learning enhances students' abilities. According to Harkavy, "The students who are engaged in this work are much more active and engaged in collaboration and creating courses. And they are doing creative work." He discussed further, "Students are more active, faculty are more engaged in problem solving, in terms of how it impacts on the west Philly stuff, faculty are more involved, student ideas are getting taken much more seriously." Professor Lee Bensen noted, "Engaging undergraduates in the research experience, it seems to me, has an enormous power for the students because you give them the skills to solve real problems and also do very serious study. And that seems to be another real benefit." Of course, Bensen refers to skills that will enhance students' effectiveness in the job market.

However, Bensen was very candid when asked about the degree to which service learning benefits communities and the distinction between public relations for the university and community partnerships that work for both the university and the community. He said, "Our public relations is now 'four thousand Penn students during the course of an undergraduate career who volunteer here.' Sounds very impressive—has remarkably little effect, remarkably little effect. It's useful to the students. In some cases, they do it because it looks good on their resume. They're told by career placement service, 'Show that you've done community service.' It makes them feel good—eases their conscience and the like. It's not that they're not good-hearted or well-intentioned; we don't have the structure so that this would actually operate [a structure that would ensure that service learning benefits that commuity]." The issue of structure is critical. Bensen and Harkavy believe that the entire university should see community partnerships as a priority in order to bring about the necessary structure. The center appears to be working toward this goal, but Bensen's quote suggests that they are a long way off. The important point is that the internal structure of the university is a central factor in determining the impact of these partnerships on communities. Penn can justify partnerships academically and economically for their purposes, but the structure and culture of the institution hinder the effectiveness of partnerships in challenging the very issues in the community that they were designed to address.

While the benefits for the community, outside of jobs and contracts for local businesses, may be less clear, the improvement in the Penn/West Philadelphia relationship has been noted in many circles. According to a *Philadelphia Inquirer* editorial, "In the past, some residents charged that the university wasn't doing enough for the area, and in fact was disparaging the neighborhood to both students and faculty. If that ever were true, it isn't any more."[26] Scheman noted the change as well: "There's a substantial difference [in terms of] coming together to talk about issues. It's not that everything's terrific, but that the relationship is there. We're meeting together to work through problems. So that, for instance, this community library that's on the corner of Fortieth and Walnut— four years ago, you know, I would have been coming in to these people screaming and yelling. Now the meetings are, 'OK, now how can we get this done?'" If anything, communication has gotten more productive and healthier relationships are being constructed. These are positive outcomes in themselves. They are the necessary precursors to truly making a difference in the life circumstances of local residents.

Community perspectives on Penn community partnerships are varied. However, many former local critics of Penn now work closely with the university. For a university like Penn with a once contentious relationship with the community, to enter the neighborhood offering assistance is not an overnight process. Years of relationship building are required in order to establish genuine ties.

When asked about the outcomes of Penn's efforts, resident Larry Bell indicated that the construction projects worked very hard to get community people employed. Della Clark provided another resident perspective: "I just think there's been better communication. They're informing the community better with some of their intentions and plans—what they want to do—and open[ing] up their window to the community in terms of their plans." Bell acknowledged the university's improvement in listening to the community, but he also pointed to some specific examples in which it took a different direction than the community suggested. He recalled,

> For instance, the Sansom Commons thing that they did was all internal. I'm sure they went out to the community and talked once they had the plan set. Actually the community wanted them to do the bookstore farther out to actually draw all the students out to that area. . . . But where we wanted them to put the bookstore, they're actually going to put a supermarket there.[27]

He also noted that the school project was designed independently, and the community was brought in only later. He characterized this approach as, "We decide we want to do this here, now let's get the community involved to make it happen, as opposed to the other way around." Along these lines, Clark added, "Well, when you've got an institution like this, which I refer to at times as King Kong, a big hairy vivacious gorilla, I mean what do you expect? It can swoop over anything it wants, right? So when you talk about process, the process is whatever they want it to be. And it's just a matter of where they want us to be involved in it, to be quite honest with you."

Bell and Clark speak to the power dynamic between the university and the community. Input means something different to some university administrators and community residents. Residents not only want input, they want to be involved in shaping the direction of the partnerships. After all, all of these efforts immensely impact residents' everyday lives. If partnerships truly are going to reach the stage of mutual gain, avenues for community voices to shape and initiate partnership activities should be actively encouraged. As previously stated, residents and community-based organizations are going to need a certain level of technical capacity and political savvy to engage major institutions like Penn. Clark said, "It behooves the community to try to stay up to date, stay current, to professionalize themselves as much as possible, so that when they come to the table, Penn will want to do business with the community, so that it's not just a

Penn thing, it's a two-way street in terms of the community. You know, in terms of coming ready, knowing what you want, knowing what you can offer. I mean those things; they help Penn to make a decision faster and better." Both Clark and Bell firmly believe in small business development. They would like to enhance the capacity of small businesses to deal with the university and secure contracts. Neither of them thinks enough is being done either to contract to local small businesses or to build their capacity. Bell suggests that funding be targeted to build the capacity of community organizations partnering with universities. Clark suggests that instead of facilitating summer internships for students in Fortune 500 companies, they should be in local small businesses, where their services are most needed. The Wharton School of Business, which could be a conduit for such an idea, does not do nearly enough for the community, according to Clark.

Those university staff or students who are known for being committed to local issues are sometimes viewed differently from the institution as a whole. Clark and Bell see Harkavy as the key figure in Penn's community partnerships. Both of them think that many of Penn's initiatives would disappear were he to leave. In conversation, Clark distinguished Ira's "personal mission" from any "university mission." Bell said, "Ira's agenda is whatever the community wants as opposed to putting Penn's agenda first."

Professor Spirn, from her experience of direct engagement in the same neighborhood for over twelve years, does not think the image of the university in the community has changed very much. Some community members have also seen her as exceptionally committed, distinguishable from Penn being institutionally committed. She said, "Sometimes someone will say something about the university, and they'll go, 'Oh, we don't mean you Ann.'"

Penn has developed a number of systems designed to ensure that their outreach efforts are successfully addressing some of the priorities of local residents. The university works with advisory committees, some of which allow community representatives to shape entire programs. But, as the comments of Clark and Bell suggest, some of these lines of communication are ineffective in providing a community voice. In a less formal sense, Harkavy and some others who have a long history of doing this kind of work are personally acquainted with the local leadership, enabling ongoing dialogue. Penn also sets some short term goals that can be readily evaluated a year from now.

The Center for Community Partnerships realizes the need to demonstrate explicitly outcomes of community partnership activities to residents. Not only does this build trust, but it gives everyone involved a sense of accomplishment. Sometimes the center simply participates in small activities to meet an immediate request. Harkavy said, "We deliver stuff, like, do you need volunteers for a clean up? That's important. It means an immediate response." Therefore, in order to achieve longer-term positive outcomes for the community, it is important to build momentum through various readily-identifiable short-term outcomes.

But, setting targets is itself not an easy task. How does one choose among the myriad needs of a community like West Philadelphia? Since the priorities of local residents and those of the university are not always in sync, decisions about the direction of community partnerships are negotiated processes, although it does appear that Penn initiates a significant amount of the activities. According to Harkavy, however, discussions with community representatives often take place prior to the development of Penn-sponsored activities.

Community residents learn a great deal about universities when involved in partnerships of this sort. As an exclusive world, higher education, particularly at the major research university level, is not a realm readily understood by those who have not been intimately exposed to it. In other words, many in poor urban neighborhoods do not fully know what a university has to offer prior to community partnerships. Harkavy said, "And they begin to know only when you begin to create relationships. That's the only way. We don't know what we have to offer. My own horizons have changed in these engagements." Partnerships are mutual learning processes. He continued:

> The folk know a lot, but they don't know everything. If they knew everything, things would be different. Now we don't know a lot too. So you can't bash it. It has to be together, and you have to face why would they know, and even why would you fully know? It's only in the engagement that you begin to do it. That's one of the tensions on the administration side. But people don't know the academics. They don't know what's in this institution because they haven't had experience with what these fields could offer.

Once again, the process of partnership is key to finding mutual benefit. What is the potential of higher education/community partnerships? We don't know. However, the more time spent crafting these relationships, the deeper both parties are willing to go, the more everyone will learn. The potential benefits, as well as conflicts of interest, will be highlighted when the necessary time and energy are put into building partnerships. Both the university and the community gain, but clear long-term results regarding the living conditions of residents are far off. Is a university like Penn prepared to do what it takes internally to keep partnerships afloat?

Incorporation into Long-Term Mission and Operations

The incorporation of this level of social responsibility into the campus takes many forms. One of the persistent questions surrounding the university's role in community partnerships is, What constitutes and institutional commitment? How do we know when the commitment to sustaining and enhancing community partnerships transcends the efforts and interests of a handful of especially committed faculty, administrators, and students? In complex organizations the size of Penn, it is difficult to determine which efforts are of the university rather than the initiative of specific individuals or departments. As previously mentioned, the task of Penn's Office of Community Partnerships is to coordinate community partnership activities on campus. However, this is not easy to do. The commitment of President Rodin is a critical factor in increasing the likelihood of institutionalizing these kinds of efforts, not to mention the commitment of specific other stakeholders such as Harkavy, the various professors teaching service learning courses, and the students taking them. However, coordination of all of this work into one incorporated whole has been difficult. Harkavy said of the need to coordinate the various departments, "We have a long way to go, and we have lots of departments. And even our most successful departments, we probably could be more successful. So I want to make that clear."

Internal reward systems are an important means to developing a coordinated long-term effort and solidifying an institutional mission. Penn's written mission statement includes explicit language about "practice"; however, it is difficult to determine whether internal operations actually support the longevity of community partnership activities. If reward systems do not exist for faculty members to engage in partnerships, then partnerships are not a part of their jobs. If this work is not an expectation for a faculty member, then it is not fully incorporated into the mission of the institution. Given status tiers among faculty, some have more flexibility to be involved in community partnerships than others. Full, tenured professors do not have the same pressure to publish as junior professors, therefore they have the freedom to be involved in numerous applied efforts. The achievement of tenure at Penn appears to be based primarily on research and publication, which is not uncommon for a major research university. However, in setting an example as an externally engaged institution, it would seem logical that these internal tenure criteria would change accordingly—to support the community service aspect of its mission.

Harkavy suggests that Penn still has room for improvement in this area. He said, when asked if there were cases of junior faculty who achieved tenure due to exemplary work in the community, "In one or two cases. Anthropology hires people to do this and there have been a few people who got tenure. Overall, for most of the assistant professors, it's not advisable. It's senior faculty who are the ones who do this work—high-profile, powerful individuals. But, then again, there are some associate professors in there."

On the one hand, the fact that tenured professors are engaged in this work is admirable. The local community gains access to seasoned professors with a wealth of information and knowledge. However, new ideas and energy often come from junior professors. Moreover, given the limited tenure opportunities for professors of color, particularly in Ivy League institutions, few faculty of color are involved in these partnerships, which happen to be primarily in communities of color. The West Philadelphia area is significantly of African descent. Those residents generally are not given the opportunity to interface with faculty of a similar racial and ethnic background.

The tenure issue appears to be without resolution in the near future. It is a deep tradition with high esteem, particularly in major research universities. It does appear that broader systemic change beyond Penn as an individual institution would be required for any radical shifts in the criteria for tenure. Harkavy said, "You have to change the higher system from multiple levels, so have we changed the reward systems? In some areas, yeah. In some, we've taken the lead. But overall, no. Can we do it alone? No. You have to change the system." He suggests that "civic responsibility should be measured as one of the key bases for valuing universities."

The approximately one hundred service learning courses Penn offers are an avenue toward institutionalizing community partnerships into the curriculum—an essential aspect of developing a long-term institutional commitment. Since Penn's service learning courses transcend all disciplines and involve faculty members at every level, they have the potential to influence other aspects of the university. This is where the Center for Community Partnerships has been able to make some institutional progress—by approaching the various departments and demonstrating to various faculty how their research can be applied to local neighborhood-based situations and how their students' learning can be enhanced. Conversations of this sort lead to the development of service learning courses. This continual process has been, and probably will continue, expanding the perspective of the value and potential of academic work in practice.

Through the multiple service learning courses, Penn has galvanized a cadre of faculty committed to community partnerships; however, as Cory Bowman of the Center for Community Partnerships notes, "Faculty aren't really responding to this as an institutional mission." Nonetheless, he sees this as an opportunity from which to build: "I think that they all keep doing it. I think part of the greatest success of this work is that every course that has been created—but more important, every existing course that's been converted toward this kind of pedagogy, toward this kind of teaching research—has kept doing it, is giving us a based from which to expand. It's really by building upon that circle of folks that have tried this kind of work [that we'll go forward]." In seeking indicators of institutional commitment for community partnerships, a "cadre" of faculty certainly would be near the top of the list. While, ultimately, true institutionalization would transcend a small group of people and enter reward systems more explicitly, Penn has done a good job of mobilizing faculty in different departments. Many of these faculty are the only ones in their departments harboring these sensibilities, but they are strategically placed. One faculty member in a department in collaboration with other faculty members in similar positions in their departments is progress. Through this approach, various departments have an avenue to community partnerships even if only one faculty member is involved.

Ann Spirn is an example of a faculty member who is the only person in her department involved in community partnerships. Her dean, however, is very supportive. The support of the senior administrator in her department, coupled with the overall support of the president, gives her the space to continue and enhance her research on flood plains and her service learning courses. Spirn is satisfied with the level of institutional support for her work. She said that the institutionalization of community outreach at Penn is "bigger than anywhere I've ever seen." Spirn herself was effectively solicited into Penn's community partnerships by the center. She recalled:

> I was recruited from Harvard to come here and be the chair of the Department of Landscape Architecture and Regional Planning. I showed up. Summer of '86, there's a phone call to me from Ira Harkavy and Lee Bensen, "How about lunch?" Well, I didn't know who these guys were. But they wanted to introduce themselves to me. They already knew who I was. They sat me down for lunch and both of them had read my book, which had been published in 1984. It's called *The Granite Garden: Urban Nature and Design*. It's about the designing of nature in the city. And they made this pitch to me. I remember Lee Bensen saying, "Your vision, we read your vision for the city design, you know." He said, "West Philadelphia is your opportunity to make your vision real."

As an internal educator and coordinator, the Center for Community Partnerships is engaged in an ongoing dialogue within the university. Although the community outreach initiatives are part of the strategic plan, well-publicized and generally well supported, there is still some uncertainty about why this work is important for the university. The Office of Community Partnerships is charged with the task of constantly refocusing the institution to ensure a collective understanding of the vision. Harkavy said, "I sometimes get—you know I've been doing this for a long time, since I was a student activist. I can't believe sometimes, that folks I've worked with don't recognize the why's and why *here*. I have to go back to it and have a discussion. That happens a lot."

They have their cadre, and they are beginning to win over skeptics. Bowman made reference to a particular dean who gradually warmed to the idea: "He used to [preface his opinions as] 'comments from a skeptic.' For the last several years, he's been talking about starting a presentation from a partially converted skeptic. And he would talk about it. He was very serious about this, and this year, at our campus-based conference on academically based community service, he labeled himself as fully converted and largely evangelical." Some of the changes in thinking in this dean and others emerged in response to the results of a survey of undergraduates. Only two areas received high ratings in the survey; one was study abroad, and the other was service learning. It turned out that over 20 percent of the graduating seniors took a service learning course that they found to be significantly rewarding.

Despite the gains, coordination among the various departments remains daunting. Some departments are still out of the loop. Penn's esteemed Wharton School of Business could add significant expertise and resources to the community, but it has not been very involved. Among those departments and divisions involved in community partnerships, coordination still could be improved. Harkavy said, "Our schools program, our community of faith program, our nonprofit program, our cluster program . . . we here at the center have to integrate that more, keep working toward a real aggregation."

Even the various faculty involved in service learning do not have formal opportunities to come together to coordinate among themselves and share lessons. On the one hand, the Center for Community Partnerships is the common denominator. On the other, it can only do so much. When asked about how the university had pursued opportunities for faculty coordination across departments around community partnership activities, Professor Spirn responded:

> Not as much as we should probably. I'm not really aware, for example—except through hearsay—of what's going on at other schools. I'm the only faculty member right now involved in Sulzberger. That's actually an area [where] I would welcome some more interaction. There's a kind of loose group of people that have been doing this for a long time that I talk to for advice, or just for talking about what we're doing. But it's not organized. There's an advisory council to the center. Those meetings, in a way, serve that kind of function. But it's not really sharing your experience so much. It's reporting what the center has done and asking for advice.

She said further, "It's like any big institution. You communicate with some people more than others. And some of it has to do with proximity." Like most complex organizations, Penn is a loose conglomeration of subgroups, interest groups, and informal decision-making bodies.

It may be too much to expect academic departments to be in coordination around all of the campus community outreach initiatives. Karl Nass reflected on what he has seen in other institutions of higher education through PHENND:

> Regardless of the size, those institutions that have coordination of their outreach efforts between the more traditional volunteer activity out of campus ministry, or whatever else, and then a faith justice institute that might be a bit more academic

based or service learning based [have] the constant tension that happens . . . and yet, the best practices we've seen are those where they have acknowledged the tension and worked to overcome that.

Among those campus-based units involved in outreach, there may be overlap. Nass suggests that whether or not they actually are coordinated, those who get through such tensions most effectively are those who acknowledge the nature of the situation. Dialogue among the various outreach activities on campus is central. One of the general complexities of most institutions of higher education, especially major research universities, is the entrepreneurial nature of the environment. When outreach initiatives are tied to outside funding, particular programs, departments, centers, and institutes ultimately may be vying for the same pool of resources—vying for the right to be the community liaison. Acknowledging these institutional realities, Harkavy notes that funding for community partnerships is not all funneled directly through the center and that he sees the Center for Community Partnerships as an advocate for all outreach activities on campus, regardless of affiliation.

Challenges Confronting Partnerships

With the wealth of resources at an institution like Penn, it is easy for someone external to the institution to imagine it has unlimited possibilities. If Penn is making overtures to the community, it might especially appear that community residents might have their pick of faculty, materials, facilities, programs, and so on. Unfortunately Penn has limitations despite its large endowment. While significant internal resources have been designated for community partnerships, a great deal still must be raised from outside sources. Many foundations will fund only specific programs with particular goals or themes, so it often is not the case that universities can develop programs off of a blank slate. Such dynamics are great challenges for the Center for Community Partnerships because they cannot answer every request. Furthermore, external grants often do not allow for the necessary time to build relationships with various external parties. Joann Weeks said of her experiences with WEPIC, "Things were happening, but never at the level and intensity that we wanted to see. Because you've just really got to get to know the people and build the trust, and if you're not there on a fairly consistent basis, it doesn't really gel."

A central factor impacting the relative longevity of these partnerships is consistency on the part of university representatives. As previously discussed, Penn has improved its relationship with the community; however, the memory of the previous nature of the relationship remains. In order to build trust and demonstrate a genuine concern for the interests of local neighborhoods, Penn must prove its commitment. If grants from external sources do not cover the cost, then the university must look to internal sources—as, apparently, Penn currently is doing.

Potential dependency appears to be another important challenge. To what extent does a local community become dependent on the resources of a major university such as Penn? Indeed, a potential negative effect of a partnership of this sort might be that skills are not transferred to community-based institutions—that communities don't become self-sufficient. The relative capacity of local organizations is a central issue. The Center for Community Partnerships has created a program to build the capacity of local nonprofit organizations, but it will take some time before this work demonstrates substantial outcomes. It is often the case in community partnerships with major institutions that the few politically savvy and resourceful community-based organizations tend to be the ones in communication with universities and corporations and public officials. Getting grassroots organizations in the position of brokering their own relationships with major institutions is persistently difficult.

Conclusion

To briefly summarize, Penn has been able to find compatibility between its sense of social responsibility to the surrounding community and its mission in an academic and economic sense. In general, partnerships make sense for this major research university. However, it only has begun structurally and culturally to create an atmosphere supportive for the long-term continuation and enhancement of community partnerships. The level of institutional commitment required to enhance and expand community partnerships is not known. But the Penn faculty and administrators implementing partnerships for the most part recognize that much more internal work must be done to make community partnerships central to Penn's mission.

The key to these partnerships is ensuring that community residents actually benefit along with the institution. As a major, local economic institution, continually expanding into the local neighborhood, Penn explicitly is suggesting that these business practices adhere to a certain ethical creed. Efforts to gentrify are accompanied by assurances that lower income people have access to home ownership, and business ventures are ensuring that local residents and small businesses share some of the benefits. These clear examples of mutual gain are at the essence of "enlightened self-interest." On the academic side, service learning courses have become the conduit through which faculty are tied to community work. Not only are the faculty directly involved in community-based issues, their involvement is directly tied to their academic research. Residents have been able to use research and gain the assistance of eager students. The mutual-gain approach transcends the academic and economic aspects of community partnerships. However, a great deal of improvement is needed to ensure greater gains among community residents. Communication between Penn and the community seems to be the one area many would agree has improved. Not only is it important for Penn to change internally to create an atmosphere conducive to community partnerships, but it must continue to build relationships with local residents and organizations. Because of the tense history, it could take several years before genuine trust and candor exist on both sides.

Enhancing the conditions in which local residents live might not seem an appropriate goal for a private university. On the one hand, as a private institution, the University of Pennsylvania does not adhere to any formal governmental mandate. However, as a nonprofit organization, the university receives significant tax breaks, which does connote some expectation of responsibility to a locality. Adding one more economic incentive for higher education/community partnerships is what has become known as PILOTS (Payments in Lieu of Taxes), the formal recognition of the need for major nonprofit institutions like universities and hospitals to give back to their communities.

With the increasingly corporate nature of private, major research universities, these institutions also are beginning to be scrutinized about their nonprofit status. This is the context in which even an "ivory tower" institution like Penn increasingly will be expected to engage in successful community partnerships. Is Penn prepared to move down this path? The beginning pieces appear to be in place, but it will take a much deeper institutional commitment to forge the kind of long-term partnership that will socioeconomically enhance the life chances of local residents and transfer power into their hands. Penn appears to be moving in the right direction (as long as the path might be), and it certainly is one of the better examples among universities of its size, but like the higher education/community partnerships movement as a whole, the seeds merely are being planted.

Chapter 3

Living Up to a People's University

San Francisco State University
and the City of San Francisco

Images of long-haired student activists from the late 1960s and early 1970s pop into my head when I think of San Francisco State University (SFSU). I think of Angela Davis with an Afro and a clenched fist running from authorities while a faculty member. The socially conscious, protest-minded culture really was the hallmark of SFSU. People went there as students or faculty to be engaged in a political, challenging, questioning environment, where acceptance of the status quo was the exception rather than the norm. However, this never has been my image of the university's administration — often the target of those protests some decades ago.

A group of scholars have been analyzing the role of what they call a "metropolitan university," which is "an institutional model committed to be responsive to the knowledge and needs of its surrounding region, and dedicated to create active links between campus, community, and commerce."[1] Ideally, SFSU fits the model. Student, faculty, and community activists historically have been holding SFSU accountable to the fulfillment of its responsibility to the city of San Francisco, particularly its poor and disenfranchised residents. In this instance, expectations are high because a part of the mission of public urban universities like SFSU is to engage in partnerships with local communities. The current administration has supported various recent community partnerships to help the institution live up to its responsibilities in the context of gaping inequalities in the technology-based economy shaping the direction of San Francisco.

Clearly a city of the future, San Francisco is overrun with construction projects, eking out the remaining space on an already densely inhabited piece of land. Poor communities, especially communities of color, are being pushed beyond the municipality. With the obvious economic boom, poor communities run the risk of falling prey to gentrification, which may have been initiated in the name of "community development." The residential housing market is indeed skyrocketing in San Francisco, pricing the poor out of contention. What can SFSU do in the face of these challenges?

San Francisco has a wealth of resources and services to guide residents through a changing socioeconomic environment; however, as the community building movement nationwide has demonstrated, these services usually are fragmented. Between welfare reform and the advent of new businesses and a luxury residential market, poor residents need issues such as employment, training, child care, transportation, education, and health care addressed simultaneously. While a public institution, SFSU effectively is an external well-resourced entity which can serve as a critical adviser and broker to and between both the local government and the city's residents.

Compared to Penn, SFSU's student body is far more representative of local communities. However, the university itself is not in dire need of revitalizing its neighboring area for the survival of the institution.[2] A number of quaint residential streets surround the campus, not to mention a nearby shopping mall. Nevertheless, San Francisco State is a critical player in the social, economic, and political circumstances in a number of communities citywide. As an institution founded with the mandate to be responsible to the city and to maintain a widely representative student body, its local roots spread widely. SFSU may be involved in citywide community partnerships, and that may be the expectation of a public urban university, but what do community partnerships have to do with the academics or economics of the institution? Is SFSU equipped to manage the level of community engagement that so many would like to see? As in the case of Penn, questions of this sort are dependent upon a number of internal and external factors. SFSU's historical mission, public image, internal capacity, external support, and demographics are similarly influential. On the community side, avenues for residents and local organizations to shape the direction of community partnerships and the capacity of community-driven initiatives are also essential.

> SFSU is a part of the California State University system, the largest in the country, which includes twenty–three campuses, serving 360,254 students. The degree of the autonomy of SFSU, therefore, is partly shaped by the state's university system[3] as well as its legislature. In 1899, SFSU was founded as the San Francisco State Normal School, which was a two-year teacher-training college, and the first normal school[4] in the country whose admission requirements included a high school diploma. The current stated mission of the university is:
>
> - To create and maintain an environment for learning that promotes respect for and appreciation of scholarship, freedom, human diversity, and the cultural mosaic of the City of San Francisco and the Bay Area.
> - To promote excellence in instruction and intellectual accomplishment.
> - To provide broadly accessible higher education for residents of the region and state, as well as the nation and world.[5]

This mission reflects a clear combination of responsibility to the local region and a commitment to academic excellence. Not uncommon for a university of its type, San Francisco State promotes its urban mandate by providing access to higher education for surrounding communities. A majority of the student body are people of color, and the average age is twenty–five.

Brian Murphy, director of SFSU's outreach arm, the Urban Institute, said of the mission, "In that deep level, the university understands its mission to be about the public good, public things, public space, and serving people who are excluded from the sort of dominant institutional structures of power and privilege. And it's proud of that fact."

Its mission statement, however, does not explicitly challenge the university to engage in local politics or community revitalization. The only discussions of the local region in the mission statement pertain to access and an appreciation for the city's culture. Looking inside of the institution, what emerges is the university's responsibility to help solve the problems facing San Francisco communities.

Evolution of Current Outreach Initiatives

SFSU was originally a teacher's college with the mission of serving democracy through teacher preparation. It evolved into a comprehensive state college and ultimately into a comprehensive state university, always maintaining some level of formal public accountability. The designation of a public institution, however, does not automatically foster deep commitment to poor urban communities. Nevertheless, SFSU has been evolving into an institution that is locally responsive and socially responsible. The land grant tradition significantly influenced this direction. Brian Murphy maintains, "And so the model in the university's mission is urban land grant university. And the model, therefore, the land grant tradition, is self-consciously appropriated by the institution."

For decades, SFSU had been known as a haven for progressive idealism. Indeed, the presence of faculty such as Angela Davis gave the university a reputation for being concerned about the issues facing poor and disenfranchised populations. However, this progressive atmosphere has not always been consistent with the broader mission envisioned by senior administrators. The administration had not been an exceptional sponsor of community partnerships. But, the current president of the university, Robert Corrigan, marked a change when he brought, over eleven years ago, his strong beliefs in applied research and community outreach from the University of Massachusetts at Boston into the administration's vision for the institution. Corrigan believes that community partnerships would have evolved in the same direction without him because the university "would have selected somebody as its president who reflected that [attitude]."

Corrigan boasts a long history of activism, including involvement in the civil rights movement. It was his commitment to social change that led him to leave the major research university atmosphere in which he once worked to enter the presidency of the University of Massachusetts at Boston. He stated, "My decision to go to UMass Boston was a desire to get much more involved in the kinds of institutions, largely but not exclusively urban institutions, that were really trying to work better with their communities; and Boston was a marvelous opportunity for me."

Corrigan by no means created the outreach initiatives at SFSU. A great deal of momentum preceded him, but his presence apparently was a catalyst in advancing community partnerships to new heights. He described a recent, three-year, university-wide strategic planning process, which involved three hundred faculty, and said, "Community outreach, community service, community partnerships are a fundamental part of how the faculty now view their mission." As discussed in the last chapter, forging agreement across the various faculty and departments is a mighty task. The strategic planning process involved a significant number of tenured and tenure-track faculty members. Corrigan remarked, "Extraordinarily, a commitment to outreach came from that; essentially we got buy-in from virtually everybody on campus."

Corrigan is right to point to the extraordinary nature of such a productive process, but strategic plans have a tendency to generate a lot of energy in the beginning. The real work is after the dust settles, when everyone realizes where community partnerships will fit in their schedules and the administration wonders about the balance between teaching loads and community-based initiatives. Corrigan does stress that outreach does not detract from academic excellence: "We want to say that we're the best at what we do, and the best involves scholarship as well as first-rate teaching as well as community involvement." Conceptually, many at SFSU believe in the compatibility between community partnerships and the core work of the university, which, in this case, is teaching.

But if SFSU's administration initially had not been highly supportive of community partnerships, why the shift? Obviously, Corrigan's leadership has made a difference, as has the historical expectation surrounding public urban universities. Corrigan suggests that "a renewed commitment on the part of the American population as a whole" is a significant factor as well. As discussed in earlier chapters, the overall atmosphere of increased external participation among institutions of higher education is encouraging all colleges and universities to think more seriously about their community involvement. Corrigan situates SFSU in the context of a broader national movement. According to Corrigan, the land grant legacy especially is influencing this renaissance. He maintains:

> I am hearing a certain nostalgia now that I was not hearing ten years ago. Nostalgic presidents are talking seriously about community involvement, picking up on the old land grant tradition. But in modern times, they may not be the economic engines any longer to drive those large states. But places like Michigan State, and others that are really in tune with their communities, are beginning to articulate a role for faculty in community development, community linkage, etcetera, that I was not hearing fifteen years ago.

As Corrigan suggests, SFSU is not in a vacuum. It is influenced by national trends in higher education as well as local trends and policies. Whichever direction SFSU takes, one thing has been true since its founding—it has a responsibility as a public institution to the state of California and the city of San Francisco. According to Brian Murphy,

> The pressures under restricted public funding are to manage 27,500 students and get them through in a responsible [period of] time. But that remains the kind of fundamental driving center of the thing. So here's the way I think of this. I see the institution representing a significant public investment—that it's part of a public infrastructure, that it's the grandest example in the United States of America of a public investment. Public higher education is the only significant area of social investment of the United States that's larger than its companion investments in other advanced [capitalist or socialist nations]. But, I look at this and say, here's this phenomenal anomaly, the state's invested this incredible amount of money in resources, public resources. What's our public purpose? What do we serve in terms of the public? And I don't disagree with people who believe that the centerpiece of what we do is educate men and women.

Many faculty and administrators at SFSU see community partnerships as an extension of the mission of a public university. They mentioned a sense of social responsibility that derives from being a part of the staff in such an institution. Murphy stated:

> The fact that his [in reference to another professor] and my salaries, which are quite grand by national standards, are paid by working people in effect . . . There's kind of a visceral, in your stomach, obligation, you know, that you should have when you realize that people-who-are-behind-the-counters' taxes are paying for all of this.

In addition to the general sense of responsibility that comes with working in a public institution, SFSU seized upon political opportunities to advance community partnerships. According to Corrigan, the election of Willie Brown, an SFSU alumnus, as mayor of San Francisco was an essential component due to Brown's understanding of the potential role of higher education.

Public institutions carry this expectation in part because many believe they are ultimately the more trustworthy agents for community involvement over private major research universities. Murphy referred to a meeting where foundations sought advice about investment strategies from various community leaders:

> All of us basically said that the real institutions who are delivering the goods are the public institutions and the community colleges. The partnerships that matter are the ones between these big public institutions and the not-for-profits at the community base. If you're not going to pay for demonstration projects and not imagine how it leverages into big public institutions like us, you're wasting

your money. And that included people from the nonprofit sector who depend on these grants.

The expectations for community involvement on the part of a public institution such as SFSU hinder the recognition received for their work. In other words, when SFSU reaches out to local communities, it's not news; it's what they are supposed to do. In contrast, private research universities that have recently forged community partnerships capture the headlines. Corrigan said of the University of Pennsylvania as compared to SFSU:

> I was a graduate student at Penn when they practically destroyed West Phila-delphia and created University City. Now they've got Ira Harkavy on staff leading the charge to restore those relationships. So Penn does it and it's great news because there were so many decades of lack of involvement in the community. . . . You know, abandoned its lab school, pulled out its teaching, pulled its practice teachers out of the urban schools, put them in suburban schools. You know, all that stuff went on at Penn in those days. So they can get big publicity out of it. San Francisco State has been doing it for forty years in an area of the state in which the public has been led to equate quality with Stanford and Berkeley, Nobel Prize winners, outstanding grantsmanship—and so they kind of ho hum.

SFSU's reputation as an activist institution indeed has shaped external perceptions of the university. Thirty years ago, a strike on campus significantly affected the internal climate. Apparently, the legacy of this period remains influential. Said Corrigan, "I still hear all these stories about the strike. Although it grew out of a commitment of community and faculty and students to change the institution, it also became a wedge between the faculty and the community. We were perceived as this crazy, strange, sort of wild group." Corrigan suggests that limited state funding for the institution is related to this perception:

> If the governor's got the opportunity to put money someplace for a chancellor of the whole system or the president, you can reward your friends and not do any-thing for your enemies. So we have the highest faculty/student ratio in the California State University system. We have the lowest numbers of dollars per faculty, full-time student equivalent in the system. Is this a pattern over the years of people not responding to how we perceived our mission? I think so. Are our people, faculty here, aware of it? Yeah.

Funding dynamics are reflected in the distribution of SFSU's resources. Once having received 90 percent of its funding from the state, SFSU is approaching something closer to half state funding and half outside resources. The College of Science has already reached a fifty-fifty ratio. According to faculty member Jerry Eisman, "We have projected out that we [College of Science] eventually will be a state-assisted program run by soft money. Well that entirely changes what people do. And so in certain places now, external funding becomes the meritorious activity." The implications for community partnerships are that they are more likely to survive if they can drive funding. Therefore, the role of private foundations and other external sources of funds becomes critical to the development and longevity of broad institutional commitments to community throughout higher education.

The additional challenge for SFSU is the assumption of inferiority among potential funders. Indeed, due to the image of major research universities as the most effective of institutions of higher education, public institutions like SFSU often face limited funding opportunities even in areas such as community partnerships for which they are well known. Felix Kury, a faculty member in ethnic studies with fundraising experience in a number of different institutions, notes:

> One of the expectations that I [found] coming out of San Diego State and going to Stanford is that there's an assumption about the size of your library and whether you can handle research at San Diego State. When we submitted the same proposal out of Stanford, and it just got funded . . . We just put new borders and sent it on and it was no problem. That's the same thing we face here at San Francisco State—sometimes serious money. I think that they are just not sure, because it's a state institution, that we have the capacity or the faculty.

For San Francisco State, this perception took form in other relationships as well. Through the Urban Institute, SFSU had been involved in a collaboration with other Bay Area universities. There are not too many examples of successful initiatives encouraging different types of institutions to work with each other. A public urban university like SFSU in collaboration with a public major research university like Berkeley and a private major research university like Stanford on the topic of community partnerships is not common—and not easy in its implementation.

While one aspect of SFSU's reputation may have hindered its state funding and the state's overall perception of the value of the institution, another aspect of its reputation probably advanced the current community partnerships. If SFSU is reputed for progressive politics, then progressive faculty and students and administrators who are interested in community will pursue such an institution. For example, Kury notes that he always was attracted to SFSU, "especially since the strike. I wanted to be in ethnic studies and chicano studies, and so I saw this as the place to be."

Vision for Community Outreach

Increased support for the San Francisco State Urban Institute, the university's community outreach arm, demonstrates the current senior administrative commitment to partnering with local neighborhoods. According to Corrigan, "The Urban Institute exists in large part because of a lot of things that we had seen happening in the sixties." Urban Institute staff member Susan Alunan said of Corrigan's financial commitment to the Urban Institute, "I think that the monetary commitment of the president has been very zealous. It started with a small commitment six years ago, and now we are heavily funded by the university and also by the Chancellor's office for our service learning. And, you know, that's a message that gets sent to the vice presidents and to the deans that this is a priority of the president." Alunan speaks not only to the explicit financial commitment, but to the symbolic nature of it all. Gestures of presidential support, particularly financial ones, demonstrate the significance of community partnerships internal and external to the institution. Internally, it helps faculty, administration, and students see the importance of community partnership. Externally, it demonstrates to the public the priority the university has placed on partnerships. Currently, Alunan estimates SFSU's support for the Urban Institute at over $1,000,000.

The historical context of the 1960s appears to be a critical factor in stimulating the magnitude of SFSU's involvement in the community, since many of the central administrative and faculty players have long histories in community activism spawned in the 1960s. Indeed, members of the '60s generation have now become decision makers in this country, which is changing the way things are done at major institutions like universities. Corrigan believes that the combination of the beliefs of those with activist backgrounds and the social consciousness of today's college and university students has contributed to the current increased civic engagement of higher educational institutions. He maintains, "I think that this generation of students and my generation of faculty have a renewed sense of commitment to what the university should be doing." He does not agree with those who have cast the current generation of students as apathetic. "I thought that the community outreach efforts of universities were a public relations attempt to get away from the sense that elite institutions were educating a narcissistic generation of students who didn't care about community." However, upon further thought, he pointed to various movements in recent decades, as examples of the involvement of today's students. Current student pressure to make universities reconsider their role is reflected in the movement against sweatshop labor.

Brian Murphy, the director of the Urban Institute, is himself a veteran in the field of university/community partnerships as well as an alumni of the '60s generation. In his former capacity as director of external affairs, Brian redrafted the state of California's plan on higher education, insisting on the incorporation of greater public engagement among universities. Corrigan said, "Brian came to the university from an interesting job that he had with the state government, and we decided to not necessarily replicate, but take the concept of the McCormick Institute at Boston[6] and try to put together something similar here." The combination of Corrigan's and Murphy's historical involvement in the issue is critical to the continuation of SFSU's community partnerships.

Another important internal personnel decision was to hire Tom Erlich, former president of Indiana University, and a leading national voice on service learning. Corrigan served on the board of Campus Compact, a national trade association of university presidents in support of greater civic engagement in higher education. Corrigan joked with Erlich, "Why don't you just get out of the rarified air of the Stanfords and Yales of the world and come to where the action really is." To Corrigan's surprise, Erlich actually did come to SFSU and has been instrumental in promoting community service learning on campus, winning over skeptics and creating "converts."

In a broader sense, Corrigan believes that in the past ten years, the overall nature of the faculty has changed, impacting the sense of community: "Seventy to seventy-five percent of our annual faculty hires for the last ten years, tenure track, have been people of color or women and women of color. You do that year in and year out for ten years and you change the face of this campus." Brian Murphy reflected upon the significance of Corrigan's faculty recruitment strategies:

> The overwhelming majority that's non-white faculty were in ethnic studies, ghettoized perfectly. There was literally one tenured member of the faculty who was African American in the entire college in the behavioral and social sciences when Corrigan got here. So he came in and said, "That's not OK. And we're going to do a series of other things." And, you know, we begin. And over the last decade the hiring record of the institution probably is the best of any comprehensive institution in the country in terms of our ability to attract and get non-white and women hires. And this has meant Latino biologists and, you know, people who don't fit the stereotype of black folks in black studies, and the Asian folks in Asian studies and engineering.

Race and ethnicity are major factors in developing successful community partnerships. Students from communities of color in San Francisco, those with whom the Urban Institute tends to work, are often a necessary bridge between the university and these neighborhoods. White non-Latino students comprise only 30 percent of the overall student body. Ninety–three percent of the university's 21,044 students come from the state of California. As Victor Rubin of HUD mentioned, "One of the reasons that Corrigan has been so supportive of the Urban Institute is because he sees the connection to the health of the city—the relationship to where the student body comes from. That's how they are going to make their mark."

In ethnic studies, for example, Felix Kury explained that they "emphasize the community-centered aspect of training students to go back and work in the community. Because of the make up of the department and the faculty in the department, there was a significant connection with Central American agencies as well as refugee and immigrant organizations." SFSU's outreach extends internationally. Given the countries of origin of many of the students and community residents, international connections have been justifiable within the institutional mission. Kury spoke of connections to Latin America:

> One international component of our community service learning was when two of our faculty members went to Cuba and established relationships with folks at the University of Havana with the idea of establishing some kind of faculty and student exchange. Well, so we developed this program where students study community organizing, Cuban organizing, and community organizing in Cuba. We may learn some things about community organizing with limited resources by looking at a situation like Cuba where resources are absolutely limited.

The Various Elements of SFSU's Community Partnerships

The compatibility between SFSU's mission and its community partnerships is undeniable. The idea of reaching out into local neighborhoods is wrapped into the ethos of the institution. Academically, access to SFSU for diverse and disenfranchised populations is a priority. Economically, the SFSU de facto depends upon San Francisco communities for its survival, even though the institution is not physically situated in a poor area. SFSU needs tuition for its survival, and its students come from the local communities. Development of the local communities is the development of past, present, and future students, their families, and the conditions in which they live. The incentives are clear. But what do the community partnerships look like in practice?

Programs of the SFSU Urban Institute

The SFSU Urban Institute describes itself as "a non-profit project of the San Francisco State University that provides the umbrella for the university's urban projects, encouraging interdisciplinary approaches in partnership with school districts, community-based organizations, labor, and local, state and federal agencies."[7] It is designed to help address specific local problems as well as to be engaged in national policy initiatives. Formed approximately five years ago, the institute shares governance with an external board of directors, including the mayor of San Francisco and other influential locals. The community board holds veto power over decisions related to the institute's involvement in the city, and an interdisciplinary faculty board was also created. Some of the institute's activities include brokering relationships among diverse groups, as well as developing comprehensive partnerships among a number of local stakeholders to address critical needs. The Urban Institute engages faculty, students, and staff in addressing issues such as job creation, training, access to higher education, environmental restoration, literacy, health, violence, drug prevention, and keeping middle school students in school. The institute's approach is to draw upon the myriad skills and resources in the university on behalf of local communities.

One example of an institute program is the *Career/Pro* initiative in the Bayview/Hunter's Point neighborhood, which helps to build the capacity of nonprofit organizations through on-site training. The various nonprofits with which the institute works address issues ranging from various job and job-search skills to tutoring for youth. Technical assistance provided also includes computer training on units provided by SFSU, and career counseling and development.

SFSU also has a Community Outreach Partnership Center (COPC) grant from HUD, which is used to provide technical assistance to the Mayor's Office of Community Development. University-based professors in housing, economics, and sociology are a part of the team of advisors, which also includes community organizers and graduate interns.

Service learning is a significant component of SFSU's outreach initiatives. In collaboration with the City College of San Francisco, the University of San Francisco, and New College, SFSU has been involved in a three-year demonstration project, called the City of Service Higher Education Consortium, which provides curriculum-based internships in critical areas of need in the city. These include urban environmentalism (particularly lead poisoning), academic challenges facing immigrants in k-12, and programs for the elderly. The City of Service, which is housed in San Francisco State's Office of Community Service Learning (OCSL), places five hundred students in seventy different community-based organizations each semester. The mission of the consortium is "to respond to the fragmentation and alienation pervasive throughout American culture by building a sense of civic responsibility among students enrolled in the four institutions in our consortium."[8] This collaboration stresses the mutual gain for students and community-based organizations: "Students learn practical and interpersonal skills and are able to apply the information learned on campus to 'real' situations off campus. Students receive credit for the learning derived from the community experience and not simply the number of hours served."[9]

OCSL has provided financial support for sixty-three service learning courses, which involve seventy-five faculty from forty departments.[10] OCSL currently is operating within a five-year plan designed to ensure that every SFSU student enrolls in a service learning course before graduating. Student volunteers are provided training in community service learning through the Community Involvement Center (CIC). Founded in 1974, "CIC enables students to integrate classroom-knowledge, self-knowledge, and community-knowledge."[11]

Faculty member and Urban Institute staff member Jerry Eisman reflects upon his involvement on the strategic planning committee and the role of service learning at SFSU:

> That year Tom Erlich came to campus and held a faculty colloquium represent-ing this academic campus on service learning. At the same time, service learning and strategic planning came together. Our main recommendation in the strate-gic plan was created off of service learning. We needed to find funding to offer faculty opportunities to grow courses in service learning. We got the offer through Tom's work with the chancellor. We got the money to fund over three years. About twenty-five new courses each year were added to the curriculum that did service learning. They now have over eighty courses and forty departments that do service learning coordinated through my office, reporting to Brian.

The theme of coordinated services, as in the case of Penn, resonates through-out much of the Urban Institute's programs. San Francisco Together, a project in formation, is one example. Through this project, community, business, civic, and labor leaders collaborate in a series of discussions regarding various critical issues confronting the city, such as economic development and the city's budget and charter. Drawing upon the research capacity of the university, the Urban Institute is serving as a significant informational resource to the city, particularly with respect to economic development and employment. The city's Department of Human Resources contracted the institute to research existing and projected employment opportunities for low-income and unemployed residents as well as welfare recipients in the city. Studies underway collect and analyze data on employment opportunities in citywide construction projects, analyze likely job opportunities in specific industries, and analyze likely areas for occupational growth to determine the types of potentially available jobs and their skill require-ments. The institute also collaborates with a consortium of public and private organizations, the CityNet, which is creating a computer-based information service for the San Francisco community. The service will provide free elec-tronic services including municipal and county information, educational oppor-tunities, library holdings, museum displays, social service information and referral, public forums, and others. Users will have a common entry point for the service through dial-up service, internet access, and direct online terminals. Also in the area of economic development, the Urban Institute cooperates with a number of community-based organizations through the Community Workforce Collaborative (CWC), which monitors ongoing construction projects in the San Francisco Unified School District (SFUSD). Factors such as workforce diversity goals, wage status, gender goals, and resident goals are all examined by CWC.

The Urban Institute publishes a quarterly magazine, the purpose of which is "to widen the public discussion beyond any one event or political moment, to give voice to a wide variety of voices, to stand for both the idea and the reality of building common life. We aim to capture—in the limits of print and picture, image and phrase—some of what makes this city worth fighting for."[12] Indeed the publication has been profiling various neighborhoods and the initiatives of community-based organizations within them for the past three years.

Overall, the Urban Institute acts as a clearinghouse for the various dimensions of SFSU's community partnerships. With direct support from Corrigan, the institute is situated to be a significant player on campus. From the community's perspective, the Urban Institute is the conduit between the university and the city. This aids in addressing the issue of limited coordination on campus and mitigates the university culture tendency to promote individualism, which can result in the development of disconnected community partnerships. As previously discussed, this sometimes can be confusing to communities if they are partnering with a variety of university-sponsored projects that don't tie together. The Urban Institute has developed into the glue that joins the various initiatives on campus, bringing SFSU closer to a university-wide commitment to community partnerships.

San Francisco Policy Center

The San Francisco Policy Center (SFPC) is another important partnership involving the institute along with the San Francisco Information Clearinghouse. Formed in 1997, the SFPC convenes academics and community activists to collaborate on policy analysis, strategic planning, and technical assistance. Generating multiple benefits, the SFPC brings education to the staffs of community-based nonprofits and community development experience to SFSU faculty and students. The initiative emerged from Mayor Willie Brown's 1996 San Francisco Economic Summit, which brought together a diverse constituency in discussions about various public policy issues.

This kind of an effort takes the research and analytical skill of academics and joins it with the experiential knowledge of community activists. Because it focuses on policy, it does not seek merely to provide services, it is engaging broader issues of social change. The cooperative nature of the SFPC stimulates critical dialogue on policy matters among people who would not necessarily have worked together otherwise. No one actually knows what can emerge in conversations among diverse groups about particular policy issues. The original conversations, as exemplified in the following extract from the SFPC position paper, illuminated the importance of these types of forums and underscored the need for "synergistic discussion leading to broad dissemination of findings":

> The mission of SFPC is to create a set of common projects between community
> members and SFSU with the following goals and objectives:

Goals

a. Conduct sound and clear analysis of major policy issues and programs affecting the future of San Francisco's diverse communities with a view for long-range strategic planning;

b. Provide quality technical assistance and continuing professional education for San Francisco CBOs; and,

c. Offer SFSU students and faculty greater opportunity to learn the strategies and practices of community empowerment from skilled and experienced community-based practitioners.

Objectives

a. Build capacity to conduct original research and analyses, and produce studies, evaluations, and policy proposals about the City's economy, government, and residential communities;

b. Establish a program of educational offerings for the skill development and professional training of community-based activists and non-profit staff;

c. Conduct, in conjunction with other organizations, lecture series, workshops, and public debates;

d. Publish a SFPC Journal to include analytical studies; and,

e. Work with SFSU faculty to create courses of study in urban community organizing, and cooperate in developing university-based curricula that integrate students in community-based organizations.[13]

The SFPC is making clear use of the added value that San Francisco State University can bring to the city. The research and analysis that are embedded in faculty life are being put to use in a specific and practical fashion. Moreover, research capacity is being transferred to community activists. Community representatives, because they were engaged in dialogue from the beginning, have been able to assist in designing the goals of the effort. Although the SFPC initiates its projects, they "originate by direct interaction with community groups," according to the position paper.

The SFPC comprises various components: Its Board of Fellows disseminates publications and the findings of the SFPC research designed to influence public discourse and potentially advocacy as well. The board is convened as a result of discussions between community activists and academics in order to identify critical policy issues. Working committees are created to develop workplans around specific policy-related issues. The board meets quarterly to coordinate the activities of the working groups and organize resources as well as identify new issues.

The *Comprehensive Economic and Employment Development Initiative* focuses on business and employment opportunities for low-income neighborhood residents. This initiative helps the city assess opportunities stemming from the numerous local construction projects and other emerging economic developments. This SFPC initiative enables comprehensive labor market analysis and business feasibility studies, which exceed the capacity of the existing government infrastructure. Again, the centrality of coordination and comprehensive service delivery pervades every dimension of SFSU's community partnerships.

The *Comprehensive Economic and Employment Development Initiative* has five goals that currently are being implemented. The first goal is to research trends in the future labor market and to assess the characteristics of the workforce in the various economic development and capital improvement projects. A working committee of academics, community representatives, and SFPC staff is developing a work plan regarding the city's economic future. The second goal is to create a network of community-based organizations. The third goal is to implement short-term strategies to address deficiencies in the system. Specific hiring agreements related to current projects in development are one example. The fourth goal is to assess the capacity of various San Francisco neighborhoods, identifying technical assistance needs. The fifth goal is to link community-based organizations with existing major economic development projects as in the Mission Bay Development Agreement, which involved community-based organizations in its planning, oversight, and development.

Another component of the SFPC is the *Curriculum Project*, which has two interrelated programs—civic education and community capacity building. The civic education program is a combination of service learning courses of SFSU students and community-based courses for students and younger staff members in nonprofits. Community-based projects require students to address issues such as welfare reform, housing, transportation, and economic development. Another set of courses is in development, which brings together junior staff members in community-based organizations with matriculating SFSU students to engage in seminar discussions about issues such as social, economic, and political history, and the impact of global trends on local conditions. University students who participated in service learning courses will be in this second set of courses, all of which will be held off campus and cotaught by university faculty and community leaders. Not only do these courses bring university students back into their communities, but they also broaden the intellectual environment for young people in the community-based organizations who have already made the commitment to work in the community. The final aspect of civic education will include various public events, where the analytical work of the various SFPC working groups will be shared with the public. Community partners, students enrolled in the urban curriculum, and a cross section of other city representatives will be among the invitees to such events.

Community capacity building, the other half of the *Curriculum Project*, is designed to enhance the skills of staff in community-based organizations. The SFPC is developing, in collaboration with SFSU's College of Extended Learning, a program of preprofessional and professional education in the areas of fiscal and personnel management, program design and evaluation, long-range strategic planning, and economic and community development. One of the courses from this project was a junior level political science course on San Francisco development politics from the postwar to the modern period. The composition from the course included twenty-two community-based persons who were not university students and twelve matriculating university students. According to Brian Murphy, "This was a heavy-duty course. Three of the Hayes Valley organizers—African-American women on public assistance—were in that course. And so for two of them particularly, it has been a deeply significant move in their lives—in the sense that they had access to an institution that they either had thought of as alien or had no relationship to them."

Building the capacity of communities is the ultimate goal of this initiative. Susan Alunan said, "And we think that perhaps by helping them build their personal capacities, their own personal development, then it will lead to increased professional development in their neighborhoods and in their lives, which will help them keep things together better." Alunan further discussed the issue of community capacity. She said, "The nonprofits in San Francisco are funded for programs. Capacity is a big, big, big issue. And I mean the CDBG[14] go just so far with this part." Alunan refers to the fact, which is nationwide, that nonprofits often do not receive external financial support for infrastructural or staff development. Rather, most funds are available for specific programs. This limits the actual capacity of community-based organizations in particular to actually implement their programmatic activities. Alunan added, "When that grant goes away, if there's a gap . . . before the next grant, and they don't get the other grant from San Francisco Works or Cal Works, then they're really in trouble. I think that capacity is the biggest issue." This is one area where university resources can be of assistance. The idea of capacity takes many forms, from organizational capacity to technological capacity to policy capacity, and so on. Because of their comprehensive nature, universities house the skills that communities can use to enhance their life circumstances. This is one important reason why higher education/community partnerships make sense in theory. When fashioned with community interests in mind, community partnerships can build the knowledge of local residents.

One way in which SFSU has been addressing this concern is through expanding community access to its coursework. The director of admissions and the Urban Institute are creating a program to enable access for nonuniversity community organizers to one or two courses free of charge with full university credit. Ultimately, the Urban Institute wishes to gain access to university-based coursework for adults as well as children. If the adults are in the classes, they can show their children the campus, giving them early exposure to the idea of higher education. Ultimately, the effort has long-term consequences. As admirable as the goals of this program may be, it remains one of the most difficult to fund. Said Murphy, "There's a tremendous reluctance for the federal government or for the foundations to fund curricular development stuff."

Finally, the SFPC's *Data Project* focuses the expertise of SFSU faculty on local concerns. Regarding issues from geographic information mapping to social and demographic transformations, faculty will be engaged in raising critical questions and providing helpful analysis. For example, the Urban Institute has been contracted by the city's Department of Human Services to conduct a workforce analysis of specific major construction projects initiated or scheduled between March 1, 1998, and February 29, 2000. The analyses of SFSU faculty in this effort include the identification of employment positions at all levels, which will be incorporated into a "master schedule" of job opportunities within a twenty-four month period. This information will be posted on the SFPC's research and database web site.

In addition to its various projects, the SFPC is fostering dialogue between communities and academic sectors regarding changes affecting the city.[15] Involving community participants in every stage of decision making, this dialogue will be extended to town hall meetings and other venues, and will inspire articles and analytic studies.

SFSU and San Francisco Neighborhoods

Apart from its citywide efforts, the Urban Institute has developed projects in some of the poor and disenfranchised neighborhoods in San Francisco. Again, the institutional incentive for SFSU's involvement at the neighborhood level rests partly with the composition of its student body. These initiatives can improve the conditions in the neighborhoods, but they can also benefit the university. Hayes Valley, Visitacion Valley, the Mission, and Bayview–Hunter's Point are some of the neighborhoods where SFSU has had a presence in recent years.

Hayes Valley

The federal government's Department of Housing and Urban Development's Hope VI program is designed to redefine public housing as we know it through the construction of new low-rise developments in urban areas nationwide. Four Hope VI sites are coming to San Francisco, the first of which is in Hayes Valley. Based on the profiles of current SFHA (San Francisco Housing Authority) residents, approximately four hundred and sixty people will live in the two hundred units at the site. Most will be families headed by single mothers. Fifty percent of the residents are projected to be black; the remainder is projected to be twenty five percent Asian and Pacific Islander and seventeen percent white. The average household income without assistance is projected to be $10,135.[16]

The Urban Institute and the SFHA partnered to discuss various ways in which the resources of the university could be used to assist with Hayes Valley development. The initial institute effort focuses on ensuring access to advances in information technology for the low income residents who will occupy the Hope VI buildings. The institute is assisting the SFHA and the Hayes Valley Resident Management Corporation in connecting all residential units to the internet through local area networks (LANs).

Computer science students from SFSU will tutor residents who will attend classes at the SFHA computer learning centers throughout the city. The Urban Institute currently is using software donated by Microsoft to train and update families who will move into the Hayes Valley development. Computer science students will serve as system and network administrators, once the LANs are operational, for residents. Under the supervision of staff from the Personal Consulting Group (PCG) and faculty, these student-administrators will train a group of Hayes Valley residents to provide some assistance to the complex as well. Much of the students' time will be spent on troubleshooting, network maintenance, account maintenance, and system installation and upgrading. The technological aspect of SFSU's community partnership was influenced heavily by the work of computer science faculty member Jerry Eisman. Eisman said of the development of this current focus:

> As chair of Computer Science, I was active in bringing the internet to campus, and along the way somewhere about five years ago I said, you know, the community is the internet. The internet changes boundaries; it changes borders and it changes what we do. And they need communications. So I created an organization called SSS Net, which is our campus community electronic communication project. We have courses in computer science that send students out into the community to help them set up their networking, their web, their way of operation, their database, advise on networks, etcetera. I created that and SSS got funded from the university budget annually to continue its operation.

The Hayes Valley Computer Learning Center, which will be located in the main community building at the site, will house ten to fifteen workstations; the internet will be accessible by every computer. The center will be staffed by an SFHA computer training specialist along with computer science students and particular residents who are computer-literate, who will be paid stipends to tutor and train other residents. Not only will the university add skills to the environment, but it will be transferring skills to residents, who can in turn train their peers. Faculty member Gib Robinson further described the set-up:

In all those new Hope VI projects, our intent is to wire them with 100 megabytes, wiring to each of the units. And to also augment that with the Computer Learning Center, so that kids and adults, in their own units, have immediate access the same way you do in an office. And to bring together public and private partners; we coaxed Microsoft out of its little shell to give us $15,000 in cash and all the software we needed. We coaxed a couple of other local players to help us shape this.

Current training activities will be expanded upon the opening of the Computer Learning Center and the launching of the LANs to include web research and website design to help residents make use of their access to the internet. The Urban Institute particularly wishes to use the web to build community among the residents and provide marketable professional skills in the technology field. "In partnering with SFHA to create a Technology Campus in Hayes Valley, SFUI has four primary goals: enhancing community, encouraging economic self-sufficiency, augmenting educational opportunities, and creating a model for other public housing sites."[17] Highlights of anticipated activities toward these goals include websites and email addresses for intracommunity communication, internet research and web surfing workshops for children and youth, a website to link residents to educational institutions, and a website designed to enhance the education, training, and employment of residents. Robinson noted one of the advantages of this sort of partnership with SFHA, "We can put wires in their walls; we can put high speed networks in; we can connect them to employment and training opportunities and educational opportunities within the city or anywhere using electronics. And we don't have to pay the rent; we don't have to pay the lights; we don't have to pay the mortgage." This particular initiative brings educational services directly to residents in their community rather than bringing the residents to campus. Robinson continued, "So whether it's schools that become venues for community revitalization or housing authority buildings that become campuses of learning, in some sense it's at least as easy to deliver educational services in those locations as on our own campuses."

Visitacion Valley

A neighborhood of 18,000, Visitacion Valley was once a deteriorating urban neighborhood, known for its massive public housing complex, Geneva Towers. Geneva Towers became notorious for crime and unsanitary conditions. The western regional administrator, Robert Demonte, foreclosed on the private developer of the complex for failure to maintain livable conditions. HUD took it over in 1991. Due to the exorbitant cost of rehabilitating the property, the administrator at the time, Art Agnos, encouraged the residents to form a residents' council to assist in the planning of a replacement for Geneva Towers.[18]

Construction is well underway for a total of three buildings, which will contain 330 units. All of the residents are temporarily relocated.

Over the past few years, the Urban Institute has been helping the Visitacion Valley Task Force create a center for training and employment at a multi-service community center for local residents called the Village. The Village is a rented building across from the Geneva Towers site designed to house various community-based initiatives. HUD provided the site after the residents requested a physical space, that would keep residents together and enable meetings and other activities.

Resident control is a central aspect of the effort in the Valley. Local activist, Larry Fleming said of the resident-based housing effort,

> These are three housing developments going on simultaneously, and the tenants that got evicted from the Towers have the right of first picking of all three. So we are guiding them now. They are designing it. We're going to get back in; and eventually we hope to actually own it, and to manage it. And eventually to set up a four-way council. It hasn't been up yet, but there's another housing project here in the Valley that's been isolated. We're connecting with that housing project, Sunnydale. The four of us hope to set up a housing development council that takes care of all of the counseling in the Valley—all of the housing in the Valley.

The SFSU Urban Institute has been working closely with the local task force, harnessing resources both within and outside of the university. One of the advantages of the Urban Institute is its numerous connections within city government. Consequently, the Urban Institute is well situated to broker relationships between neighborhood-based initiatives and public officials. Fleming discussed this reality, saying, "The Urban Institute has been the connective piece to all of these pieces. All these connection pieces and the city departments have been done through the Urban Institute."

The Urban Institute facilitated the involvement of a variety of external institutions in the Visitacion Valley initiative. Local activist Judith Sandoval said, "There are four or five city departments that meet monthly now about us. They never talked to each other before." The institute is able to convene unprecedented meetings due to its numerous connections to city agencies and other institutions. Susan Alunan understands the significance of these institutions to the residents of Visitacion Valley. She said:

> Without the cooperation and the real commitment of HUD, all the community groups, the city and county, the mayor's Office of Community Development, the mayor's Office of Children and Families, and the Human Rights Commission.... They're all out there. And they have, you know, moved it along as much as we have or as much as the community itself has. We have Visitacion Valley planning meetings, strategic planning meetings around Visitacion Valley as a

whole. And theirs is a biweekly village planning meeting for the collaboration of organizations that are in the Village. And that group includes the mayor's Office of Community Development, the Office of Children and Families, as well as the community-based organizations in the Village.

This comprehensiveness and extensive communication, on the one hand, requires a great deal of patience, but on the other, the community's connections to important policy makers ultimately eases the red tape and bureaucracy that often stifles community-based initiatives. The Urban Institute introduces community residents and organizations to various important officials and steers them in the direction of certain resources. Vernon Long discussed one specific example, "If there was a proposal that we needed to get out ... I mean writing the proposal ain't worth nothing if you don't know who to give it to. They kind of guided us. If you write a proposal for this, you need to talk to this group first to find out what they want you to do. But we do nothing of that. We go the long way around."

Apparently, the added value of a university in community partnerships extends beyond the internal resources of the institution. Indeed, SFSU may have more significant connections to public officials than most. SFSU alumni tend to facilitate relationships between the university and city agencies. Many SFSU alumni enter positions in public administration. Alunan's observations of the public administrators involved in Visitacion Valley are favorable: "They're committed! A lot of them are alumni of San Francisco State. And so we've all formed friendships and real, trusting relationships around these community projects. The same trust we have with the community, we have with the city. And I think other cities would die ... other universities would die to have that kind of relationship with their cities." Public universities may tend to be more tied to city agencies and the like. However, it appears that, in general, institutions of higher education take on a perceived neutrality that may foster a brokering role, particularly among other large institutions. SFSU has made significant use of this convening power on behalf of residents in Visitacion Valley.

Other work in the neighborhood includes the resident-created Visitacion Valley Jobs, Education, and Training Project (VVJET), which provides jobs development and training to help the community benefit from the $50 million worth of construction taking place in the area. During 1997, VVJET trained 185 people and placed 182 of them in jobs. The Urban Institute participates in "Thursday Nights at the Village," which is "a mix of team building, proposal writing, problem solving, and community outreach."[19] The Thursday program brings together a subcommittee of volunteers and the director of the Village, Vernon Long, in creating a jobs program for local unemployed adults. Part of the idea of the work is to tie social services to housing. The original residents' council merged into the Geneva Valley Development Corporation for this purpose. According to Long, the most significant needs for residents in Visitacion Valley are "economic opportunity, economic development, and education."[20] The Urban Institute's Words Project, also in Visitacion Valley, piques children's interest in reading. "After consulting with the kids themselves, the program started teaching youths to write rap, glided into poetry and soon the participants were reading on their own. Two from one family were reading two years below grade level. After one semester both had improved by two grades."[21]

The Mission

In the Mission district, the Urban Institute works with youth who face a variety of challenges. Mission High School is the site for the Mission Health Center, which delivers health services and primary care for the school's 1,400 students. Depression, sports injuries, colds, and sexual and physical abuse are all common areas of treatment at the center, which is a collaboration between SFSU, the University of California at San Francisco, Mission High School, the San Francisco Unified School District, and city agencies.

The health center began serving students and their parents, but it ultimately served the entire community. Susan Alunan said, "They didn't care whether they were immigrants or whether they were legal or not legal. They got MediCal clearance so that they could accept MediCal. And they really went into the community." The health center workers faced a number of challenges to their work, at one point finding themselves evicted from their Mission High School location, where they based their activities, due to various internal conflicts.

According to Alunan and Murphy, many people in the community wanted them back. Alunan said,

> When they were pulled out of Mission High School the community was just up in arms. And now the community leaders at the last meeting were in tears. The former friends of the people who sort of forced the center out are [saying], "How can we get this back up and running? How can we serve the students of Mission High School and the youth groups?" Because we brought in [services for] mental health, conflict resolution, referrals for counseling, AIDS, HIV, STD. So it was a full range of services and referrals for the kids and their parents and the community at large.

The health center has since been relocated into a brand new, tailor-made site.

Also in the Mission, SFSU is involved in developing a Mission District Academic Complex to include an elementary school, a middle school, a high school, community-based organizations, businesses, SFSU, and the City College of San Francisco. The philosophy guiding this planned initiative is to provide "a seamless continuum of services from one institution to another."[22] This continuum would enable services to follow students from kindergarten through 16 and beyond. Students would be able to understand the links between these various stages in life and would have the benefit of coordination among primary, secondary, and higher education, as well as the business world.

Bayview–Hunter's Point

Faced with the highest concentration of hazardous waste in San Francisco, residents in Bayview-Hunter's Point have been organizing to improve conditions. The Southeast Alliance for Environmental Justice (SAEJ) formed in response to the proposed development of a third power plant in the neighborhood. They successfully blocked the power plant and subsequently developed into a permanent community organization addressing existing contamination and advocating for environmentally safe economic development. The San Francisco League of Urban Gardeners (SLUG) is taking another approach to the environment in the neighborhood through gardening. SLUG mixes economic development and community empowerment with environmental beautification. They turn vacant lots into gardens and provide entrepreneurial opportunities for residents. For example, their Urban Herbals project allows youth and young adults to produce, manufacture, and distribute a line of gourmet food products and gift baskets.[23]

Among the environmental hazards in the neighborhood and other parts of the city are "brownfields," defined by the Environmental Protection Agency (EPA) as "abandoned, idle, or under-used industrial and commercial facilities where expansion or redevelopment is complicated by real or perceived environmental contamination."[24] Since 1993, the EPA's Brownfields Initiative has been supporting and raising awareness of the clean-up of brownfields around the country. The actual planning process for cleaning the sites rests in the hands of local governments. San Francisco's approach focuses on cleaning up military bases that are closing, including the Hunter's Point Naval Shipyard.

From education to health care to housing to technology, the Urban Institute has been finding ways to be useful in addressing the priorities in various neighborhoods throughout the city. This extensive approach to various local communities highlights the public responsibility to which so many SFSU faculty and administrators refer. They are fulfilling the public mission, but also creating avenues for the voices and interests of community residents to influence the nature and direction of the community partnerships. This level of dialogue with community residents increases the likelihood of achieving a sense of mutual gain. As opposed to the Penn situation, the idea of mutual gain may not be as essential. If the mission of SFSU is public, then it need not necessarily expect any returns. However, given that community partnerships hardly have been treated as essential aspects of higher education at many public universities, it is easier to justify the long-term development of community partnerships when a university has clear incentives.

SFSU as Incubator

The various efforts discussed up to this point have focused on explicitly university-sponsored activities working in partnership with community initiatives. SFSU can also house community initiatives without officially sponsoring them. The Urban Institute's environmental restoration and job-training work around military bases, for example, is managed by a semi-external entity. In Visitation Valley, residents are being trained to clean up closed military bases; the Pentagon has supplied $750,000 in support of the effort, which is called CAREERPRO (the California Economic Recovery and Environmental Restoration Project).[25] It is based at SFSU, but it is not a university program. This is another potential role for universities—as incubators of what would otherwise be independent nonprofit organizations. Activist Lenny Siegal, a nationally renowned expert in cleaning up military bases and the director of CAREERPRO, described how the project developed in response to multiple base closures in the Bay Area, including Alameda, Treasure Island, Mayer Island, and Moffett:

> The Bay Area was really impacted by that. And initially [CAREERPRO] was formed to look at what was going to be the impact on workers. Not only base workers who worked for the Navy, but people whose livelihood depended on these installations being active and lively. . . . And so we convened a lot of round-tables and discussions on this, and how you could transition people from one work force into another. And the idea being that we would use the capacity of the university—people who dealt with worker retraining issues, education of the work force, and stuff like that . . . to take the expertise out into these areas where those issues were right on the surface. . . . And a component of that was environmental clean-up, because all of these bases were going to have to go through environmental clean-up to be transferred. A lot of the studies or the roundtables that we convened came up with the fact that there wasn't going to be a lot of job growth in the environmental clean-up industry. Most of those people have their people in place, you know, and it was more like construction work.

Being based at the university has enabled CAREERPRO to access SFSU's resources, which have bolstered the effort. Similar to the strategy of the Urban Institute as a whole, Siegal's approach has been to improve communications in order to get the work done successfully. Through this sort of a path, "you end up with a program that everybody thinks is better. And that became the model. There are now three hundred advisory boards in military bases around the country based on what we did." The success of this approach is affected by the particular demographics of various communities. Since each community is different, each will require a board that intimately understands the interests and needs of local residents. Siegal maintains, "This model works best, most easily, in the Silicon Valley, where you have a lot of educated and empowered people. It's a lot harder to make it work from Bayview–Hunter's Point. And so to a large degree what we try to do is take what's been successful in the easy communities and export it to the entire nation where you've got a variety of communities, people who don't have that knowledge, that can't read technical documents that are there."

The $750,000 from the Department of Defense started the program and allowed for the initial exploration of the issues. Other government sources from divisions such as the Air Force, Navy, DOE, and EPA eventually were secured. The affiliation with the university was a significant factor in raising these funds for CAREERPRO. Siegal said,

> One of the nice things about being affiliated with the university is that we are in many ways . . . an independent program, but because we have the affiliation, the infrastructure with the university, it makes it much easier for the federal government who would want to do these community partnerships. But it's much easier for the federal government to fund money through a university than it is through a CBO.

The project's marriage of university affiliation and independent management means that on the one hand, it does not have the direct tie to the internal operations of SFSU, but on the other hand, it does not experience the same juggling of demands that would face an academic department. CAREERPRO has a specific mission, which is enhanced by the support and advice of SFSU and, especially, the Urban Institute. Being based at a university also enables an external perception of neutrality. As Siegal noted, "The fact that we're part of the university, one of the world's largest universities, makes it easier for people who don't know us to be OK with what we do. And it makes it easier to bring in speakers representing different points of view. It's a balanced program."

Of the military, Rene Cazenave, also of CAREERPRO said, "They feel comfortable with us because we can criticize them, but we don't throw tomatoes at them." This is important because "a lot of our work really relies upon being able to work with the community people and the Pentagon and the Air Force and the university." In addition to forging connections with high-level government officials, CAREERPRO can "alert community members of issues that are on the horizon that they should start thinking about, and sort of introduce them to people, you know. A lot of what I do . . . is just take community folks around and introduce them to people who have flown out from Washington who may be able to answer their questions or be a resource down the road for them."

Gib Robinson spoke of the kind of benefits that can accrue to the university as the result of this particular kind of partnership: "And part of what Lenny and

Renee [another CAREERPRO staffer] do is also provide a vehicle for faculty members who have no idea how to take their students or their work into a community." A close working relationship with a staffed nonprofit organization allows SFSU to draw on the knowledge and skills of experienced community activists. Robinson continued, "And that's part of the partnership. It's got to be reciprocal, and it's got to be among other things a conscious effort to change the limitations of the university side as well as enhance the community side."

Robinson speaks to what we have seen as the essence of higher education/ community partnerships — mutual gain. With SFSU's extensive array of initiatives, what is the impact on the campus and the community? Despite SFSU's public mission, as we've discussed, it would be difficult to imagine the university being so engaged in communities across the city without realizing some concrete benefits. In the last chapter, the degree to which community residents actually benefited from community partnerships with the University of Pennsylvania was not quite as clear as it could be. Is this also the case in San Francisco?

The Impact of Community Partnerships on the Campus and the Community

Impact on the Campus

As many institutions of higher education pursue some self-interest through community partnerships, interviewees at SFSU reflected on the degree of benefit accrued to the university as a result of their outreach. As one example, Corrigan stated, "I am not sure I can measure that the institution itself has received material benefit as a result of this. I think our students have. I think our faculty are better for what they are doing. Those sixteen faculty who take the service learning seminar with Tom Erlich come out of these seminars understanding the relationship of their discipline to community. I don't know how to quantify that."

The very existence of the Urban Institute at SFSU is an important factor in engaging the campus. As with the community partnership office at Penn, the Urban Institute is the internal champion of community partnerships. It engages faculty in service learning; it shows faculty and students precisely how they can be helpful, and how their teaching, learning, or research can be enhanced through applied experiences. However, centers of this sort run the risk of isolation. Both Penn and SFSU are fortunate to have explicit presidential support for their outreach offices. The internal politics, however, often run even deeper than the connection to senior administration. The connection to faculty, particularly tenured faculty, may be the most critical aspect to incorporating outreach into the mission of an institution of higher education's mission. Jerry Eisman, as both a senior faculty member and a staff person of the Urban Institute, takes on the role of liaison to faculty. He said of this role,

I really believe that if you've got a senior faculty member in your service learning office, somebody who has been active in a lot of different ways, it makes a heck of a lot of difference. My predecessor in the office was a staff person [but not a faculty member]. And she was quite bright, but had few contacts. The dynamics change completely for me to be there. Because, you know, there's a lot of work that we do in the hall or at the lunch table. And I've been on the strategic planning committee for the university. I was on several faculty committees, including right now I'm on the faculty affairs committee. Without being in a faculty position, how do you get into the DNA of the institution?

Another recurring challenge found across the country regarding campus relations to community partnerships is the distribution of interest among departments. It is not uncommon to find the bulk of outreach work contained in a single department. What is cast as a university-wide commitment may well be a departmental one, or in some cases, an individual one. SFSU has the good fortune of numerous faculty and administrators interested in the work, but consistency across departments still has not been achieved. Eisman pointed to his own College of Science as well as the College of Business as some of the more difficult departments to get involved in community partnerships. It is often the case that some academic disciplines more readily identify possibilities for direct application. For example, Urban Studies and the School of Education at SFSU have a number of service learning courses.

Again, part of the charge for the Urban Institute is to stimulate creativity among the varying disciplines and give faculty members a particular idea of how their work can be helpful to communities. Although Eisman has found it difficult to influence those in science and business, he mentioned a few examples of courses. Eisman's own work with technology is one. In marketing, a faculty member teaches a course in broadcast communications that pairs marketing students with broadcast students to develop public service announcements for nonprofits. In the sciences, Eisman also pointed to a course that takes students to waste dumps to conduct soil testing. But overall, Eisman struggles with engineering and physics as well as more traditional business arenas, such as finance.

As in the case of Penn, one of the most critical gains for institutions of higher education that are involved in community partnerships is student learning and skills building. Not only do students gain invaluable exposure through service learning, but they concurrently develop marketable skills. Several SFSU students secured jobs as a result of their experiences in working with communities. Brian Murphy went as far as saying, "More and more, folks who have an understanding of the community and connection with the community are going to get the jobs."

Impact on the Community

Given the general public image of institutions of higher education in urban neighborhoods, it may take several years before the outreach efforts of certain universities or colleges are received favorably. We may never accurately know the degree of impact of higher education/community partnerships until long after their inception. However, what continually emerges from these case studies is that the process may be even more significant than the outcome. In speaking with Vernon Long of Visitacion Valley, it became clear that SFSU's continued and at times unofficial presence—regardless of funding availability or fanfare— has been integral to sustaining the partnership. Long said:

> When we left Geneva Towers, we were pretty much left out there by ourselves. And, you know, the people that lived in the building—[Geneva residents] set up a system for them to find someplace to live. But the services . . . we were on our own pretty much. And a group of us got together; really, four of us got together and created ways to do things. And so my key point is collaboration, and that's where the university came in. The university came in and they stayed even after the grant that they were trying to get didn't happen. So they stayed. So that to me showed a commitment—that they were here for free. For a year or so they gave us their expertise and helped us build what we have now. None of this was done by any single individual, you know. It was done with the strong collabora- tion of people that actually cared about the situation. And the Urban Institute was one of them.

Another community activist in Visitacion Valley, Judith Sandoval, also spoke of the issue of commitment: "In the very, very beginning we moved over here, it was a mess. Things were depending on all sorts of stuff. And it was Ricardo Gomez of the Urban Institute and two of his students, graduate students, who came in here and just did everything. They were here opening night. . . . They painted the whole building."

Sandoval went on to discuss her prior feelings about major outside institu- tions in general—from city agencies to universities—and the obstacles to be overcome in order to build trust between the two sides of a partnership. She said, "All my life, we picketed against these people" but said that now she has more faith in such institutions due to the commitment they have demonstrated in the neighborhood. "Not only has the Urban Institute but the city as well have not only been working with us, they have become activists." But the institute had to win Sandoval's support. She said:

> When [the Urban Institute] first came out here, it was negative. They came out with a proposal already written, and the old style . . . you come into the commu- nity, and individually, you have each organization sign up on a support paper.

They come in; they get the money; they run it. Well, it didn't work—big time fights and arguments. We worked, and then what happened, the proposal didn't get funded. But they came back. So it did come in originally old-style, but it didn't last that way. And that's why it's been so important. They were our first antagonists; now they are our primary advocates.

Not only does it take time to develop trust in partnerships of this sort, but this example demonstrates that a certain clearing-of-the-air may be necessary before any progress can be made. Evidently, the antagonism characterizing the early part of the partnership gave the community the opportunity to voice their opinion based on prior exploitative encounters with major institutions. This helped carve out a culture of accountability. Instead of scaring away the Urban Institute, the community response helped forge a trusting and communicative working relationship.

Sandoval's statements exemplify some of the suspicion of universities that exists in communities. Because the university world is open to only a few, the possibilities for working relationships between institutions of higher education and communities may not be readily apparent. When asked if they ever expected helpful assistance from SFSU, the Visitacion Valley activists further demonstrated their prior lack of faith in the commitment of major institutions to neighborhoods such as theirs. Larry Fleming maintained:

The university has always been in my mind: shut its doors. They were there and the rest of the world was over here. You know, and nobody messed with the university capitalist. That was just an oasis that's in the city ... and this is not speaking for San Francisco State in San Francisco; this is almost in every community. . . . Wherever the university is, the grass is green, but the surrounding community is chaos; there's no grass at all. I mean, it shouldn't be that way; there should be overflow—an outflow of whatever they're teaching inside these walls should better benefit the people that's out there. And that's always been my case.

Vernon Long continued on this issue, "And it was known to the outside world that San Francisco State wasn't going to do nothing for you."

Evidently, it took the development of the working relationship between SFSU and the Visitacion Valley neighborhood to establish faith in the Urban Institute's integrity. It can be concluded that the relationship-building process is essential to improving the possibility of achieving long-term, concrete community revitalization. Some community constituents will sign on to proposals initiated by universities, maintaining little control over the direction of partnerships. However, that does not mean that trust has been established between the two parties.

The fact that the Urban Institute did not receive the grant to work in Visitacion Valley—a $3,000,000 grant from HUD with a $3,000,000 match—yet continued to work with the community ultimately boosted their credibility inside Visitacion Valley, and in other sectors as well. Susan Alunan said, "But what has happened is that community has given us so much credibility in the mayor's office, in the Human Rights Commission, [in] the mayor's Office of Community Development [and Office of] Children and Families. I mean it's that kind of grassroots credibility that's really helped us build our great reputation in the city."

Few evaluation methodologies can fully capture the varying dimensions of community dynamics. In judging the impact of SFSU's outreach programs, one can look at a number of angles—how the university is impacted, the community, and so on. Alunan speaks to ripple effects—the power of symbolism. The Urban Institute made a critical statement by continuing to work beyond the grant proposal, and word of mouth boosted SFSU's reputation and credibility as a genuine community partner. Public image, in this instance, is an essential driving force in fostering sustainable community initiatives. Therefore, a university must pay attention to the various symbolic acts that will clearly demonstrate its genuine commitment to community. These acts enhance public image, which brings forward other important stakeholders in support and, potentially, collaboration. A positive public response helps an institution of higher education see the value of community outreach, helping unconverted internal faculty or administrators see the potential of higher educational resources in practice. As previously mentioned, many faculty members with a predisposition to community involvement were attracted to SFSU due to its reputation as a socially conscious institution. Therefore, as SFSU continues to build a socially responsible image, not only will existing faculty better understand the significance of community partnerships, but history suggests that prospective faculty, administrators, and students who believe in community partnerships will be attracted to the institution.

Incorporation of Community Partnerships into Long-Term Mission and Operations

But what does any of this say about the ability of a university to build the ethos, commitment, culture, and structure conducive to the expansion and enhancement of community partnerships? While the natural tie between a public urban university's mission and community partnerships has been established, it does not necessarily mean that universities of this type are better equipped to support long-term community partnerships.

Many of the faculty members at SFSU have had experiences with major research universities and are well attuned to the distinctions. Gib Robinson recounted his experiences at the University of California at Berkeley versus his current San Francisco State experiences. He attempted to push Berkeley to engage in community partnerships: "When I went to San Francisco State from Berkeley, I had already hit that administration and realized that Berkeley wasn't going to change because of its rigidity." Robinson suggests that the backgrounds of administrators at San Francisco State play a significant role in maintaining community partnerships: "There are lots of chairs, both deans and chairs, whose resumes include this kind of work, but it's not evident because when you see them, you are seeing somebody who's been named chair of this or that. But their backgrounds are I think part of what makes the fabric of this thing work."

While the question I am addressing is focused on institutionalization, Robinson suggests that the backgrounds of individuals can impact the institutional culture. Since administrators and faculty with particular sensibilities are attracted to public urban universities like San Francisco State, a mutually reinforcing pattern develops—SFSU develops a reputation for being socially responsible, which attracts socially responsible people, which makes the institution socially responsible. Nevertheless, despite the prominence of ideas about social justice, the actual institutionalization of community partnerships is a monumental endeavor. Brian Murphy speaks of the complexity in institutionalizing these initiatives: "We have a comprehensive urban university whose charter originates in the sort of teacher education, normal school history, but whose faculty are recruited overwhelmingly from research one[26] universities. But that's where you get doctorates. As young faculty members without tenure, these people balance the overwhelming demands to teach at this institution and their wish to remain intellectually alive." On the one hand, faculty who are trained at major research universities are not trained to work in communities. Some may be activists or community organizers in their spare time, but graduate school does not prepare people for engaging in community partnerships. Secondly, the demands of being on the faculty, especially at institutions like SFSU with very high teaching loads, can be limiting, and ultimately detrimental, to community partnerships.

In addition to teaching and research responsibilities, it is difficult for faculty members to fully engage in community partnerships absent of specific reward systems for applied or nontraditional academic work. At the least, release time from coursework could facilitate greater community involvement among faculty. But according to Corrigan, while faculty will receive rewards for a diverse combination of activities, they also are given the option of focusing on specific aspects of their work, so that community work is not necessarily emphasized. "Our faculty are judged in all three areas of scholarship, teaching, and community involvement. But they can emphasize one to the exclusion of others. They have to show quality in all three areas, but they can emphasize one of those." However, he particularly stresses teaching in saying, "Everybody has to show excellence in teaching. I mean, we are a teaching institution."

As is often the case in most institutions of higher education, consensus about issues such as faculty recognition is elusive. Jerry Eisman sees the limitation of faculty recognition around community partnerships as one of the most significant challenges to their work. He said, "The part where we're having the biggest problem is in faculty recognition and lack of tenure in hiring and promotion. And all I can say is we're working diligently on that issue. What's happened in the CSU is that there has been a real struggle over a contract. We don't have a contract." He continued, "That's probably our biggest problem—lack of recognition. We're doing things sort of indirectly in terms of celebrations—recognition ceremonies—this kind of activity. And through that way, for example, a few weeks ago we had a celebration of service. Last year it was a celebration of faculty teaching and the year before that, the celebration of faculty research." The issue of rewards in relation to outreach activities is not consistent within the administration either. According to Eisman, "On the tenure and promotion side, the vice president is looking at traditional faculty activities of publication in particular.

While stressing teaching, Corrigan is cognizant of the necessity for senior administrative support for rewarding community involvement. He said of the longevity of community partnerships, "If it's only grassroots—only from the bottom up—it only gets so far. If the institution itself—whose presidents, provosts, and deans are not committed—and the reward structure do not reflect the values, then it doesn't go on."

This institutional support for community partnerships is an outgrowth of years of interrelated decisions. The hiring of personnel with an interest in community eventually impacts internal committees and institutional structure. For example, Corrigan said, "If the curriculum committee has on it people who are concerned about community and community building and involvement—hey, maybe the reward structure begins to change as well." But it takes a significant number of personnel as faculty and administrators to achieve in-depth institutionalization: "You've got to replace an awful lot of folks at the dean's level, the provost level. You've got to have senior faculty who respond." He continued, "If I'm here five more years, for argument's sake, on top of the eleven that I've been here, and each year the faculty that we bring in are more or less like the faculty that we brought in over the last eleven years, then there's no doubt that it will be institutionalized." Corrigan suggests the lack of institutionalization of any initiative at an institution of higher education is often related to "the failure of presidents and chancellors to stay put."

One of the major criticisms of university/community partnerships over the years has been the sheer sporadic and temporary nature of the efforts. Apparently, if few university-based stakeholders are interested in the work, then the chances of institutionalization will be significantly reduced. Many institutions of higher education are recognizing that, as discussed in earlier chapters, colleges and universities cannot simply pack up and leave their surroundings, thus more appear willing to put resources toward more sustained attempts at community outreach. Jerry Eisman suggests,

> The key concept around responsibility is that we're not going away. We're not coming in to do a project, get a flash, get some publicity, get some research, and then go away, go back to our other studies. We are not an academy using the community as a research means or laboratory, or a place for us to do our thing and then retreat back in the walls. We go, and we go to meetings, and we sit and we stay. And we come back to the next meeting no matter how frustrating it is.

Many would agree, throughout the different types of institutions of higher education, that presidential support for community partnerships at institutions of higher education enhances longevity. Brian Murphy suggested:

> I would venture to say that if you talk to any one of a number of other players who do this kind of work, if they don't have the support of the president in the first ten years of doing what they're doing, they're not going to be around in the fifteenth year. If they've got that support, they built the infrastructure, they get credibility, they're legitimized, if you will, within the institution, which is another set of questions, they might be around. I think Portland State is really going to be interesting to look at five years from now because a colleague of ours, Tom Erlich, just got back from Portland State where they got a brand new president. Maybe he's committed to the urban mission, but probably not exactly the way Judith Romilly was. Well, there are members of the faculty there, a very large number of them, who believe she destroyed their curriculum with this notion that they had to have public service everywhere and they had to have public commitment and civic education.

This particular book is not based on a longitudinal study of the evolution of university partnerships over time. My cases also do not include any examples where the president is not supportive. However, the evidence in the case of SFSU does indicate that President Corrigan's influence has been significant to the expansion of outreach initiatives. In general, it is too early to tell the depth of the significance of presidential support, particularly in a contemporary context. Many of the current outreach efforts are driven by a relatively unprecedented presidential commitment, maybe brightening the prospects of long-term institutionalization. But, as Corrigan mentioned, given the attrition rates of presidential posts nationwide, presidential support for these initiatives might not be as significant as it readily appears. The pervasion of various stakeholders with similar interests throughout the institution may be the ultimate prerequisite for institutionalizing a commitment to community partnerships. An individual, committed president might spearhead a move in that direction, but achieving that common, internal institutional sentiment is at least a ten-year project in itself.

Challenges Confronting Partnership

Absent of the involvement of outside institutions, community-based politics can be inconsistent. Universities face their own brand of inconsistency, as students cycle in and out and faculty research tends to follow dollars. Eisman spoke of some of the challenges on the community side of the equation:

> As you well know, community relations are a difficult avenue to pursue. We go through changes of the guard. We're there for internal politicking. We're there when faculty come and go. We establish relationships with the community that will take a while to establish, but we gain their trust. And we gain the trust because we're there to work as a partner—as a full partner.

Eisman places high value on the need for universities to dig deep roots into communities—to stick around and maintain consistency. Community residents, organizations, and public officials need to see a demonstrated commitment on the part of universities in order to establish trusting working relations. Eisman continued:

> It's a matter of a genuine, long-term, action-oriented partnership that we partici-pate in. And that's what makes us work. We've been working in the housing authority for years. We work with the public human services for years. We've been working with the schools and the libraries and the police departments, etcetera. We watch mayors come and go. And we're still there.

Another critical factor, which Eisman stresses, is the need for university-based stakeholders to listen. He maintained, "We don't dictate to them, we listen." The obvious gap between the privileges of tenured faculty and the circumstances of poor people of color in urban areas can create uncomfortable situations. But the more effective outreach initiatives get beyond these difficulties. It is often the community people who are very receptive of external offerings of assistance even in situations where there is little reason to trust outsiders given historical exploitation. Brian Murphy said:

> I marvel at the generosity and the good spirit of community partners who can sit with me at a table and know that I've got tenure, you know, and still be my friend and talk with me about let's do this; let's do that. And not just be consumed with annoyance.

But, intertwined with the challenges of institutionalization, are resource con-straints. Whether external or internal, the availability of the necessary financial support for community outreach initiatives is limited. Indeed, if significant time is required for successful higher education/community partnerships, and if urban public universities generally receive less and less government support, then the prospects for longevity may be grim. Murphy spoke of the need for a greater understanding among foundations and government funding sources regarding the dynamics of community work:

> And the more broad point is the inability of foundation or government funders . . . to pay for the hanging out time that's required. The months, and in my judgement, years it takes of being at the Thursday night meetings. And so, now universities — if they care about it if their leaderships cares about it — they can put up some of the resources. They can give faculty release time; they can do other things that give you the time to hang out. It typically, in my judgement, works hugely better if you actually already have tenure because then you are not always trying to think through, "What's the connection between things I'm doing and next week's article?"

In the philanthropic community, resources are much more likely to be funneled into specific program areas rather than general support or infrastructural development or the community organizing/"hang out time" needed to build relationships at the neighborhood level. Staff at the SFSU/UCSF health clinic in the Mission spoke of their learning process in doing the work, and the concurrent limitations in funding. As Charlotte Ferretti, the director of the Mission Health Center, put it:

> Money comes down categorically for different kinds of things, and you're interested in community organizing. I might not have thought I was interested in community organizing, especially six years ago; that was the furthest thing from my mind. But for six years I have been on a community grassroots organization that was just now turned into the Mission Planning Council. And I was at a meeting until 9 over at [the Urban Institute] on Wednesday night. And then back on Thursday from 12 to 2 at the Mission Planning Council meeting seeing the same people, talking about a different subject. But you have to do both; you can't run your clinic and not be a part of the community. You absolutely have to do that.

Indeed, Ferretti discussed the incredible learning curve facing any academic wishing to do the work. The funding constraints are more of an overarching external challenge; however, the faculty do not automatically know how to engage neighborhoods in such a grassroots manner. It seems as if funders should pay for training faculty to understand the range of dynamics that should be understood in order to be effective in community partnerships. The presence of the Urban Institute partly alleviates the learning curve question through its experience and internal connections within SFSU. Ferretti mentioned that she could go to the Urban Institute for information and advice when she had some difficulties in the community. One could easily conclude that it helps to have faculty members with preexisting ties to local communities and experience doing the work. As previously discussed in this chapter, some of the current faculty at SFSU already bring that. As Murphy suggested, "I think what's really fascinating about the state faculty, and it's been that way all along, is a lot of grassroots folks who became faculty."

However, if the goal is to expand the level of involvement among institutions of higher education and stimulate comprehensiveness and longevity, then faculty who do not have those connections (often most faculty do not) should be brought into the fold. Part of the task for institutions like SFSU is to build upon the outreach experiences and community ties of existing faculty in order to galvanize the rest of their peers.

One of the great challenges lies in who tends to be awarded tenure. While a diverse contingent of faculty may be on staff at SFSU, most tenured faculty tend to be white and less representative of the grassroots/activist mindset. This is hardly exclusive to SFSU. According to Murphy, "Given generational trajectories within the academy, the great majority of non-white faculty are either not yet tenured or very early in their careers." He continued, "There just has to be some awareness of the fact that the people who are under the worse pressure to publish, to get their tenure, are precisely the same men and women that we would like to have more in the field, faster."

Prior relationships between institutions of higher education and communities are another important factor challenging partnerships. Indeed, this may be less of a problem for those colleges or universities that have historically enjoyed healthy community relations. However, partly due to the limited resources and support for outreach, it is often the case that local communities have not received very much assistance from universities. This may be true across disciplines. Although certain departments are, by definition, clinical, outreach and internship programs may only be designed for the short-term benefit of a particular student—to fulfill a requirement. In the case of a faculty member, it might be to complete a study. According to Feretti, "All those faculty people that had their grant money went out to the community and when the money was gone, they were gone too. And that's the perception that the community has about medical care, too." Indeed, not only do some community members feel they have been threatened or policed by institutions of higher education. They often feel as if they have been the exploited subjects of study. The study of the lives of the urban poor is important, but some feel that they do not in any way benefit from such research. These experiences help shape community-based expectations of higher education. Even if SFSU or any other university invests significant resources into outreach initiatives, the pre-existing perception of the institution may not change for many years. People have a need to see that the particular college or university is seriously taking a new approach.

Higher education is not generally a foreign concept to most San Franciscans. In fact, one in six San Franciscans is enrolled in a college or university at any given time. However, many of San Francisco's poorer communities feel they have been wronged by a higher educational institution at one time or another. Even in the midst of a successful partnership, certain dynamics may weaken the position of community residents. For example, although partnership includes two distinct parties, funding often directly supports institutions of higher education rather than both the institution and the community-based stakeholders. Ferretti said, "What percentage of the money is going into the community? And also what percentage is staying on campus. I get sick to my stomach, frankly, and I'm an academic, of money that stays with faculty at the university and doesn't reach the community."

For many institutions of higher education, funding for community partnerships from outside sources can be a means for raising "soft money." Given the aforementioned funding constraints for institutions such as SFSU, more flexible funding is needed from outside sources.

Analysis

A number of lessons emerge from the experiences of SFSU and its Urban Institute. Indeed, the category of public urban university both advances and hinders community outreach. On the one hand, SFSU tends to attract a number of faculty and administrators with activist backgrounds. This population also tends to be relatively diverse, including some with previous grassroots work experience. The student body tends to represent some of the communities in which the Urban Institute works throughout San Francisco. These factors play a critical role in the level of depth and creativity in community partnerships. The sheer number of people interested in this kind of work on campus, from the president to the students, fuels the direction of the work and apparently enhances its prospects for survival over time.

On the other hand, as a public urban university, SFSU draws upon limited financial resources. As exceptional fundraisers, those at the Urban Institute have managed to extend beyond existing resources and creatively access funds from a variety of external sources. However, the dollars are hardly guaranteed. Public urban universities also face high expectations regarding their role in community outreach. Therefore, publicity and recognition for the current initiatives may be limited due to not only the expectation, but the fact that SFSU actually has a reputation for community outreach and activism. Now that major research universities are making a greater effort to partner with local communities around the country, the competition for resources has intensified. Indeed, SFSU already has been relatively victimized by its perceived inferiority in comparison to major research universities.

SFSU does not face the immediate economic concern of ensuring the revitalization of its surrounding community in order to protect or attract students and faculty. It does draw some concrete self-interest from its diverse student body, which represents numerous San Francisco communities. Community partnerships involve many of these communities.

Overall, partnerships with local communities are apparently consistent with the mission of SFSU. Although the written mission statement does not fully capture the outreach interests of central players within the institution, the general internal perception is that SFSU should be involved at the neighborhood level, although it should not be assumed that community outreach efforts enjoy complete internal agreement. Despite rhetoric or perceptions, the true signs of institutionalization rest in operations. SFSU has been grappling with developing reward systems for applied activities among faculty, but this conversation appears to be evolving. The lack of consistent involvement among departments also speaks to an evolution of institutionalization rather than a reality. It does not appear that the entire university embraces the work as an extension of the core academic mission. To do such would require that most departments have some sense of the specific ways in which their disciplines can serve communities. Through the Urban Institute's service learning efforts, various departments are beginning to find their added value in addressing pressing challenges facing local communities. This too, is evolving.

As in most complex organizations, an effort can survive regardless of unanimous or even majority-based support. However, it appears that SFSU actually is moving in the direction of broad support within its own ranks. The more difficult issues of faculty rewards and coordination across departments are unresolved, but given the type of institution, SFSU likely will move more rapidly in this direction than will a major research university. Ties to local communities and activist backgrounds at SFSU far surpass what one would find at most major research universities. With the notion of access being a major driving force of SFSU's mission, the university is and has been in the position to draw upon those connections to further community partnerships.

Chapter 4

Community in the Roots

Xavier University and New Orleans

The campus of Xavier University swells with pride. One can feel it pulsating from the students to the president to faculty to administrators to staff to alumni and beyond. People come to Xavier for a reason—to be a part of the production of outstanding citizens. Xavier is an HBCU (historically black college or university). It is small and private and very much like its host city, New Orleans. New Orleans is the smallest big city that I have ever seen. Six degrees of separation are more like two and people are friendly. Consequently, word gets around fast. In an environment like this, it is difficult for any institution to be isolated. The community activists could be good friends or relatives of the leaders of many of the major institutions in the city. Yes, Xavier is the place students can attend to launch successful professional careers, but they can't ignore New Orleans, even if they are from very far away.

Like San Francisco State University, Xavier draws students from local areas, though not exclusively. Like Penn, Xavier is private. It is not, however, a major research university. Teaching is the priority at Xavier, and it is taken very seriously. It is not only an HBCU, it is religious, founded by missionaries. Community partnerships have always made sense for Xavier, but it also has not perfected its institutional commitment to or management of them. As in the case of San Francisco State, community expectations for Xavier's local engagement are high. Sometimes Xavier has met them, sometimes it hasn't. Have Xavier's current partnerships brought them any closer to mutual gain between the university and the community?

The Mission of HBCUs and Xavier University

HBCUs were created to be resources for African-American communities throughout the American South. They have been instrumental in developing a black middle class, however persistent socioeconomic disparities within the African-American community may be. HBCUs vary in size, prestige, and resources, but images of campus buildings, grass, and trees encircled by deteriorating, poor, usually African-American, communities often characterize the context of many urban HBCUs.

This close proximity of HBCUs to African-American neighborhoods is a func-tion of segregation. They were expected to play a significant role in developing the predominantly African-American communities in which they were located. But during segregation, these neighborhoods included middle-class African Americans and numerous locally owned institutions. When desegregation pro-vided middle-class African Americans the freedom to relocate, the flight of a tax base gradually withered the socioeconomic circumstances of these communi-ties. Rendered much less desirable, these urban communities faced declining public school systems, public health, and economic opportunities. While corpo-rations and individuals with resources often opted to leave these areas, HBCUs had to remain. Facing their own set of obstacles as relatively under funded insti-tutions, HBCUs in these urban areas were increasingly challenged to think even more deeply about their survival both as academic institutions and as conduits for local community development.

The city of New Orleans is plagued by some of the highest concentrations in poverty and unemployment in the United States. Known for its restaurants and tourist attractions such as Mardi Gras, this historic city grapples with a concur-rent infamy for racial tensions and high crime rates. Vigilant community-based initiatives, such as All Congregations Together and others, have begun to address some of the city's challenges. Xavier University has been positioning itself as one of many central players in these improvement efforts.

New Orleans remains a predominantly African-American city. Indeed, most of the aforementioned issues confronting the city as a whole are disproportion-ately impacting African Americans. As institutions founded with the goal of improving the educational status and life chances of African Americans, HBCUs continue to live with an expectation of addressing the issues of African-American communities. However, an HBCU's firm commitment to engaging in local African-American neighborhoods is not automatic. An HBCU, like other insti-tutions of higher education, must cultivate the will to be involved in local con-cerns. It has to identify the interdependency between the institution and the community, and find mutual benefit between its overall institutional aims and the needs of local neighborhoods.

Xavier University's campus is contiguous with three different neighborhoods, each with its own set of priorities. Of the three neighborhoods, Gerttown most closely resembles the characteristics of urban poverty. The university is involved in partnerships in Gerttown and other nearby neighborhoods. However, Xavier, along with Tulane University, is partnering with impoverished neighborhoods throughout New Orleans, such as the Earhart-Tulane Corridor and the C. J. Peete housing development. Most at the university would agree that such outreach is merely the furtherance of the institution's mission, which reads as follows:

Xavier University of Louisiana is Catholic and historically Black. The ultimate purpose of the university is the promotion of a more just and humane society. To this end, Xavier prepares its students to assume roles of leadership and service to society. The preparation takes place in a pluralistic teaching and learning environment that incorporates all relevant educational means including research and community service.[1]

Not only is Xavier an HBCU, it is explicitly Catholic. Xavier was founded in 1915 by Katherine Drexel, founder of the Sisters of the Blessed Sacrament, and is the only historically black Catholic university in the Western hemisphere. In 1915, Xavier was a high school. A normal school was added in 1917, and by 1925, Xavier had become a four-year college. Basic notions of social justice are clearly stated within the mission. This student-centered mission statement discusses community service in the same sentence as teaching and research. Sybil Morial, a university administrator, said of the mission statement, "So we don't talk about a liberal education, we talk about service to society. That is our mission."

Throughout its history, Xavier has grown and excelled. It added a College of Pharmacy in 1927, which has become one of the premier departments of its kind in the country, particularly for African Americans. Nearly 25 percent of African-American pharmacists practicing in the United States graduated from Xavier.[2] Since 1994, the college has offered a Doctor of Pharmacy professional degree. Xavier is also the premier institution in the nation conferring undergraduate degrees to African Americans in biology, physics, and the physical sciences overall. Xavier places more African Americans in medical school than any institution in the country. In 1998, Xavier placed ninety-five African Americans in medical school; the next institution on the list, Howard University, placed forty-three.[3]

The university admits students with excellent academic records; however, it stresses the need to provide access to underprepared students as well. Therefore, Xavier's student body spans a wide range of academic and socioeconomic backgrounds. Scholastic Aptitude Test scores at Xavier, for example, range from 510 to 1460. They have a 78.2 percent retention rate from the freshman to sophomore years. A number of developmental courses to raise the level of achievement among underprepared students helps Xavier continue to be both prestigious and accessible. Enrollment at the university has been rising steadily over the years. In the fall of 1998, Xavier had a record 3,655 enrolled. About 47 percent of the university's students are from outside of Louisiana. Of the remaining 53 percent, most are from the New Orleans area. African Americans comprise 89.7 percent of the student body, while 5.1 percent are white, 1.9 percent are Asian American, and 3.4 percent are Hispanic or other.[4]

Xavier is not a wealthy institution, but it is rapidly raising funds. The endowment stands at $27.7 million, a number that has more than tripled over the past eight years. The university is continuing to receive national attention and noto-riety for its preparation of African-American students from all backgrounds. Another written version of Xavier's mission statement reads, "Reaffirming its Black heritage and its Catholic tradition, Xavier offers opportunities in educa-tion and leadership development to the descendants of those historically denied the liberation of learning."[5] Xavier's commitment to disenfranchised populations is rooted in its history. With access to learning opportunities and leadership development for African Americans at the center of Xavier's reason for being, current community partnerships with New Orleans neighborhoods can be understood in historical context.

Evolution of Current Outreach Initiatives

During the 1960s, the university, like any institution in the South, was situated within the context of the civil rights movement. Federal funding for partnerships between city governments and communities and Model Cities resources became available, and the university began to take advantage of some of these resources. At that time, Xavier forged partnerships with surrounding communities. As previ-ously mentioned, the nearby Gerttown neighborhood probably most resembles urban poverty and the lexicon of associated problems, including drugs, aban-doned housing, and crime. Immediately adjacent to the university is a small resi-dential enclave, which could be classified as "a much more stable working-class, lower-middle-class, lower-middle-income neighborhood."[6] According to John Pecoul, a university administrator and longtime faculty member, "Gerttown had a more stable community base of leadership and neighborhood infrastructure." Another local neighborhood is called Zion City, which although small, takes on many of the characteristics of Gerttown. Most of the federal resources received by the university were targeted toward engaging Xavier in revitalizing Gerttown. Pecoul remembered, "This was a remarkable period of community coming together, planning, tapping some of the federal resources to rebuild the infra-structure of Gerttown." Having emerged only recently from segregation, this predominantly African-American area was significantly plagued by the legacy of Jim Crow. Bus lines had not run through the area, and roads were unpaved. Community partnerships with Xavier directly addressed these problems.

While various elements of Gerttown's physical infrastructure improved as a result of the partnerships, other problems increased. The neighborhood's econ-omy had been driven by its ports and railroads, and a drug-related economy was not very significant during the '60s. Pecoul noted:

> The things that have gotten much worse, I see as having to do with the external
> economic forces that are much larger than can be addressed by the community
> and the neighborhood and the school: the loss of jobs on the docks, the shift to

containerization, the decline of the railroads as freight and passenger-hauling vehicles, which was a big part of the economy of the neighborhood. The rise of drug trafficking . . . and that correlated with the rise in unemployment and the decline in the quality of the public school system after desegregation.

Notoriously one of the worst in the country, the New Orleans school system had been "abandoned by the state white power structure at the time."

As the '70s emerged, a number of African-American middle-class households had left the city. Not only did this lead to the deterioration of housing and the loss of small businesses, but it weakened community-based leadership structures, which according to Pecoul "did not remain as coherent and as strong." Xavier found it difficult to partner with a number of disparate groups claiming leadership in the community. It was not until the 1980s that the university found greater opportunities for partnership. Pecoul suggests that it is difficult to partner with a community when there is not a true, consolidated, community-based leadership body. He notes:

> Politically and economically, we [universities] have self-interests as institutions. And if we're honest, some of them will conflict with some interests in the community. But until the community's leadership is defined and emerges, and the community reaches a consensus in its interests, then what you have is a babble of voices, each claiming to articulate and represent the interests of the community, and the university having to decide, well, who do we work with?

If, during the 1980s and '90s, Xavier was going to engage effectively in community partnerships, a certain degree of cohesion on the community side was going to be required. The commitment to partnering locally has been essential to Xavier's mission since its founding; however, the sporadic relationship with the community was due partly to factors inside of the community rather than the university.[7] According to Sybil Morial, any cohesive community leadership had been especially difficult to identify. To a certain degree, this holds true today. She said, "Well, you know, for years we were very active in Gerttown. Gerttown is a neighborhood that had a million churches and a million organizations and schools and homemade leaders and, you know, all kinds of people who had their own little power base. And so it was much more difficult to reach out. Morial contrasts Gerttown with the neighborhood immediately adjacent to the university where the Xavier Triangle (to be discussed later in this chapter) is located. She said, "The beauty of the Xavier Triangle, our immediate area, is that there are not institutions there. There are no schools; there are no churches. There was nothing to bring those people together, so they were ripe for coming together."

Nevertheless, Xavier's approach to community partnerships has been evolving. Nedra Jasper Alcorn, the Associate Vice President for Student Services, has been at Xavier for eleven years and has been handling various campus-based volunteer initiatives. Since she came to Xavier, she maintains that the university's approach to the community has changed in that "we've moved from just basic direct service where somebody says, 'I have a need,' and 'OK, I'll provide the service.'" Xavier still does meet specific needs, but they are looking to collaborate with the community in strategically addressing a broader set of problems facing the community. Alcorn said, "Rather than just the direct service and looking at the need, we identify what type of systemic causes are involved in the service that's provided. And how we can work with the community so that the resources of the university are matched with the resources of the community so that all may thrive. I think that's been the difference over the last eleven years." In fact, Xavier's overall self-interests as an institution have been shifting over time.[8]

Sporadic community partnerships continued throughout the 1970s and '80s without much coordination inside or outside of the institution. Where the community and university interests seem to have converged over time is more in the economic arena than in the academic one. As Pecoul notes, "The self-interest is: the healthy community helps the neighborhood and the university." In other words, the university and the community both depend on the economic health of the community. The university has been physically expanding, acquiring local property. If some of these properties, particularly commercial ones, are abandoned and deteriorating, the university is helping the local economy and upkeep. However, if university acquisitions are displacing residents or outbidding small businesses, the interests conflict. "We have not had a policy where we went in and bid up prices to get people out or anything of that type," Pecoul noted.

Norman Francis, president of Xavier, does see a relationship between the academic aspect of the university's mission and the community partnerships. He suggests, "The young people we serve come out of communities that have not provided them with all of what we consider to be the opportunities and the legacies to totally fulfill their capacity and potential." Teaching students from this background, according to Francis, is a long-term community development strategy: "Well the long range is then go back into those areas from whence those youngsters have come and see if you can't help those communities or those school systems in your community to make sure that the system does a better job. We get involved because we're talking about saving human capacity, capital, and the like and we want to make sure that when those youngsters come to see us, they are prepared as well as possible with their potential to move forward." These ideas are consistent with the concept of HBCUs, which were designed to develop the capacity of African Americans, many of whom come from distressed or low income areas. Xavier's academic mission is to prepare students. This is connected to the community development mission because those students likely will either return to or do something for their home neighborhoods.

Xavier's work in local schools is another aspect of the connection between academics and community development. Xavier's expansion into the sciences, for example, was an outgrowth of community partnerships. Francis recalled summer programs from twenty-five years ago where Xavier students went into elementary schools to demonstrate how science can be fun. The philosophy was "OK, we've come to you, now you come to us." In other words, in introducing elementary school students to science, it was preparing future applicants to Xavier in the sciences. Those same programs have been expanded and enhanced and continue today. They were a major catalyst in building Xavier's ultimate reputation in the sciences. In twenty-five years, Xavier's enrollment has gone from 1200 to 2800 with 60 percent majoring in the natural sciences. Xavier benefited, and neighborhood residents benefited by gaining increased access to a prestigious institution of higher education and, for some, access to medical school.

Community activist and executive director of All Congregations Together, Joe Givens, provided an example of the mutual self-interest from a community perspective: "If I come to a university, and on the way to that university, I'm riding in a taxi and I see drug addicts and buildings falling down and trash and garbage and misery—and then all of a sudden I see a wall and then beautiful landscaping and lawns and stuff, I've got to ask the question, 'What kind of people go to this school?'" This image is all too familiar in urban areas around the country. It is part of what prompted higher education to develop a greater sense of social responsibility for neighboring communities.

Although a centralized community voice was lacking during the '70s and early '80s, the urgency and saliency of drugs and crime during the late 1980s began to bring residents together. Local properties were increasingly abandoned during this period. Additionally, the oil economy of the entire state collapsed along with the broader recession facing the country. According to Ron Mason of the Xavier-Tulane partnership, universities in New Orleans had to get involved because they are "driven by the need of the city to survive and thrive. About ten years ago, before this new mayor came in, things had gotten about as bad in New Orleans as they could possibly get on a citywide scale. On a scale local to Xavier, that neighborhood was always one of the worst neighborhoods, that is, Gerttown across the canal in the city, because it had always been a mix of light industry and poor black folks."

Xavier responded to these conditions by creating volunteer programs, which would simultaneously address some of the pressing problems facing local neighborhoods and provide experiential learning opportunities for students. In 1988, Xavier became one of the first HBCUs to establish and staff a campus volunteer center to coordinate and encourage the volunteer activities of various students. Still in existence, the center not only engages students directly in community outreach, it expands their career goals. In its early years, the effort still was not grounded within a broad-based community agenda. It did provide tutoring services, for example, in order to help primary and secondary school students who were depending on a crumbling public educational system.

However, the volunteer trajectory was also influenced by national trends. The "me generation" of the 1980s, characterized by raw individualism, was being challenged as a departure from social responsibility. Some suggest that young people were opting out of political involvement or any form of civic engagement. But it is equally important to place these tendencies within a broader political context. The federal government was opting out of activities once considered strictly its domain. The nonprofit sector and volunteers were placed in the position of service provision like never before. Therefore, both the public sentiment and the economic and political need in civil society had shifted. Jasper Alcorn discussed this context in relation to Xavier:

> In the '80s—when they talked about the Generation X, and when the federal dollars stopped flowing into communities—this was the resurgence of the community service movement. Of course, when you have more resources, you have less need of people to be involved because you've got folks that are working in more agencies. But in the '80s when they cut out and cut back so drastically the funding for social help and programs, then there was a resurgence of what it is that we do. And we knew because nobody else was doing it for us. We had to go back and do it for ourselves. So it's more or less an economic need that precipitated us going back to what we do know. And that was in the '80s when Reagan first started cutbacks for social help programs. And that lasted for about twelve years, and we haven't recouped from that yet.

However, Alcorn added that the sense of stewardship and volunteerism emerging in a more structured format in the '80s was not a departure from the preexisting spirit in African-American communities. "The way black communities have always survived is by helping each other," she said. Urbanization had, in fact, withered that traditional sense of community. She added, "So that was the history of our culture. And as we moved from familiar neighborhoods, and moved to urban areas and everybody goes into their garage with their automatic garage opener, we became less familiar as communities. And so what happened is that even though we may do that, we have a need now to get to know each other." Consequently, Xavier draws on numerous traditions in its approach to community partnerships. As an HBCU, it is steeped in African-American communalism established over centuries. It is similarly influenced as a Catholic institution. The Sisters of the Blessed Sacrament, who founded Xavier, built the institution on a foundation of service.

As New Orleans continued to confront multiple social challenges, a number of activists and public officials inside and outside of the city considered innovative strategies to meet local needs. For example, an assessment of the local assets and deficits in the tradition of community building led to increased recognition of the various local universities as important, yet underutilized, assets. The Department of Housing and Urban Development, for example, has looked to both Tulane and Xavier to address issues from housing to employment and training beyond the capacity of city and state public authorities. The assets in Xavier's immediate neighborhood include the university, an elementary school, a high school, a seminary, two nursing homes, an elderly housing complex, sixteen churches, and numerous local businesses and community-based organizations.[9] Xavier historically has been involved in improving streets, public transportation, the construction of a new elementary school, a health center, and an indoor swimming pool.

Vision for Community Outreach

As Jasper Alcorn explained, Xavier's community partnerships seek to provide "efficient and effective community problem solving rather than just providing direct services" and to be "involved in advocacy on the part of the community, working with them side by side, looking to what their needs are and trying to work toward legislation, funding and all of those kinds of things, and using university resources to assist them." Alcorn further discussed the idea of "advocacy": "Assisting them and going to community meetings, talking with legislators, with elected officials on their behalf and with them. So that they know that they aren't alone in the struggle." Welfare-to-work was mentioned as an area around which they have advocated for local residents.

It seems that the outreach efforts of Xavier take on various dimensions. One is the Xavier Triangle Neighborhood Development Corporation, which is a local development corporation jointly managed by Xavier and the community. Another is the volunteer work at the university, which engages students and faculty in addressing a wide range of local problems. Another is the partnership between Xavier and Tulane, which is a community development effort centered on public housing.

Another important collaboration involves the Deep South Center for Environmental Justice, which, along with Xavier, promotes the right to live free from environmental harm. Taking a holistic approach to the environment, this center addresses the issue in relation to jobs, education, housing, health, and other issues. Workshops educate local residents about methods "to protect and defend themselves against environmental inequality."[10] The university itself is equipped with a Center for Environmental Programs, which promotes campus-wide environmental literacy. This center's Environmental Communication Lab and Geographical Information System (GIS) Lab train students and interns in video and GIS technology.[11]

When asked why the institution is involved in so many community partnerships, Norman Francis said, "We got involved in it because we are corporate citizens. We're not just an educational institution, we're corporate citizens. We have a responsibility like anybody else, and our mission is to create a just and humane society. We have an additional responsibility as an institution serving a minority population." Francis is able to justify community partnerships within the framework of the mission as well as corporate citizenry, but as with San Francisco State, a sense of responsibility does not necessarily naturally flow from the historical commitment of the institution. SFSU happens to have a number of people with strong activist traditions shaping the direction of community partnerships. This is somewhat the case at Xavier as well. Xavier is also a small institution. Francis notes, "We're small enough. We have a bureaucracy, but we're small enough not to have the bureaucracy interfere with our ability to get things done." Presidential support, as is the case in the last two chapters, helps. Said Francis, "As a CEO of this institution, I see myself as a cheerleader; I see myself as a supporter." Not only is he a supporter, he is a consistent force, having been in the position for thirty-eight years.

The vision for Xavier's community partnerships is rooted in its historical mission. The institution benefits academically as well as economically. Not only have past community partnerships led to increased enrollment, they have developed some of the more deteriorating surrounding areas. Xavier has both the self-interest in drawing students from poor and disenfranchised communities and in developing its physical surroundings. The university's larger community partnership activities incorporate service into the learning process and stimulate large-scale economic development.

The Elements of Xavier's Community Partnerships

Mobilization at Xavier

Xavier's "philosophy is that the strongest education integrates classroom learning with practical application in the world beyond college"[12] All student-centered outreach activities are under the umbrella of Mobilization at Xavier (MAX), designed to "rebuild New Orleans." Numerous activities ranging from adult literacy tutoring to homework clinics for local k–8 students to various service learning programs fall within MAX.

Jasper Alcorn stresses the fact that students are not blindly dispatched into communities to conduct service. Student Services has developed a system of training and orientation to ensure that communities will gain. For the students, service is a part of the learning process, helping them understand complex social dynamics and inequalities. She said:

> What we ask them [students] to do is look at, basically, the system versus the individual. And to analyze that. Then we bring that in and we translate. This is where the whole concept of service learning comes in—that you tie theories and what

you get in the classroom to practical experience. And it starts to create questions of power dynamics and what's actually happening, how people vote. If [someone is] concerned about what's happening in the classroom, [students might try to find out] "Did you vote in the last election for school board members?" and those kinds of things.

Essentially, Xavier is teaching civic participation through community service. Alcorn went on to say that the volunteer efforts are a "part of the total educational process. We wanted to make certain that the volunteer program was a part of the educational process for students so that they learned that you're not just helping, you're not just giving, it's part of learning about working with people — about what happens in other communities, how legislation may affect folks' lives — and having some understanding of how all of those things connect." Ideally, the mutual benefit is the experiential learning experience for students on the one hand, and the services into the community on the other, as is the case at Penn and SFSU.

Volunteer Services at Xavier attempts to coordinate the numerous community-based projects in which university students are involved, similar to Penn VIPS; although while Penn's initiative targets the entire university community, Xavier's focuses only on students. That said, Jasper Alcorn's office not only helps to establish some internal cohesion to potentially disparate piecemeal efforts, it takes a proactive approach to encouraging involvement among students, rather than merely coordinating existing efforts. Those students without a predisposition to community service, therefore, can be influenced. Alcorn said of their orientation process:

> When freshmen come in, we introduce what's called a community plunge. So when they come in that weekend, they sign up to participate in one-day service events on the Saturday of the final day of orientation. And that's, first of all, to orient them to the city of New Orleans, but also to orient them to the culture of service. And this is something that they'll be expected to be involved in throughout their college career. And so the way it changes the campus is that there is the town/gown relationship, and the separation is not there because . . . the community belongs to all of us and the university belongs to all of us.

For local neighborhoods, Volunteer Services acts as an "agency clearinghouse," where schools, health care agencies, and nonprofits can provide a list of their needs and the university can respond accordingly. Alcorn said of this function:

> When we work with the schools, all the principals and either head teacher, ranking teacher — whomever they want to bring with them — will be our point person

at the school. They come to a meeting at the beginning of the semester. Over the summer, they send us a list of things they'd like us to work with them on. But basically, at the meeting they give an orientation to what our expectations are; they tell us what their expectations are, give us a wish list, and then we sit down and say, "OK, what can we do?" And then we send them back correspondence and say, "We can assist you in these areas for this academic year." And then they know whatever things we identify [that] we can't assist them with, they can try to get elsewhere. So that's part of the strategic process for working with schools—same thing with other agencies.

Many smaller agencies also call periodically, and the office determines whether or not it can meet their needs. When Xavier receives requests that cannot be met, Student Services arranges for a referral to someone else, or attempts to develop the internal capacity to be able to meet the need at a later date.

A couple of new initiatives at Xavier have some implications for community partnerships. One is the announced plan for a Center of Excellence for Middle School Education, which targets deficiencies in performance at the middle school level in public schools. Dr. Francis said, "The new center will pool the research and experience of veteran educators in a collaborative effort to determine the most effective way of preparing teachers in math and science."[13] This is one area where Xavier continues to combine its mission of leadership development of students with its proficiency in the sciences, and ultimately with the needs of public schools. Another important area in which Xavier could become an important resource is through the national American Humanics program, which prepares students to work in the not-for-profit community. The program was just recently introduced; it will help introduce students to careers in not-for-profit management and provide formal certification of proficiency in the principles of managing not-for-profit organizations. With the increased reliance on not-for-profit organizations in service provision, a great need for effective staff persons has ensued. The national American Humanics organization (based in Kansas City, Missouri) estimates that fifty thousand entry-level professionals are needed nationwide to work in nonprofits.[14] Students will be exposed to a new career option, and the nonprofit community will benefit from hiring skilled and trained entry-level staff. If graduates of the program remain in New Orleans and work in local nonprofits, the city will benefit.

Xavier Triangle

A number of foundation and federal government initiatives are targeted toward building the institutional capacity of HBCUs. Recent programs have focused in particular on strengthening the roles of HBCUs as both educational institutions and vehicles for community development. The Department of Housing and

Urban Development, for example, recently has increased its budget for supporting HBCUs. One of the more notable initiatives in this area, spawned by Ford Foundation funding, is an organization called Seedco's HBCU initiative, which assists HBCUs in creating Community Development Corporations (CDCs). During the early 1990s, Seedco, a national organization providing technical assistance to community development initiatives, approached Xavier University about developing of a CDC together with local stakeholders. Prior to Seedco's inquiry, Xavier had bought a building near to the surrounding community. Xavier officials and leaders of local community-based organizations had already been in conversation about a joint effort to address critical social and economic issues. These conversations led to the creation of the Xavier Triangle Neighborhood Development Corporation (XTNDC), officially founded in 1991. "Triangle" stems from the geography of XTNDC's original target area, which is bounded by Howard Avenue, South Carollton, Washington Avenue, and South Jefferson Davis Parkway—a twenty-five square block, triangularly shaped area.

The target area has since expanded to four times the original size, with a southern boundary on Walmsey instead of Washington Avenue. Based on 1990 U.S. Census data, the target area contains 4,500 residents. Since 1980, population in this area had decreased by 12.8 percent or 1,373 residents. Many moved due to insecure safety, limited job opportunities, and high housing costs. Between 1970 and 1990, the suburbs experienced an increase by 76 percent of employed residents, while the city experienced a 25 percent increase.[15] Between 1980 and 1990, New Orleans' population as a whole decreased from 557,927 to 496,938. In other words, this particular neighborhood of New Orleans has followed national trends of divestment from urban communities, which have adversely affected many urban African-American neighborhoods nationwide.

XTNDC is an independent entity with university representatives comprising no more than one third of its Board of Directors. The university provides the main office and various meeting spaces as well as fiscal and personnel management. According to Pecoul, the board of XTNDC "doesn't purport to be the umbrella community organization, but it does purport to be open to input from the community and provides channels for input and participation. But the corporation is set up as a partnership of residents, the university, and other major stakeholders like businesses and churches. And the board reflects that profile."

It is important to note that although university stakeholders are on its board and the university assists with its infrastructure, XTNDC does not have any direct decision-making power regarding the university's overall community agenda. However, Pecoul notes that the XTNDC is a good example of the community and university collectively determining mutual interests:

The way we approached it with the Triangle is the best way. We went through a false start I would say within the Triangle framework as Seedco presented it to us. They were very strong on the university being a partner, but a minority partner. So the board was structured with the university having a minority of votes. I don't know whether it was five or six—five or six seats out of twenty-five or thirty. I don't remember exactly, but we were a minority partner. They also said that because the university was coming in probably with a lot more of a clear-cut agenda and so forth, that they gave the planning grant to the university. But the specific assignment was to develop a plan, which minimized the leadership of the university and maximized the community leadership. We took that very seriously. And we hired a staff person and organized it and it's structured that way.

It turns out that many local stakeholders actually wanted the university to play a more significant leadership role. Brenda Davallier said of the early process of incorporating XTNDC, "I know that I wasn't there when they incorporated, but all the original incorporators were residents. Nobody from Xavier—they were all residents. They had included in their articles that Xavier would appoint up to one third of the board, but not more than six. And the board could be as many as twenty-five. And they really did; they wanted the name Xavier included in 'Xavier Triangle.'"

Brenda Davallier is the current executive director of the XTNDC.[16] Because XTNDC is an independent not-for-profit 501c3 organization, the director is an independent staff person. Given the structure of the organization, the director ultimately is accountable to input from a number of directions. Without any formal status within the university, departmental or otherwise, the XTNDC appears to be in a vulnerable relationship with Xavier. Davallier, however, has never felt any such insecurities. She notes, "For one thing, and I have always felt this, we've been treated like another department of the university—not a step child or somebody that's in the way. And one of the things that I hear among other colleges, and it's been in several places, the competition for space for instance. That seems to be a very big thing on most campuses."

The XTNDC is equipped with spacious offices in a building on Xavier's campus. The site happens to be in an area that is closest to the neighboring community, giving it a physical presence both at the university and in the community. Early in the development of the XTNDC, the university had to be cognizant of the potential perception that Xavier was looking to use the XTNDC as a means of taking over the community. It was critical for Dr. Francis to publicly dispel any such ideas, if indeed Xavier was interested only in revitalizing the neighborhood. Davallier recalled, "And what Francis did is, he called a meeting of all of the residents in the area, not in Gerttown, but in the area, from our side of the canal. And we had eight or nine people come, and in fact we had occupied Xavier south [the southern part of the campus] at the other end, and he wanted to assure them that we wanted to be good neighbors. That we weren't going to take over the whole community."

The fact of the matter is that community partnerships never will involve the entire university. Community-based constituents primarily will communicate with specific representatives of the university. Successful partnerships tend to be characterized by healthy relationships between specific university-based stakeholders and community representatives. One of the more critical figures is the president. If the president supports the partnership activities internally, and is trusted by the community, then prospects for future relations are brightened. Community activist Joe Givens does distinguish between supportive and non-supportive university faculty and administrators. He happens to be encouraged by President Francis. Givens said, "There's such a thing as community-minded presidents and then there's such a thing as ivory tower presidents." Givens is excited about the prospects for Xavier's involvement in community partnerships partly because he knows and respects the players at the university. He said, "Sybil Morial has been a supporter of this work for a number of years now. And I've worked with John Pecoul in the past. So, I know they're serious about it."

The university's involvement in the XTNDC also consists of fiscal and personnel management. Xavier University is the fiscal management agent for XTNDC. Davallier commented on this topic, "That's also very significant because then, for our new CDC, especially when I started, you need good, sound financial management to be able to get funding." Both Xavier and Tulane often engage in joint plans and proposals with XTNDC regarding issues within the geographical target area. The initial board members were all community residents who requested a greater presence of Xavier staff on the board. The XTNDC promotes issues such as economic development, home ownership, and overall neighborhood revitalization. Its historical focus on housing issues has earned XTNDC the designation of a Community Housing Development Organization (CHDO).

XTNDC works with a Resident Advisory Committee (RAC) comprised of any residents or businesses from the target area who wish to be involved. RAC meets monthly to identify local priorities and develop and implement strategies to address them. It provides an avenue for continuous resident input into the work of XTNDC. This committee works closely with the preexisting Enterprise Community Committee—one of eight in the city. Since its inception, RAC has demonstrated a significant commitment to developing the necessary strategies for improving local conditions. Rona Marshall, the board president, said of the RAC meetings, "We average I guess about twenty-five or thirty people a meeting, and that's not bad when you are looking at the fact that these are people who have no cars to get from their neighborhoods. And there are no buses that run, so, you know—and this is the reason why we try."

Residents either walk or catch rides from others to attend the meetings. But it is important to note that home owners rather than renters tend to come to the table. According to Marshall, the home-owning population has a greater sense of investment in their neighborhood. They tend to feel a personal stake in the future of the area. In order to get renters more involved, the XTNDC is stressing strategies to foster home ownership. Another strategy focuses on "making owners of these rental properties more accountable." As discussed in previous chapters, developing genuine lines of communication with residents is difficult. It takes a great deal of time, and, as Marshall notes, those of higher means or sense of entitlement tend to come to the table. Even the poorest communities have some level of economic diversity. Maybe store owners or politicians might be the most likely to partner with a university. Community partnerships must constantly ask themselves, Who is the community? Who are we trying to impact? The home owners do have a stake in the neighborhood, and need to have their issues addressed, but the renters probably are the residents who stand to gain the most from the resources of a university.

Nonetheless, the XTNDC is addressing access to housing for both home owners and renters. For home owners, it currently is rehabilitating twenty-four occupied homes and four units of cooperative housing. According to Rona Marshall, "We've begun a lot of rehab, meaning that we've certified a lot of home owners to actually have major renovations done to their homes. Again a lot of the Xavier Triangle boundaries, people that live within those boundaries, are homeowners. A lot of them are elderly, which made that program very successful." Cooperative housing "affords an awful lot of people, particularly in our community, an opportunity to have a home that they would not have been able to afford," said Marshall. She continued, "And what I also love about it is the fact that these homes are extremely attractive. They're very comfortable; they bring an upgrading to the neighborhood." XTNDC recently received a grant of $365,898 from HUD to provide "extensive training on cooperative homeownership."[17] In promoting home ownership, XTNDC's Zion City Housing Cooperative provides affordable cooperative housing. All residents of Orleans Parish may qualify.

The need for small business development also has surfaced on the XTNDC's list of priorities. The Micro Enterprise Loan Fund is providing seed money of up to $5,000 for small or start-up businesses. Those who qualify either already operate small businesses or have the desire to do so. Small businesses, in XTNDC's definition, are those with no more than ten employees and annual incomes at or under $250,000. Half of the funding from this initiative is designated specifically to the Xavier Triangle community; residents of all other parts of Orleans Parish can qualify for the remaining half. The XTNDC also has held housing forums, cooperative training classes, and public safety initiatives on campus. Francis, the president, has attended all of these activities along with various New Orleans public officials.[18]

Prior to the XTNDC, Xavier University already had been involved in local economic development. Since 1983, for example, the Xavier University Economic Development Center has been providing technical assistance to small minority businesses throughout the Greater New Orleans area. The center serves as a clearinghouse of information for the business community and economic development agencies, and conducts various applied research projects. Both the Economic Development Center and the XTNDC are projects without time limits. As discussed in previous chapters, one of the complaints encountered across the country among community-based stakeholders about institutions of higher education is their inconsistency. Oftentimes, these inconsistencies are the direct result of terminal projects. As established in previous chapters, the work necessary to simply forge relationships with community-based stakeholders may span several years. Sybil Morial distinguishes the XTNDC from previous time-limited projects in the area. She reflected on the Model City era:

> There was an opportunity. The people in that community [Gerttown] really needed things done. A lot of the streets weren't even paved. There was no bus line. The school, Daniel School, was falling down. There was no health clinic. No recreational facilities. So the people in the community—although the Model City provided an opportunity to get some funds to do some things in the community—they approached Dr. Francis. Then people with the city, other civic leaders, and community people came together, and Dr. Francis said, "What do you want to do?" And so they had a list of a lot of priorities. They wanted to replace the schools. They did get a new school. They got streets paved, they got a bus line run. They got the day care center. They got the health center and the indoor swimming pool right there on land that Xavier made available. And that particular effort was just a project, you know, it was just related to that project and that goal. When it was accomplished, the goal was accomplished. They got everything they set out to get. Then the cohesion that was there before kind of lost its purpose. There was no longer a purpose for them being together. And that's the difference with the CDC (XTNDC). It's not just project oriented.

Therefore, the XTNDC is an attempt to build an ongoing university/community partnership that can be self-renewing once a particular set of goals are met. Davallier added, "It's a real partnership. It's an ongoing relationship where you move from project to project or activity to activity, goal to goal. And you keep revising the goals to keep up with the nature of what's going on in the community."

While XTNDC has focused largely on housing, it galvanized the community in the development of a comprehensive revitalization plan in 1997, which discussed issues ranging from education and youth to poverty and unemployment to the environment and health. Demographics, land use, zoning, infrastructure, resources, and assets are other critical issues addressed in the plan. As a result of the extensive planning process, which engaged a broad cross section of stakeholders in the target area, XTNDC emerged with a revised mission statement and a specific action plan.

> The mission of Xavier Triangle NDC and this comprehensive plan is to stabilize, revitalize and beautify the community with particular attention to upgrading housing, encouraging home ownership, improving the physical and service delivery infrastructure, creating opportunities for increased employment and economic development, and establishing solid links to citywide and area agencies and organizations.[19]

During the planning process, six teams each developed strategies to address six priority issues, including beautification, education and youth, economic development, public safety, funding for housing and human services, and health and environment.

The plan for beautification proposes to impose fines for littering and to maintain sidewalks, including a proposal to tow cars parked on sidewalks. They proposed to require the state Department of Transportation and Development to maintain and landscape along state-owned roadways. The creation of green spaces along abandoned railroad tracks and vacant lots was also included in this category.

Under education and youth, the development of a peer ministry was suggested along with the need to create structured activities and recreational facilities for youth. Strategies to increase local youth's responsibility for the community were also discussed.

Plans for economic development call for a general discount store, continuation of the microloan program, and participation in a business association. The need for effective job training and placement and the improvement of traffic circulation, parking, and land use were also suggested. The majority of the target area has an average income of $11,000 per year. Over 40 percent of households in New Orleans are in poverty; rates exceed this level among African Americans. These rates are reflective of those in the Triangle target area, which has a 12.4 percent unemployment rate. Higher paying technical jobs are increasing, but most residents are not trained for such positions.[20]

In the area of public safety, they proposed to arrange meetings between residents and the local public safety committee, to enforce truancy, to publicize the names of drug offenders, to develop a neighborhood watch, and to call for more police patrols at night.

The category of funding for housing and human services included greater financing for property repairs, the further promotion of home ownership, the prohibition of the use of "fireboard" and OCS board on the exterior of buildings, and the use of NHIF funds to purchase vacant houses and lots for development. Partly due to the work of the XTNDC, housing conditions have been improving in the target area. After two years, during 1997 there were sixteen fewer vacant or blighted houses, fifty-nine fewer "substandard" occupied homes, and only twelve houses in need of demolition (compared to seventy in 1994).[21] In the target area, 94 percent of the renters and 93 percent of the homeowners are African American.

Health and environment suggestions included the need for laws prohibiting car repairs on streets and driveways, and parking on sidewalks and other unauthorized places. They also called for noise ordinances. They suggested health screening for the ill effects of chemical pollutants, as well as further discussions with federal and state officials regarding the Thompson Hayward Plant, as the chemical company's grounds had become recognized as a hazardous waste site.

A community advisory board has been monitoring the implementation of the plan. Throughout the planning process, various local stakeholders had given input toward the ultimate construction of the current strategies. Community residents, businesses, and various local organizations and agencies were solicited regarding their ideas for local improvement. Initial contact was conducted by mail; twelve hundred questionnaires were sent to residents, two hundred to local businesses, twenty-three to churches and other organizations. One hundred fifty surveys were completed, some of which were aided by one-on-one contact.[22] After synthesizing the responses, results were summarized and distributed at a public meeting at which working committees were developed to address some of the critical issues.

The XTNDC is a unique partnership. Its independence actually releases it from the university bureaucracy and any limitations in the culture and structure of the institution. Nevertheless, it is still an extension of the university's commitment to community partnerships. Community residents, although they may not be the most disenfranchised, are sharing governance of the effort, and a broader community-based constituency shapes the priority areas that XTNDC should address.

Center for the Urban Community (Xavier and Tulane)

Using an approach called "holistic intervention", the National Center for the Urban Community, founded in 1998, is a joint initiative between Xavier and Tulane Universities. It emerged from the Campus Affiliates Program, the original partnership between the two institutions founded in 1996. Ron Mason,[23] one-time head of this effort and a senior advisor to the presidents at both institutions, sees the center as a national model for using university-based resources in solving problems facing urban communities. Tulane and Xavier, while having been historically collaborative with each other, are very different institutions. Tulane is a predominantly white, major research university. According to Mason, this difference is beneficial to both institutions. He said, "It's good for Tulane to be able to say we partner with an HBCU, and it's good for Xavier to be able to say we partner with a research 1, top 100 institution." This effort grew out of an external need in the city as a whole, but also a commitment on the university side to extending the idea of community partnership. Mason notes, "So it's the need that drives it from Xavier's point of view, though it is also Catholic — sort of the Catholic tradition of service. And I think they rightfully see service as part of the learning experience and they tie it together that way. For example, what we call service learning at Tulane is when you do service connected to a class-room course that you get credit for."

The National Center for the Urban Community began as a Tulane University initiative when it had been commissioned by HUD to manage the Housing Authority of New Orleans (HANO), which was notoriously one of the worst in the country. HANO is the sixth-largest housing authority, officially with 30,000 residents. Unofficially, HANO deals with 50,000 residents, which is more than one-tenth the population of New Orleans.[24] New Orleans public housing residents' average income is $5,000 per year. What is interesting about public housing in New Orleans is that it is dispersed throughout the city, often in close proximity to wealthy areas. Therefore, the initiative is essentially citywide.

Through the process of working primarily on housing issues, Mason said they realized, "We couldn't just do the housing work and not start to address or work with people to help to address the other problems that affect the strength of the family and community." A part of the original "Cooperative Endeavor Agreement" between Tulane and HUD was to "work with the people and families of public housing through university-based, family self-sufficiency initiatives."[25] This thinking led to expansions from housing into welfare-to-work and public education. The very process of engaging in community partnerships is knowledge development. By working on the ground with communities, they realized that a single-issue approach would not capture the full scope of challenges facing residents.

They developed a "comprehensive family-focused case management system." As a result of this more comprehensive strategy, seven hundred people are employed and five hundred have left public housing for single-family home ownership arrangements. Public schools in close proximity to public housing now are equipped with GED programs, ACT prep courses, and tutoring services. They provide shuttle buses for residents and students between public housing sites and the university campuses. The public housing, therefore, remained the centerpiece of the initiative, but numerous interrelated activities were developed in order to meet the multiple needs of public housing residents. Other activities in which the universities became involved include drug interventions, tutoring, service learning courses, and remedial education. A barter program, and an Individual Development Account (IDA) program[26] are also essential to the effort.

The idea of managing housing authorities may seem a bit external to the broader mission of any institution of higher education, even in reflecting on Xavier's charge to create a humane and just society. Mason believes that the work of the center is in harmony with the missions of both Xavier and Tulane:

This is the theory upon which the center was built, and that is that you can't be an academic without bringing value to the process. And the reason we do the services, the reason we help manage public housing is because it establishes real relationships with people who we want to work with academically. We would be duplicitous if we just did the research and didn't provide the benefit as well, if we have the wherewithal to do it. And what we're finding is that by doing the work, we create the opportunities for the academic endeavor.

It is not uncommon for university-based research projects merely to study the poor without providing any assistance toward the problems faced by the poor. "Poverty pimps" has been the popular reference to researchers who build lucrative careers based on studies of impoverished communities without ever having been involved in any efforts to address poverty. Neil Goslin, a staff member of the Tulane/Xavier partnership at the C.J. Peete housing development,[27] notes, "You have researchers set up grants and they use the problems of neighborhoods like this to get attention to those grants and to get money for those grants, and they may get some people involved in the research process, but usually what happens is after the money is finished and their papers have been written, they disappear. People are left thinking, 'Well what did this do for us? We still have these problems.'"

Mason speaks to the broader administrative responsibility to make use of the university's resources on behalf of poor communities up front. Research projects on those communities will be conducted whether or not they have any connection to the center's initiatives. But if both universities are engaged directly in these public housing developments in advance, then they will have created an atmosphere in which researchers must connect their studies to the long-term development of these communities. The center is the vehicle through which research can be made relevant to the communities, and the center's work in itself stimulates new, yet responsible, research projects.

Housing residents are involved in these efforts, but it has not been perfected. Jocqueline Marshall, a C. J. Peete resident, is very involved in the initiative. She indicates, "And I find that's the biggest challenge that I have been having: a lot of people are looking at me as just a resident, and just as a parent, but they don't realize we're the people who have insight into what's going on. You can sit here and say, 'Yes, I can help you.' But you can't help me unless you're walking in my shoes. You need information from me to help me." Marshall highlights the two-way nature of this work and one of the central themes of this book: community partnerships are compatible with the higher educational mission. Marshall points to the knowledge production that naturally emerges out of these partnerships. Taking her ideas to the next logical extension, community partnerships lead to smarter research. If academics have closer relationships with public housing residents, for example, they have greater access to knowledge about the state of public housing, the circumstances of poor people, and so on.

The center's work is a beginning. It has the support of the presidents of both institutions, and it intends to continue expanding its boundaries. A small grants program is supporting the development of resident-driven efforts. The partnership is giving individual residents grants to work on their own projects. For example, many of the residents have hobbies that can be profitable businesses. The grants will allow some of them to get started. The center is also in discussion with the school system about the possibility of handing over ten schools and creating two inner-city k–12 Urban Academies that would be connected to all of the other work of the center. This would complete the picture of what Mason calls a "holistic community development demonstration project."

The center does work with a community advisory board, called the Executive Monitor Resident Advisory group (EMRA), which meets about every other week. This group is comprised of the presidents of the various resident councils that are elected representatives of public housing sites. EMRA acts almost as a board of directors for Mason. It has taken some time for the relationship between EMRA and the center to develop. Mason indicated that early meetings between himself and EMRA were more like complaint sessions than productive meetings. Augusta Cary is the resident council president of the C. J. Peete housing complex, where the center works extensively. Cary has become the first resident in the country to sit on a housing authority board. According to Mason, "She is determined to carve out the residents' pieces of what's going on over there."

The latest incarnation of the Xavier/Tulane partnership is the Crescent City Collaborative, which targets the heart of the city, commonly known as the Crescent. About 38,000 people reside in this area, which also includes three universities, a hospital, and three large public housing developments.[28] The effort is in a planning phase at this time. The goal is to create a ten-year plan, which will include a demonstration school district and a health program. The health program will involve Tulane's medical center and Xavier's School of Pharmacy along with local hospitals. HANO and the city of New Orleans have committed $100 million for revitalizing the three public housing neighborhoods in the Crescent. In the area of the C. J. Peete public housing complex, for example, a private developer has begun working on creating a "model mixed income living and learning community."[29]

Tulane and Xavier are also collaborating to engage faculty in research and service learning relevant to the improvement of urban conditions in these neighborhoods. The National Center for the Urban Community has recently moved its offices to Xavier's campus. It will provide technical assistance to and support for various urban-related university-based initiatives. Overall, the center will analyze policy around myriad issues facing urban communities such as welfare to work, child care, poverty, education, and race. The link to faculty has not been very strong up until this point, but the will has been established. Longtime

Tulane Professor of History Larry Powell is the new director of the center. Few Xavier faculty have been involved in this particular effort to date.[30]

Faculty and Departmental Involvement

While MAX, XTNDC, and the Center for the Urban Community are the major community partnership activities, faculty and departments have found their way into some of these efforts. Unlike Penn or SFSU, Xavier does not have one central coordinating office that will solicit departmental and faculty involvement. Each department does, however, seem to incorporate some aspect of community partnership into its curriculum.

The College of Pharmacy is one of the most reputable departments on campus. It is also one of the few graduate programs. Ann Barlare, Professor of Pharmacy Administration, is a Xavier graduate who returned to the institution twenty-two years ago. She is a New Orleans native who returned with a purpose. She said, "I could work someplace else, but perhaps my contribution would be different if I were at Xavier." The School of Pharmacy has been brought into the Center for the Urban Communities efforts at the C. J. Peete housing development, where Barlare conducts health screenings and monitorings, and medication review clinics. She holds "mini-presentations to a number of people at Peete about different diseases or health conditions and what they can do in terms of maximizing drug therapy and making lifestyle changes that would be conducive to their health. We work with health fairs that Peete holds twice a year. Last year we went every week to do blood pressure screening, cholesterol screening, diabetes screening, and to conduct medication review clinics. This year, we're going twice a month because we found we were just overwhelming them."

They also conduct similar activities in local high schools. To Barlare, this is not charity work separate and apart from the mission of the department: "It's so much a part of our instructional program that we don't separate it out in our mind." Barlare suggests that training in pharmacy in general has been moving toward self-medication, so teaching community residents how to monitor their health is very much in line with the thinking in her field. Now that word has gotten out about their efforts, they often are contacted by local organizations to give seminars, particularly at local schools. Many of the students who they encounter ultimately become Xavier students. Although the efforts are known within the school and in the community, Barlare mentions, "People in the university don't know what we're doing." For Barlare, incorporating service into her academic work has not been a problem, due to the nature of teaching in her field. But while the efforts are connected to community partnerships sponsored by the administration, like the Center for the Urban Community, they do not tie to the efforts of other departments.

Chair of the Art Department Ron Bechet spoke of the Community Arts

Partnerships, in which Xavier works with three community-based organizations. Students are trained to work with these partners and provide "reciprocal things that will help those partner agencies become stronger." Longtime art professor John Scott promotes an interdisciplinary approach: "We're functioning as a fragment of the whole, you know. What I can bring from the arts community will benefit art, but also chemistry, biology, and anybody else." The art department historically has worked in local communities, particularly with youth. The Audubon Art Center, for example, was an outlet for youth to come and learn about the arts. Programs of this sort become of great benefit to the department because they attract future students. They introduce the arts to people who otherwise might shun art as insignificant or not a viable career option. Scott characterizes departments at Xavier as collaborative, partly due to the small size of the institution. He likens it to "improvization." Rigid structures may not be in place to get departments working together, but "we can react very rapidly to a developing situation to take total advantage rather than having a meeting scheduled a month from now to see about the possibilities." He is opposed to the concept of a big umbrella entity that would impose a "rigid structure," suggesting instead that "if there are opportunities for synergy . . . they can be taken advantage of, but not try to package it under one big umbrella."

Xavier is more than a university to Scott. The commitment to community will persist at the institution in his eyes, and departments will continue to transcend turf boundaries. This is partly due to the culture of New Orleans, as well as the historical ethos of the university. Scott notes, "What people don't understand about this is that Xavier to us was not just a school, it was a life raft. So without this place now, we're in the ocean with nothing. It's not only about a job, it's about the survival of a people." Both Bechet and Scott are New Orleans natives as well. These comments speak to the ownership and pride throughout the Xavier community. One aspect of the HBCU is that it was designed to develop the African-American community. What these institutions have been able to do, simultaneously, is to preserve certain cultural traditions. To varying degrees, a spirit of community partnerships is rooted in the very idea of an HBCU. The African-American community has become increasingly diversified, changing the context in which HBCUs operate, but Xavier has been able to preserve a tradition of stewardship toward one's community.

Another New Orleans native and Xavier alumnus, Rosalind Hale, is the chair of the Division of Education. She also believes that service is the norm at the institution. With a public school system in dire need, I was compelled to ask Hale about the role of the Division of Education in enhancing the capacity of the local schools. They have been working with middle schools. They are training minority teachers to teach advanced placement courses. They have concluded that teacher training is the one area where they can make a difference in the quality of schooling. This work takes Xavier back to its roots as a normal school, designed to train African-American teachers. They are also providing counseling, since very few counselors are available in the schools. Graduate students carry out much of this work. I asked her if students, especially undergraduates, could really benefit communities. What can they provide, I wanted to know? "An ear" and "a voice," according to Hale: students can be a sounding board, especially in a counseling role, for those who want to get out their story. Students can also be a voice, referring community members to faculty or other experts who can directly address various issues.

Entering the New Orleans school system, however, has been difficult, Hale said. Many principals have limited or blocked their access, but Xavier has found ways to enter, primarily through direct relationships with teachers. This work requires a great deal of personal contact. Hale notes, "That's why you see my hair all over the place. . . . Any one day you'll see my calendar is, I don't have time to breathe, you know, because I feel very strongly that the personal contact is very important, and I try my best to be the initial liaison and then the faculty member takes over." As confirmed in other chapters, community partnerships are most successful with long-term relationship building. In order for partnerships to be done well, people like Hale need the time to develop those relationships, to be in constant conversation. The Xavier ideology around social responsibility is impressive; however, if the institution does not have the necessary institutional support systems, partnerships run the risk of folding.

Although some faculty have been able to incorporate service smoothly into their work, we can see that Hale may be overcommitted. Similarly, Associate Professor of Business Michael Taku provides technical assistance to local small businesses but can't find release time from his four-course-per-term teaching load. Overall, faculty seem to be very interested in community partnerships. Some departments, such as Art, Education, and Pharmacy, have found ways to incorporate service into their work, but it is still a struggle. Institutional commitment without formal interdepartmental ties may be achievable in a small institution like Xavier, but it leaves a lot to chance. The broader community partnership activities sponsored by the administration do not necessarily connect to departmental efforts. However, the Center for the Urban Community's expansion may change that situation.

Impact on Campus and Community

Impact on Campus

Clearly, the campus is driven by a service-based philosophy. How much has this survived the current community partnerships? Have the partnerships changed anything about the campus? As previously mentioned, experiential learning opportunities are clear ways in which the university is positively impacted by community partnerships. Omar Buckner, a Xavier alum and current staff member of the Tulane/Xavier partnership, reflected on his Xavier experience: "As a student at Xavier, we started this organization, MAX, Mobilization at Xavier, and it's a student-run volunteer organization. I know for the past ten years, it's [been] the largest organization on campus. I spent five years—a little more than five years—at Xavier, and I without a doubt learned more from working in the neighborhoods and working in the community than I did in any class I took."

As in the other case studies in this book, engagement with communities affects the overall way of doing business at Xavier. Because real world problems are not neatly divided into disciplinary compartments, universities that bring community partnerships into their curricula begin to promote an interdisciplinary approach. Ultimately, this fosters greater internal communication among academic departments. Although some disciplines are more likely to be involved in applied teaching and research, they may bring other disciplines to the table to meet community needs that fall outside the boundaries of their expertise. Xavier promotes what they call a "co-curricular" experience, which suggests that all disciplines play a complimentary role in the academic environment.[31]

Community activist Joe Givens said, "I can't think of any disciplines that don't have practical application right now in our neighborhoods." He feels that universities have not done enough to get multiple disciplines involved in community partnerships. Students, according to Givens, are not being challenged in all disciplines to think about practical application:

> So I think what's absent is imagination when it comes to creating opportunities for students who participate in this. I also believe that any student in any discipline that makes anything of that discipline, does it with imagination. The most imaginative science majors, the most imaginative lawyers, the most imaginative social workers, the most imaginative community workers. So imagination is an essential part of that. So the question ought to be asked to university students in English, "How can you help this neighborhood with the things that you know now?" Biology major, "How can you help this neighborhood?"

From the outside, Givens is not witnessing a shift toward interdisciplinary involvement in community partnerships. He is suggesting that each discipline reflect on its methods and goals in relation to practical application. While departments could be collaborating at the university, however, they may not be effectively weaving practice into the central priorities of the disciplines. Indeed, Givens refers to issues that transcend specific universities and ultimately call on disciplinary associations to revamp their expectations.

Jasper Alcorn stresses the internal collaboration that ultimately could lead to greater involvement. Alcorn credits the collaborative nature of her co-workers as a principle ingredient in the success of Xavier's community partnerships.

It's whatever it takes to get the job done. And people collaborate. They cooperate. Programs are worked together and they compliment one another. And that's across the university, across academic and student affairs, and whatever division. Folks are just working together. And so you had that working together on campus, and then you bring that out into the community, and people don't see the fractionalizing. They see all these areas coming together, so it's easy when they're talking as a unit. They're not talking to one area of the university and, you know, they're fighting for turf. We've got some resources, and some people with expertise. We recognize . . . how can we compliment each other to make sure that we all survive, we all thrive.

This degree of collaboration is partly due to the size of the university. Both Penn and SFSU have a greater struggle to get multidisciplinary involvement in community partnerships. "In larger institutions, it's easier to compartmentalize your life; I think at smaller institutions, it's a bit harder," notes Jasper Alcorn. Dr. Francis also has been taking an increased responsibility for establishing consistent internal communication about the university's community partnership efforts. In the past, he has convened meetings among various university stakeholders on the issue. In looking to the future, Morial sees the Center for the Urban Community as "the umbrella that's going to pull it all together." But already, she sees the community partnerships as a means of sensitizing the entire Xavier community to the needs of the adjacent neighborhoods.

According to Alcorn, the culture of New Orleans is an asset to brokering cross-sectoral relationships. Although a city of about a half a million, New Orleans is culturally small. She said of New Orleans, "It's small; it's really small when you think of the communities and neighborhoods and who knows whom." Xavier's student body happens to be drawn from across the country, but situated in New Orleans, they become a part of the tight network. It is probably easier to build collaborations among the larger institutions with community-based organizations in a city where so many know and know of each other. Xavier's developing partnership with All Congregations Together, for example, was significantly facilitated by the preexisting relationship between Joe Givens and various administrators at Xavier. The prospect of a Rockefeller Foundation grant was the external catalyst that helped both Xavier and ACT develop a very specific joint initiative.

Although Xavier's student body is essentially national, many of the students are not disconnected from the realities of poor and working-class urban areas. Service has a special meaning for these students because they are taught how they can be helpful to their home communities. In Alcorn's words:

Many of our students may come in and may be from communities just like Gerttown, but they're on scholarships or on aid and they get an opportunity to come to a place like Xavier, where we assist in being able to help that student, give them a springboard from one economic class through its educational pursuits to another. And that student can then go back and help the family, the community that [he or she] originated from or one that [he or she] migrates to upon graduation. That's the broader way that we assist.

Impact on Community

While an HBCU with a socially responsible mission statement located in a predominantly African-American city and neighborhood, Xavier has not always been perceived as a good community partner. Although Ron Mason sees Xavier as opening doors to the community in its partnership with Tulane, he has come to realize that Xavier is not necessarily treated as a more committed or responsible institution. Mason recalled, "Even Xavier [receives] the same sort of reaction in the community oftentimes that we [Tulane] get when we go out there. The reaction being, you know, 'where were you when we needed you, and now you are just here because of some grant or some research to do, and if it wasn't for that we wouldn't see you.'"

The XTNDC has placed the university in a direct working relationship with local residents. Rona Marshall, who grew up within the boundaries of the Xavier Triangle, is currently the chair of the XTNDC board. Marshall works at the mayor's office as a program manager in the Office of Health Policy. She received an invitation to attend a meeting about the development of the Xavier Triangle. Marshall discussed why she ultimately became so deeply involved in the initiative:

> I felt that, number one, I've already done a lot of community work, but most of it was on a state level or city level or was in a community outside of the community where I actually have lived, and where I've actually grown up. So, well, I need to come back and do something from where I got my start. And so I was asked to think about becoming a member of the board. And, of course, I was very excited about it because it fit right into my plan of giving something back. And once I was asked to be on the board, then I was asked if I would take the honor of becoming president. And of course they voted me in as president, so here I stand.

She suggests that the university traditionally has been perceived as inaccessible and unattainable in her neighborhood. Her work with XTNDC is an opportunity for her to play a role in diminishing that mystique.

> From the perspective of the community I have heard sometimes, well it's as if Xavier was . . . on an island of its own, that's untouchable. Whereas to me, what I have tried to impact and bring into the community is that that was a myth. The school is very open to us in so many ways, and I say that genuinely. They're always involved in things that will assist in educating from whatever level. Whether it's to open doors in terms of putting the information where we can get it, or where to go for certain types of jobs. Whether it's programs where they

teach you job skills or where there are jobs that are actually available. They've opened their doors to have workshops and these types of things on campus so that we don't have to go looking. Xavier has purchased properties that they have given to the organization to develop and build homes on it so that some individuals could be first-time home buyers for single-family dwellings. I mean, to me, that's being involved.

Being an HBCU in an African-American neighborhood does not preclude Xavier from being perceived as elitist. But Marshall suggests that the perception is not backed by reality. The barrier had to be broken down. Xavier is a prestigious, private university, yet it is not inaccessible to the community. But it took being involved in the XTNDC to make Marshall aware of Xavier's potential to be a trusted community partner. Marshall, like her neighbors, had not expected Xavier to be as involved as it is. She said, "That is not what I saw as the function of the university. Anything that would have to do with education, yes. But to reach that far, no. I did not. And I probably would not even believe that something like this exists if I weren't personally involved in it." While universities have to internally justify community partnerships within their missions, Marshall suggests that they would have to make the same justifications externally. Even though community residents could benefit from interaction with the university, they may not realize that any such partnerships would be within the purview of the university's mission.

Marshall credits the involvement of the community in the XTNDC in expanding residents' expectations of the uses of Xavier's resources. Residents are placed in the position of jointly making decisions about the neighborhood's future with university representatives. But Marshall's personal experiences demonstrate that the direct contact is necessary. As in Philadelphia and San Francisco, residents don't readily think of universities as resources beyond teaching and research, particularly if they have not had much direct experience with the institutions. The world of higher education, particularly that of four-year institutions, tends to be foreign to many communities. Unless the universities make it known that they are willing and ready to work with community-based residents and institutions in addressing local problems, communities will not know exactly what they can expect from them.

Givens sees the limited expectations of universities in communities as well. He said, "In our congregations, I think they've come to expect a limited role of universities. 'This is where the kids go when they finish high school,' period. Not think of it as an active agent for change in the neighborhood—an active agent for the development of the neighborhood. It's an active agent for the development of future leaders, fine, but it is not expected to have a proactive role in community affairs."

If communities do not have the expectation of a more engaged role for universities, it is difficult to develop community-driven higher education/community partnerships. Indeed, Xavier can create a number of different initiatives, but unless community residents are informed about what they can expect, it will be difficult to forge relationships where the true priorities of the community are being addressed. The XTNDC did go through a process by which the community and the university developed a strategic plan. However, it is not a plan that proposes how the university's resources specifically will address the various challenges facing local neighborhoods.

To Marshall, the fact that Xavier is an HBCU does not necessarily lead to a stronger connection with the mostly African-American local neighborhoods. Many local residents, to her knowledge, do not attend Xavier as students. Some tend to see Xavier as "out of their reach." However, she does not see tension between Xavier's students and the local residents. Jasper Alcorn suggests that Xavier is accessible to residents of Gerttown. She referred to the university's Tuition Opportunity Plan (TOPS), which is a state program that allows Louisiana students to attend private universities at the rate of state institutions. If students who are less academically prepared attend Xavier, they are offered a number of academic support and tutorial services. Xavier's above-average retention rate speaks to the success of those supportive services.

Higher education/community partnerships of this sort are not static. Relationships between universities and local communities are not always good or always contentious. As discussed in the previous two chapters, relationships take time, and must be continuously cultivated. Marshall noted, "You might have the community 100 percent today and then next week that changes, and there are a lot of variables as to why that happens. But it's an ongoing struggle to make certain that you're in touch, in communication, and responsive to what the people want. And they've done that quite well. And I think they've done that quite well with a lot of constraints."

According to Alcorn, it is impossible to expect that everyone in the community will be pleased with their relationship to Xavier. She said, "No matter what you do, you're always going to have your detractors. I mean, you're never going to do enough for some folks." In her experience, the expectations of the university are very high. Because Xavier has offered assistance to the community through the student volunteer service initiative, local expectations have risen. The Student Services office gets more calls than it can handle. Alcorn said, "I think the expectation is sometimes higher than we can manage. You know, you hear stories about how we're taking average students and turning them out to be doctors. And so people think, well you can do the same thing. The expectation is that we can do the same."

Community residents' expectations will continue to increase the more they see Xavier working in the neighborhood. Residents also point to Xavier's overall record as a successful academic institution. In their eyes, Xavier has become a reliable partner due to its demonstrated capabilities as an institution of higher education. Additionally, since Xavier's admissions policies are flexible enough to admit students who otherwise may not have been given access to a four-year college or university, community residents likely see themselves in some of Xavier's students. If Xavier can bring success to people like them, residents have faith that the university will be able to deliver for their neighbors.

Joe Givens sees Xavier as playing a particular role among the various universities in New Orleans. He suggests that Xavier has always played a significant role in the politics of the city. He said, "Well I always knew that at Xavier University we had very sensitive people who understood community, who understood politics, who were involved in the development of African-American power in the city." Graduates of Xavier historically have gone on to become important contributors to the city of New Orleans. Givens spoke of his mother, who graduated from Xavier and spent her life teaching in the school system. Dutch Morial, New Orleans' first African-American mayor, was also a Xavier alumnus. However, Givens suggests that the preparation of students for leadership in the city was the primary means by which Xavier historically had contributed to the local terrain. He recounted an experience in 1984, during Jesse Jackson's presidential run, when Givens was a part of a campaign to register voters. He sought assistance from the political science department at Xavier. He said of the chair of the political science department,

> He was less than helpful in this process. In fact we got no assistance from him at all. We got a little resistance from him, who said that the university ought not be a part of partisan politics, but all we were saying to these students was to register to vote. We weren't telling them who to vote for. So at that point I began to compare what I saw at Xavier and Dillard in 1984 with what I'd experienced ten years earlier in college. And what I experienced was that if you weren't a part of an organization that had some connection to the community, you weren't doing anything. Remember in the early '70s and mid '70s and late '60s, students were all looking for connections to the community.

Givens highlights a similar shift in sentiment being addressed by today's broader movement around higher education/community partnerships. Campus Compact's presidential declaration, for example, heavily focuses on a lost sense of civic responsibility among students. The distinction between now and the '60s is that current community partnerships are being sponsored by higher educational administrators. Political and community activism among students during the '60s and '70s were often a point of contention between students and administrators. Even into the 1980s, when students were occupying administration buildings around issues such as divestment from South African businesses and racism on campus, administrators and students were often at odds about the meaning of social responsibility in higher education. The current anti-sweatshop movement is another area where students are calling for greater social responsibility among administrators.

But, the '60s and '70s are contextually critical to the current call for greater social responsibility among institutions of higher education, particularly with respect to community partnerships. As discussed in previous chapters, people such as Harkavy at the University of Pennsylvania and Murphy at San Francisco State were student activists in the '60s and '70s. Those experiences were among the early foundations for their commitment to promote community partnerships. Moreover, one could argue that student activism from the '60s to the present gradually helped higher educational administrators see the need to partner with local communities, particularly in urban areas. For example, student movements that addressed diversity on campus ultimately were calling for higher education to forge a pipeline to urban public schools—the places from which a diverse student body could be drawn. This current movement, therefore, is not altogether new, but, like most movements, it is an amalgamation of new thinking and previous strategies. Givens referred to the current efforts of administrators as "refreshing" and a "shift in attitude among administrators."

If higher education/community partnerships are going to proliferate, broader lines of communication will have to be developed. Givens, for example, had not been sufficiently informed about the university's various community partnerships. He said, "I am beginning to realize that universities like Xavier do in fact have initiatives that students can participate in, that brings them out into communities. I don't know why they are not better advertised or why they are not better sought, or more sought after by the students themselves." Greater lines of communication between the university and community-based organizations helps both collectively arrive at a win/win situation. If universities simply develop community partnerships absent of ongoing communication, the efforts will be unsuccessful. Each institution of higher education featured in this book has had a moment in history where partnerships did not work for this reason. As Givens said, "It takes a willingness on the part of the administration, but it also takes a willingness on the part of organizations, community-based organizations, to want to have that kind of relationship. One of the incentives that we have is that we believe that community organizing is a career."

As previously mentioned, Givens' organization, All Congregations Together (ACT), and Xavier University are collaborating on a community-organizing initiative. One aspect of this effort is to train students at Xavier in the principles of community organizing, introducing them to the possibility of a career in this area. Another is to help All Congregations Together, with the assistance of students, to organize some of the many churches in the vicinity of the university. On the one hand, students get experiential learning opportunities and an introduction to a new career option, not to mention the broader philosophical lessons that Alcorn seeks through Student Services. On the other hand, ACT could expand the network of churches as well as the network of potential employees in the community-organizing field. If the initiative is successful and achieves long-term funding, ACT, individual students, and the community as a whole will benefit. Additionally, if ACT and the students can build healthy relationships with the local churches, Xavier may be able to overcome some of its historical challenges with finding unified community-based leadership. Since ACT's mission is to unify churches citywide to advocate around critical issues, the university may soon be able to collaborate with a consolidated local church leadership in its community partnership aims.

Efforts of this sort, according to Givens, expand the overall life-goals of students. Life takes on more meaning than professional accomplishments. Givens notes, "If the university is involved, then students become more involved in the community quicker than, first I'll get my degree, then I'll do my internship as a doctor, and then I may contribute back to my neighborhood in some form or fashion." Xavier has made the decision that it is in the business of molding not just good professionals but good citizens. Involvement in community partnerships likely will change the goals and aspirations of some students. Moreover, those students who pursue more traditional and lucrative professional careers still will have some foundation for placing a high priority on social responsibility. Many Xavier students stay in New Orleans, and many Xavier staff are alumni. The motto "pass it on" has survived for decades, and the institution and many of the students take it to heart. This is great for students, and indirectly it becomes great for the community, as Xavier alumns are sent out into the world to be responsible, caring people. But what about the more immediate community residents? The underlying suggestion, particularly in the case of Penn and West Philadelphia, was that community partnerships primarily benefit various members of the university community. It is clear that community partnerships benefit Xavier and are consistent with its mission. Do higher education/community partnerships make sense for New Orleans residents?

"They make sense and they're beneficial to both partners, and probably more so in the case of students and the universities than they have been in the past to the communities," notes Buckner. "I'd like to think that's one phase that we are trying to do differently. It's not going to happen overnight." Goslin added, "We're still at the point where the universities are getting more out of it."

The Center for the Urban Community appears to be the vehicle through which communities may begin to benefit more from partnering with universities. The center places community needs at the top of its agenda. Its comprehensive approach is moving residents out of the piecemeal approaches that had been applied to their life circumstances. Moreover, residents have begun to expand their horizons. Mason reflected, "What struck me more than anything else was people who have been stuck with a limited vision for generations are starting to see past what their limits had been before we started working with them." Many of the residents could have never envisioned owning homes, for example. Mason said, "If I had to hang my hat on one outcome, that would be it—just expanding the vision of people who, for a lot of reasons, have been forced to limit their vision for a very long time."

Expanded vision may not be as easy to assess as the number of jobs or housing units, but it is an important part of process. Community change is not just about the outcomes in services, it is also a question of mindset. Previous chapters discussed the importance of trust, which is another important mental factor in this case. C. J. Peete resident Larry Hurst said, "Because this community, like any other urban community, has been oppressed, we're bitter. It takes a while before we learn to trust. And with Tulane being a prestigious university and Xavier being a prestigious university, people who haven't graduated have been able to walk on a college campus. They always feared they could never go there unless they was walking through it—be in fear that you was going to be harassed. If you go on their campus, you was either coming to steal a bike, break in one of the offices, or you was panhandling. So what the university has done was to give people here an opportunity to even discuss college."

Through the Xavier/Tulane partnership, Hurst suggests that he has learned a great deal through working with the universities, "So this year we have been going on year five. I think Tulane and Xavier have done a great job with the people that's been working down here in this community to shape that relationship, to offer their fax machines, to teach them how to sit down and structure their self and their way of thinking, and just how to get along—to move from one point in their life to the next point. So I think it's a great opportunity because I learned a lot from them. I learned how to do business, how to watch people, watch what they say, watch their motives. I learned a lot about grant proposals and how money has been allocated and never got to certain places." The partnership hasn't changed poverty in five years, but it has given residents like Hurst access to information and a certain awareness about the inner workings of the systems that impact their lives. But, as previously stated, the universities learn as well. Hurst said, "You can teach me how a university functions; I can teach you how we strive off of $138 a month, but still make it."

Another C. J. Peete resident, Darlene Poole, said, "Having the universities here in development like this has been a tremendous asset to our community. But the community has not embraced that because it's trying to get the residents to overcome their own barriers and issues—lack of knowledge and how to use that information and not being intimidated by people with a Ph.D. and a Master's degree." She sees both the community and the university as having issues to address. She mentioned that some people from the university act as if they know more than residents, and don't respect their knowledge.

The Center for the Urban Community does take regular inventory of its outcomes. Mason notes, "We have to measure the benefits to people because we have government grants. They make us track it on a quarterly basis. So we know how many people are getting GEDs. And over time, the hope is that you can actually see the communities change—you could see communities become stronger and families become stronger and children become stronger." Celeste Hannah, a center staff person regularly tracks residents and their life circumstances on a database. What she has learned from her relationships with residents has helped her be an advocate in other settings, "That's what I see—being able to go to those meetings and say, 'No, wait, you're wrong. This is what the residents are saying.' I mean, that's advocacy to me, for people to know what's really going on and what you really need to address and people don't have anywhere to live, people are doubling up in units or in houses or tripling up." The office at C. J. Peete is now equipped with a database that allows them to track vital information. Current director of the Center for the Urban Community, Larry Powell, maintains, "So everything we're doing now is becoming a lot more targeted. You know, when somebody tells us they need a GED program in this community, well we don't go rush out and try to set it up. First we want to see what the needs are. You can do that by surveying folks, but maybe it makes a lot more sense to see what the data says in your database."

The Xavier Triangle is guided by clear, quantifiable goals, such as the number of rehabilitated homes and cooperative housing units. Rona Marshall provides the perspective of a longtime resident on the impact of XTNDC's efforts on the neighborhood: "I mean, since I first became involved, we had mountains of abandoned properties, mountains of trash, mountains of just all kinds of things that you can think of.... If you look at the then and now, you will see where many abandoned houses have been torn down, demolished, cleaned up. You now see, of course, abandoned lots, however, to me that's still much more attractive than houses that can be used for drugs, they're fire hazards, and children could get hurt in them."

The relative responsiveness of the community is another means by which partnerships can be assessed. Alcorn has encountered various opinions of the university, but in her work, she continues to see the community's interest in working with the university. She said of the community response to the volunteer activities, "I think for the most part it must be pretty good because people still keep calling and asking us for assistance. So if we weren't doing something right, I think those calls would stop coming. So if the word gets out, I think that's proof positive that we're doing a good job because the calls keep coming. 'I need a tutor, a teacher referred me or I have a friend who has a child'—it goes on and on. And you get calls for tutors, mentors, for all kinds of things." This goes back to the issue of trust. When the residents begin to see the community partnerships making a difference, they have more faith in the potential of those efforts to make some difference in their lives.

Incorporation of Partnership into Long-Term Mission and Operations

Like the University of Pennsylvania and San Francisco State, Xavier has had to confront the idea of faculty reward systems. As an institution that appears to stress teaching as much as research, Xavier is not as conflicted as Penn concerning the incorporation of service into rewards. Scholarship, teaching, and service are all weighted in tenure decisions. However, it is unclear exactly how much weight is given to service in Xavier's model. Pecoul noted, "We don't weight it. No, we don't. They're all there, and clearly it is that the university's priority mission is the teaching mission." All tenure decision making is ultimately subjective depending on the composition of the review committee. Pecoul suggests that the institutional correction for any erroneous tenure decisions is the appeal process. As in most institutions, decisions can be appealed at every level. To Mason the situation is a bit more grim. Getting faculty credit for "service work, applied work, and applied research is a real battle internally, both at Tulane and Xavier."

The question of reward systems in all of the cases in this book is not to suggest that service replace teaching or research. The challenge for institutions of higher education that wish to sustain community partnerships is to find ways to incorporate service into their core missions. In Xavier's case, Pecoul notes, "You can't just substitute community service for the others, but you can make the case of the appropriateness of community service and the way it reinforces teaching and enhances it." This is the same quest at the University of Pennsylvania, but it centers more heavily on the intersection between service and research. The very concept of tenure, as it has been developed over time, may very well be an obstacle to innovation in higher education, particularly with respect to community partnerships. Pecoul says of service and tenure, "I'd like to see us do more, and the way it seems to be evolving, to do that is going to go in the direction of the non-tenured track." He refers to a "fully-legitimized, non-second-class, non-tenure track." Mason suggests institutionalization will develop with as many "chairs, academic chairs, and faculty chairs in community development at as many urban institutions as we can. Because if you are going to get the universities involved, it has to be faculty-driven, and that's just the way it goes. So what I'm working on now is trying to raise some money to get a chair, and once we get a chair, I think the process of institutionalizing the academic program is just geometrically expanded." In order to create such chairs in the academy, Mason suggested interdisciplinary centers as opposed to academic departments as houses for such positions. Mason also mentioned funding as a major need to bring about institutionalization, "If the money is there, the work will get done." Tenure decisions and other faculty rewards around service probably are more justifiable when appropriate to disciplines. As Pecoul stated, "If you're a molecular research biologist, your type of community service and what's relevant might be quite different from the sociology tenure."

As in the other cases in this book, senior administrative support is essential to the longevity of successful community partnerships. Longtime Xavier president Norman Francis has consistently promoted the service mission of the university. Sybil Morial stresses the importance of Francis' tenure to the initiatives: "Longevity really allows you to set policy, put it on track and in the right direction." It seems as if it is important to develop a cadre of committed members of the university community, with the president being one of them. Such a cadre can be the internal advocates to advance the institutionalization of community partnerships. Larry Powell said, "You need to build a constituency of self-interested faculty and students, and embed this in the educational mission of the university." Xavier seems to have a cadre of students and administrators, but at the faculty level, there appears to be a certain looseness. It is difficult to discern whether there is an organized agenda among faculty to ensure the furtherance of community partnerships. It may be that it is so rooted in the ethos of the institution that further institutionalization is not necessary.

Xavier is also faced with the same question confronting the other institutions of higher education profiled in this book: Do community partnerships transcend the exceptional commitment of a handful of people? From the president to coordinators of outreach programs to especially committed faculty members, some of these figures may be irreplaceable. Their relationships with community-based stakeholders and their knowledge of the university and community will not easily be recreated. In this current historical manifestation of higher education/community partnerships, we do not have enough examples to see the development of outreach initiatives beyond the few committed visionaries. However, Xavier will begin to address these issues starting with replacing Ron Mason, which has already been done. Larry Powell, Mason's replacement, has been very involved, but he is faced with managing a much-expanded agenda for the Center for the Urban Community. Moreover, while the longevity of Francis has been a major advantage to the university, he will retire eventually. Will his successor be an internal person who is prepared to build upon the existing commitment? Or will it be someone completely new, as is often done in presidential searches, who may or may not subscribe to preexisting support for community partnerships?

Challenges Confronting Partnership

Institutionalization remains as one of the major challenges facing higher education/community partnerships. Partnerships among different institutions of higher education constitute an additionally difficult proposition. Xavier's partnership with Tulane, for example, ideally combines a number of advantages—the wealth of resources at Tulane, and the historical community-based orientation of Xavier. As a much smaller institution, Xavier has a structural fluidity that not at all resembles anything at Tulane. However, its resources are limited. Ron Mason discussed his amazement with the amount of work that Xavier gets done despite its resources. He provided an example of the resource distinction between Xavier and Tulane: "While I might be able to get a faculty member at Tulane to head up Campus Affiliates Program by buying 75 percent of his time and letting him take a semester off, you can't do that at Xavier because there's no time to buy."

The process of partnership between these two institutions is, at times, daunting. Ron Mason noted, "The beauty of Xavier is that because they are Catholic, they have a long tradition of service, you know. And we've been able to work with them and learn from them in ways that allow Tulane to jump start its work in that area. The problem with Xavier is that it's an elite school like Tulane is an elite school, and they have institutional arrogance just like Tulane has institutional arrogance. And just getting the two to work together is a chore in and of itself." Mason continued, "Another thing we're struggling with now is to get the institutions to be comfortable with saying publicly among their funding sources—that is private donors—that we're working with poor people. I mean there is a real need on the part of the more traditional faculty to maintain an air of elitism. You know, they like working in an ivory tower behind a closed door with a pencil and paper, right."

Powell, as a Tulane faculty member, sees the distinction between the universities, but believes he has benefited from working with Xavier, "For Tulane, this has been more of a cultural shift. There's much more of a transformative experience than for Xavier. I think this kind of work is much more of an extension of Xavier's mission, which has always been oriented toward community. For Tulane, it's not that Tulane has been indifferent to the community, it's like it's had a series of one-night stands." Being a major research university, Tulane is farther from a supportive institutional environment for community partnerships. Yet, as Mason mentioned, teaching loads at Xavier aren't all that conducive to partnerships, either.

While Xavier may have the ethos, as Powell noted, most Xavier faculty involved in the Center for the Urban Community provide services, as was indicated regarding the School of Pharmacy. However, "They're really not involved with programmatic stuff. They just don't have the time, or choose not to come, and I don't push the issue." Being a tenured professor of history at Tulane, Powell himself has the time to be involved, but he also indicated that his work with the community partnerships has little to do with his discipline. When we think about compatibility between mission and community partnerships, it would seem that consistencies are most apparent in the academic arena when faculty or students make their fields of expertise available and relevant. For faculty, when they find consistency, they will be able to naturally bring community partnerships into their teaching and research. It goes back to the tripartite, yet complementary mission — teaching, research, service.

Although the Xavier Triangle has placed the university in communication with an amalgamated, community-based leadership body, community interests still vary. Over the last few decades, some local residents organized against the university and eschewed the idea of partnerships. That sentiment remains in some local circles. Pecoul noted, "They have the attitude that the university will do harm to the neighborhood rather than good. I think it's a small minority, but it's vocal."

As is the case among higher education/community partnerships nationwide, funding is a continual challenge. If institutions of higher education are going to be truly serious about establishing protracted, collaborative local relationships, they will have to reallocate existing funds or target specific funding drives to community partnerships. Although foundations are beginning to take a closer look at these partnerships, it will take years before numerous funding programs emerge in support of this field. Indeed, foundations may not even choose to take such a path. Xavier's overall reputation — as a science-based institution that produces competitive medical students — raises money. Few of these resources are specifically designated for community partnerships, but the XTNDC, for example, is finding that it can leverage Xavier's resonance in the funding community for restricted dollars. Davallier said of Xavier and fundraising, "Their science program is just fantastic. And because it's so successful, they've been able to attract money. They've been very successful." Xavier's institutional commitment to allocating funding for community partnerships is significant. However, institutionally, the XTNDC, in this case, benefits from its combination of independence and partnership with Xavier. It can use the Xavier name to raise money, but it is not prevented from various bureaucratic fund-development issues inside of the university.

Conclusion

Xavier University currently sees its community partnerships as justifiable within their mission. Rhetorically, it is not at all a stretch to imagine community partnerships fitting within an institution designed to "create a more just and humane society." Xavier's mission statement addresses social responsibility more clearly than that of either the University of Pennsylvania or San Francisco State. The combined influence of being an HBCU and a Catholic institution seems to drive this ideological commitment to partnering with local communities. However, Xavier has not been able to fully incorporate community partnerships into its overall way of doing business, either. The culture of the institution, heavily stressing teaching, can be a hindrance to faculty seeking release time for community partnerships. The institutional commitment that would ensure the longevity of community partnerships does not quite match the social justice ideals. Although the academics of the institution benefit from community partnerships, the major initiatives are not tied to academic departments. The XTNDC is a separate entity and the Center for the Urban Community is only beginning to engage Xavier faculty. MAX is a student initiative. All of these are critical, but institutionalization will require a deeper connection to academic disciplines.

As in the other chapters, mission can be addressed from the economic side as well as the academic side. For institutions of higher education, the academic side is the core mission, which is supported by the economic mission. When a sense of responsibility to community is incorporated into the core mission, it is easier for the institution to justify long-term support for the continuation and growth of community partnerships within its mission statement. The XTNDC is an interesting attempt at involving the university in economic development activities by way of a separate organization. Economic development is clearly justifiable within the long-term mission of the XTNDC, but not necessarily in the core mission of the university. Indeed, as in the case of the University of Pennsylvania, economic development is essential to the survival of the institution; it supports the core mission. If the surrounding area is revitalized, then students feel safer, and faculty want to live in the neighborhood. Economic development activities are critical in that they leverage the financial might of the institution on behalf of local residents. Gentrification, however, has been a persistent fear, particularly of poor and working-class urban residents living near institutions of higher education. But once the neighborhood surrounding a college or university is developed, what incentive does the institution have in continuing upkeep? Where is the incentive for the university or college to ensure that economic development efforts do not lead to gentrification?

A win/win situation that has at least the potential for greater longevity is one where the institution sees and understands social responsibility to its surrounding neighborhood as a part of its core mission. For Xavier University, this would mean that faculty would be required to incorporate service into their teaching and would engage in research that would have some direct impact on the local area. For students, this would mean that they would be required to engage in experiential learning, particularly in their majors. A number of institutions around the country have been developing service learning requirements for students. Faculty reward systems that incorporate practical application are more difficult to find. Xavier weights applied research and teaching in faculty reviews. However, it is difficult to tell if practice or service activities have any major significance as criteria.

Additionally, it is also unclear whether or not impact on the community is a standard by which students or faculty are judged. While there is no centralized evaluation methodology for the various community partnerships at Xavier, the XTNDC and the partnership with Tulane are assessed primarily by their impact on the community. However, faculty and student engagement does not seem to be reviewed by such standards. The win/win is when faculty get rewarded for their teaching and research, and the courses and studies yield some direct benefit to the communities. For students, a win/win is when students' grades are based partly on the degree to which their service was helpful to the community. One could argue that the longer-term benefit for communities is that students become trained as socially responsible persons. This is very important; however, it would seem logical that immediate gain for local communities should be seriously taken into account.

The process by which the XTNDC was formed is a good example of university-based stakeholders and community-based constituents collectively determining a strategy for the local community. The exclusively Xavier-based Student Services office has moved from a reactive to a proactive approach to community partnership. However, it is much more challenging to develop with the community a strategy for all student volunteer activities and service learning courses. It appears that a more comprehensive pipeline between the university and the community is in formation with respect to Student Services.

Xavier's historical relationship with neighboring areas tells us that the level of organization on the community side may be even more critical than the university's internal decisions about partnerships. This begs the question, Who represents the community? Some residents work with the university, while others are detractors. Despite its historical mission, few seem to think that Xavier has always done a good job of forging community-based relationships. Community residents have had low expectations of Xavier's commitment to neighboring areas. However, it also appears that some of Xavier's initiatives have not been well publicized to residents. Once residents do come into contact with the university's community partnerships, they tend to have a more favorable perception of Xavier and what it has to offer.

Residents have a particular perspective while local businesspersons have another. Home owners and renters have a different sense of personal stake in their neighborhoods. Public school administrators also have their own ideas. All of the stakeholders will not agree on everything, but they find synergy around particular areas. The XTNDC's strategic planning process, for example, galvanized the common interests. The struggle to find a win/win between the university and the community is only one piece of the process. Finding a win/win relationship among community based stakeholders may be the greater challenge to higher education/community partnerships. Both sides in partnerships must adapt in order to be collaboratively successful.

Xavier is predisposed to being supportive of disenfranchised, especially African-American, populations. Through providing access, the university created opportunities. And through leadership development, they trained students to be professionally successful and socially responsible. Current community partnerships challenge the boundaries of the existing mission as economic development and more proactive service learning and volunteer initiatives are the priorities. Whether or not Xavier can maintain this level of community partnership over the years remains to be seen. The new direction of the Student Services office began in 1988, XTNDC started in 1991, and the Tulane/Xavier partnership is embarking on substantial new initiatives at this moment. Xavier believes that its success as an academic institution is tied to its responsibility to the surrounding community. If it draws students from local public schools, and the quality of learning for students improves, Xavier ultimately will benefit from a better prepared student body, for example. However, the win/win is not as clear in each dimension of the partnership, and from this it appears that Xavier has transcended its self-interest and developed the will simply to act as a socially responsible citizen to the city of New Orleans.

Chapter 5

Just Getting By

Hostos Community College
and the South Bronx

In the shadows of Yankee Stadium, the South Bronx had become a symbol of urban decay in the 1970s and 1980s. As the poorest congressional district in the country, the South Bronx was exhibited to the nation as the example of everything wrong with the inner city. During the 1990s, however, a number of community development initiatives have helped to make the area a national example of another kind — that of urban revitalization. While progress has been made, the mostly Latino South Bronx community still faces an uphill climb. As a Federal Empowerment Zone, the neighborhood receives a significant infusion of government dollars to address critical local issues. However, unemployment, poverty, poor health, and declining public schools continue to be prevalent in the area. The development of the South Bronx population could enhance the self-sufficiency of residents in addressing these problems.

Walking up from the subway station on one of the Bronx's major thoroughfares, the aptly named Grand Concourse, one can feel the presence of Hostos Community College. Its modern architecture stands out in a neighborhood where very few buildings are new. Hostos occupies both sides of the street with two buildings joined by a glass-enclosed bridge. It's right there on the street, next to the subway, the bodegas (delis), the fast-food restaurants, and all the trappings of most poor or working-class New York City neighborhoods. Hostos is the community.

The atmosphere in and around the college is truly international: mostly Spanish-speaking people of every hue and phenotype, along with African-American and Afro-Caribbean twenty-somethings, occupy time between class, reading or conversing. Upon entering the cafeteria, the diversity of Hostos' student body explodes before your eyes. The vibrancy of students from all over the world seeking to better their existence is hard to ignore. As much as these students are international, they are local. They are from the South Bronx, the central Bronx, Washington Heights, and Harlem. More than any other institution in this book, Hostos is dependent on its neighborhood for survival. It draws its students and its identity from local communities. It has a responsibility to the community that keeps it afloat, and the community has an expectation. Not only must Hostos provide an education for these local residents; it is expected to provide cultural enrichment, services, and resources for the local neighborhoods. In this case, I don't have to stretch to find the compatibility between Hostos' mission and community partnerships academically or economically. It is almost wrong to imagine Hostos in a college/community partnership, since the line between the two is so blurred. It seems that the real question for Hostos is: To what extent can it manage the needs and expectations of student-residents and non-student residents?

The Mission of Community Colleges and Hostos

The contribution of community colleges has been to equip local residents with the necessary education and skills to function as employed, healthy, and educated citizens. This has been especially significant in that community college students are likely to remain in the neighborhood after graduation. Therefore, community colleges can develop local residents ultimately to work in and serve their neighborhoods. For reasons of this sort, South Bronx residents strongly advocated the creation of Hostos Community College. As stated in the *Hostos College Catalog* (1999–2000):

> The mission of Hostos Community College is to provide educational opportunities leading to socioeconomic mobility for first and second generation Hispanics, blacks and other residents of New York City who have encountered significant barriers to higher education. In order to provide its students with new academic and career opportunities, the College specifically addresses itself to their need for improving English language and computational skills. An integral goal of the College, therefore, is to provide transitional bilingual education opportunities for its Spanish dominant students, and to foster a multicultural academic environment in which all students will learn to appreciate the many cultures which they represent.

With this mission, Hostos Community College demonstrates a clear commitment to access for a particular population—a population that happens to reflect the demographics of the surrounding community. Like many community colleges, Hostos fills a particular void for those who do not have the means or the traditional criteria for four-year colleges and universities, particularly those in a specific geographic area. Community colleges ideally can serve as a springboard to a university education—providing associate degrees along with transferable credits. Consequently, the primary relationship between community colleges and their surrounding communities is rooted in the provision of accessible education and certification. Community colleges train local populations in various trades. Oftentimes, community college students remain in their neighborhoods, giving the mission an inherent community development angle. In other words, if community college students are trained in areas that can be of use to the local community, and they remain in the neighborhood upon graduation, then the neighborhood will benefit. At Hostos, for instance, many students who are trained as nurses work in local hospitals.

While Hostos is a direct local asset to the South Bronx that provides accessible education for residents, it is also the product of residents' demand for an institution of higher education in and for the neighborhood. Hostos emerged from a collective demand of Puerto Rican and other Hispanic and African-American leaders, who saw the need for a college to serve the needs of the South Bronx. An act of the Board of Education on April 22, 1968, met this demand, leading to the enrollment of the first class of 623 students at Hostos in 1970. Many of the original local activists sit on the Hostos Advisory Council today.

Housed in a former tire factory on the Grand Concourse, Hostos has faced occasional adversity in its quest merely to keep its doors open. However, over the years residents have continued to advocate for Hostos' continued existence. In the mid 1970s, for example, a fiscal crisis led to suggestions that Hostos should merge with Bronx Community College. Community leaders rallied behind the concept of an independent college, which led to legislation guaranteeing Hostos' existence, the Landes Higher Education Act of June 9, 1976.[1]

Indeed, Hostos since has grown in popularity and currently is housed in six buildings to meet the local demand. Its 1988 "Master Plan" proposed major construction in order to improve education and service for students. The East Academic Complex completed in 1994 and the Savor Manor Buildings completed in 1997 are two outcomes of the plan. The East Academic Complex houses business and accounting, data processing, and secretarial science, along with several other departments and student associations. Microcomputing labs, art and dance studios, a gymnasium, a swimming pool, an art gallery, and two theaters are also notable components of the 279,000-square-foot facility. Savoy Manor, which is about 43,000 square feet, houses the various administrative offices, including financial aid, counseling, admissions, and others. With all of its buildings located on or near the Grand Concourse and at a major subway station, Hostos' campus is a nearby resource for local residents.

Despite its growth, Hostos' ascent was dealt a crushing blow that almost closed its doors again. As a part of New York City's CUNY (City University of New York) network, Hostos is required to abide by certain regulations, including a writing examination. In 1997, Hostos substituted its own test in place of the official CUNY exam. With a 77 percent Latino student body, Hostos has identified as a bilingual institution that ensures proficiency in both English and Spanish for *all* students. Wanting to determine its students' preparedness to advance from a two-year to a four-year institution in the CUNY system, Hostos believed its own test would be a more accurate determinant of students' future success. Hostos' move brought on a barrage of criticism from the mayor, the governor, and educational officials, often under the banner of "lowering standards."[2] CUNY's trustees took action, requiring Hostos' apparently graduating class to take the official test immediately, affecting approximately 115 of the 400 students expecting to don caps and gowns. Hostos' president at the time was forced to resign in the midst of the controversial storm.

Hostos still feels the repercussions of this situation through significantly decreased enrollment. According to the current president, Delores Fernandez, "Because of the bad publicity that the school got a year and a half ago, the students aren't coming here. It's been very difficult to recruit students. We dropped 1,500 students." Some of those students were actually lost due to other circumstances, which may or may not be related. Once a Work Experience Program (WEP) site, Hostos students on welfare could fulfill their workfare assignments on campus. However, New York's Mayor Giuliani pulled the WEP program from Hostos and Manhattan Community College, leaving workfare recipients in the South Bronx to travel as far as Brooklyn or Queens for their employment placements. Six to eight hundred Hostos students were lost due to this policy change.

With the extent and magnitude of life challenges that Hostos students face, the college wrestles with simultaneously providing access and service to residents and ensuring a high quality education. The community desires both high quality education and a broader commitment to serving residents of the South Bronx. Forever a virtual extension of the movement politics of the 1960s, Hostos faces myriad local expectations surpassing those facing most institutions of higher education.

From its historical roots to its name, there is little doubt that Hostos is intended to be a community institution. Named for the Puerto Rican educator and activist, Eugenio Maria de Hostos, the college is held up to a legacy of education and service, specifically to Latino populations. During the late 1800s and early 1900s, Eugenio Maria de Hostos worked for the liberation of Cuba and Puerto Rico. He fought for educational opportunities for women in Chile, where he developed award-winning curricula. He spent his later years in the Dominican Republic, where he served as Director of the Central College and Inspector General of Public Education. High quality education, political liberation, pan–Latin America, and opportunities for women are clear elements surfacing from Hostos' life—the same principles to which the college aspires.

Evolution of Current Community Partnerships

Having started out of a community demand, Hostos always has been expected to support not only its students, but the local community. But it has not been easy for Hostos to maintain the connection, especially in a constantly changing environment. The activists who pushed for the creation of Hostos reflected the Puerto Rican and African-American population of the South Bronx in the '60s. Not only have the demographics changed, but so have the magnitude and complexity of local issues. According to longtime Bronx resident and one of the original activists for Hostos, Jesse Hamilton, the mid 1970s was a critical time for the neighborhood. In addition to the more recent Puerto Rican and African-American populations in the area, there had been a more economically stable Jewish community that was then beginning to migrate. They owned a lot of property in the area. When they were moving out, "there was a rash of fires. There was a major fire every night, buildings coming down, people being displaced. And that went on for a good ten years. So that community that we had seen as our market then, started to move. And in its place, we had empty lots, and our population density in terms of the census declined, which brought less money. It was a ripple effect."

But still, the African-American and Puerto Rican communities were stronger and better organized at that time. There were also more middle-class residents. The Black Leadership Council and the Puerto Rican Caucus were the strong groups that came together to push for Hostos' creation and survival, according to Hamilton. A lot of the buildings that were being burned down were in the African-American and Puerto Rican communities. Many of the middle-class members of these populations began to move. As Hamilton expalined, the more economically stable populations for the most part left the neighborhood.

Throughout the 1970s, keeping Hostos afloat was a struggle, but it remained a community institution, where residents were joining with students, faculty, and administrators to ensure Hostos' continuation and enhancement. Longtime professor of sociology Gerald Meyer has been a critical campus-based activist throughout the years. One of the things that Meyer has noticed throughout his years of organizing with a heavily immigrant student body is that "the students here have been involved in mass political movements in their own country." In 1972, Hostos was located in only one building, housing almost 3000 students. In order to get the state to support more space for the institution, Meyer helped organize a coalition between the student government and the union of college staff. Administrators supported these actions as well. They rallied in the Bronx and met with the Bronx borough president, and they rallied in Albany, New York's state capital. As a result, $3.5 million was appropriated for the purchase of the building across the street. Thus Hostos has been an extension of political struggle not only in its founding, but in its survival and expansion.

The biggest battle came when most of New York City was deteriorating during the 1975–76 fiscal crisis. The CUNY budget was significantly reduced, which was going to hit Hostos hard. Meyer created the Save Hostos Committee, which was also approved by the Hostos administration. Save Hostos organized thousands of people from the college community and local residents. Its petition campaign garnered 10,000 signatures. Students and the administration, however, diverged as to how far the organizing campaign should go, so the students and their supporters created the Coalition to Save Hostos, which Meyer recalled "took the school over and expelled the administration from the school."

Hostos was officially closed by the CUNY Board in April of 1976, but they were forced to rescind the motion because the Black and Puerto Rican Caucus refused to vote for that budget. Several faculty left, the Nursing School closed, and enrollment fell in the midst of this tumult. Were it not for the Black and Puerto Rican Caucus and the actions of students and residents, Hostos would not be around today. Hostos and the community, emerging from such intensity together, brought a certain spirit of unity. Throughout the 1970s and '80s, Meyer maintains that community partnerships were generally more "sustained" and "systematic." "Our protection," Meyer said, "is really the community." He went on to say that he thinks that the administration is reacting to a conservative climate today. Regarding the impact of the changes in welfare on the community, for example, Meyer feels the college is fitting itself into what they have been told to do rather than fighting it: "There's no one on the other side speaking back. And there's no one going to the sources of power that exist in order to change those actions. A lot of that is because the political climate has changed. There's a lot more the college could do, I am absolutely convinced, to connect with the community."

Against this background, consider the present situation, in which Hostos is under attack—criticized for not upholding high academic standards on one hand and not doing enough in the community on the other. Managing a situation like this is difficult and complicated. Can the current administration develop a strategy that satisfies the critics without compromising the community?

Interim President Delores Fernandez entered the tumultuous circumstances at Hostos two years ago. She has worked with her colleagues to develop a strategic plan, guided by a common vision:

> To make Hostos Community College a "School of Excellence" for students seeking a liberal arts or career education in a dual language, multicultural learning environment:
>
> - By serving as the premier bilingual/multicultural academic and career institution in the city, state and nation;
>
> - By preparing students to compete successfully in the academic and career fields of their choice;
>
> - By preparing students to participate fully in a diverse global society; and
>
> - By creating an educational and work environment that nurtures respect and understanding for cultural and linguistic diversity.[3]

With this vision, called the "Hostos Renaissance," the college emerges from the trials of 1997. For many institutions of higher education, such a vision could be implemented in such a way as to completely circumvent the priorities of residents who do not become students. Indeed, this mission does not directly address community development of the surrounding area. Although Hostos's founders intended it to be involved at such a level, it has not embraced its role as a community development institution explicitly enough to discuss it in its official mission statement. However, given the composition of the student body, issues related to preparation for Latino students are central to the advancement of the surrounding South Bronx neighborhoods. As previously stated, Hostos graduates will likely work in their home communities. This came up, to a lesser degree, in the case of SFSU and Xavier as well. But there are particularly strong similarities between a place like Hostos and an HBCU. Not only is Hostos a community college, it is a Hispanic Serving Institution. It takes more of a people-based than a place-based approach to community development. This book primarily focuses on place-based approaches, but with institutions like Xavier and Hostos, the people-based emphasis is prominent.

The Rennaissance centers on a "dual-language" goal, transcending a traditional English-as-a-Second-Language (ESL) approach, which focuses on improving proficiency in English for non-native English speakers. The dual-language approach is equally concerned with enhancing proficiency in Spanish for native English speakers. The college maintains, "Mastery of two languages adds value to the career and liberal arts training provided to students," and as suggested in the mission, the college seeks to become a national model in this area.[4]

President Fernandez elaborated on the goals of the Renaissance:

> The mission of the Renaissance itself is . . . to make the school a school of excellence. And a school of excellence where those students that are seeking a liberal arts and career education, career profession . . . do it in two languages. I think that if we maintain our goal of being a dual-language school, we're the only school within CUNY, and within I think the United States. But if we get to the point of being a dual-language school, we'll be the only one. And the school, my vision of a school of excellence, comes as a result of things that have happened here at Hostos . . . and my belief as a member of the Latino community that this is our school — in a sense that Eugenia Maria de Hostos represents so much to a minority population.

In the face of the 1997 controversy, Hostos probably needed to emphasize academic excellence in its latest vision. It probably needed a president who would push this goal. The dual-language aspect of the Renaissance, however, is unique. It emphasizes the positive aspects of being an English/Spanish speaker, and it helps to preserve the culture of the student body and ultimately the community.

Vision for Community Partnership

The overall vision for community partnerships is inextricable from the overall Renaissance at Hostos. President Fernandez said,

> I want to let [local schools] know, I'm trying to create some collaboration so that we can start to build some corridors and work with them so that we can become feeder schools from their high schools. And so that's all down the line, slowly but surely. I have different phases of what I am attempting to do with the Renaissance. I think the word community within a community college's title is very important and very significant. And I think that's overlooked many times when you hear discussions that are going on around higher education. Because I don't think it's important how long it takes anybody to get a degree, or even if you're going there for a degree. It's really what that school can do together with the community in order to enrich the community and the community [to] enrich the school.

Community is, therefore, critical on a number of levels at Hostos. The fact that the community is within the college, as well as the need for the community and the college to collaborate, is essential to the Renaissance. Many of Hostos' students are older; few attend the college directly following high school. Therefore, if Hostos, through its Liberty Partnerships program, builds relationships with the local high schools, then it will create an entirely new recruitment and enrollment base from the community. Hostos' strong Allied Health Program requires significant proficiency in math and science. The Renaissance proposes to build those areas along with elementary education in order to attract high school students. Sandra Ruiz, Assistant to the President, said of the shifting priority toward high school students, "I think it's getting the high school population to the point that they believe that we are a school of excellence." However, she speculated about the mixing of the older existing student body with high school students: "So we're going to have to see how we can play that out over the next few years, so that they can be mixed and working together without putting that other population out in the street. Because we are the only ones here for them."

The question of "Who is the community?" arises again in this vision. With Hostos' traditional student population being older, with families and maybe fewer long-term opportunities, their interests are distinct. The Renaissance could clash with the needs of Hostos' traditional student population. Younger students, coming directly out of high school, may have more opportunities and certainly different interests than the existing older student body. But this seems to be a direction that Hostos may be required to take in order to stay afloat. Having lost so many students, not to mention its academic credibility, Hostos needs a new strategy. If a pipeline between the local high schools and Hostos has not been built, Hostos should seize that opportunity. But will this take the institution away from its original mission?

With the local population as its recruitment base and the multiple challenges facing the very locally representative student body, Hostos' version of "outreach" is more akin to "inreach." Its vision for community outreach must require a commitment to providing comprehensive supportive services in order to help its students through the educational experience. Oftentimes coming from relatively impoverished backgrounds, Hostos' mostly female students may be single parents trying to balance workfare assignments with childcare and coursework, while struggling with domestic violence and potential eviction. With this hardly uncommon profile of a typical Hostos student, the idea of completing an associate's degree in two years is often unrealistic. According to President Hernandez, Hostos should not be referred to as a "two-year" institution. She prefers the term "stop out," which suggests that students will complete their associate's degrees, but probably in about four or five years due to the complexities of their lives. The use of such a term does not belittle those who do not complete the degree program in two years. From Hostos' point of view, sensitivity to the needs of the student body is integral to a healthy community partnership. If the institution is not tailoring its educational programs and services to the characteristics of the local population, then it is failing to build a healthy relationship. From another angle, as a community institution, Hostos is primarily dependent upon the community for its survival. If any students are going to enroll at Hostos, they are going to be from the neighborhood. If the neighborhood is not pleased with Hostos, students will not enroll. The scandal of 1997 still haunts Hostos, and enrollment is still falling. The community is not standing by the institution in the same manner as in the 1960s and '70s. Therefore, the future of Hostos is significantly dependent upon the success of Fernandez' "Renaissance."

Supportive Services for Students as a Form of Community Partnership

As previously mentioned, the education of the local population is in itself a form of community development, especially if students are trained in areas that provide them greater access to employment or to four-year colleges or universities, and they ultimately remain tied to the neighborhood. The career advisement, health services, and other supportive mechanisms offered at most institutions of higher education take on a special meaning at Hostos, given the nature of the student body. For example, given the number of single mothers in the student body, the Hostos Children's Center is essential to the quality and continuation of the educational experience. The Children's Center, which "provides a safe, nurturing, stimulating environment for up to 60 preschool children during the day and 20 children during the evening," is open Monday through Thursday from 7:30am to 10pm, and 7:30am to 2pm on Fridays.[5] A Learning Environment Responsive to All (ALERTA) is a bilingual, multicultural, child-centered curriculum within the Children's Center. It includes day trips and social and cultural activities. Through the center, parents are also taught parenting skills and prepared to be advocates for their children. Unfortunately, the City Department of Health–sponsored program is far too small to meet the needs of the student body; through it, waiting for child care could take as long as three semesters.[6]

A number of Hostos's students depend upon public assistance. Due to the transformation of welfare into workfare, as a result of federal and ultimately state and local legislation in 1996, these students were required to take jobs to receive their benefits. Hostos traditionally has provided supportive services to its students on public assistance, but the wider political circumstances have required Hostos to adapt accordingly.

The College Opportunity to Prepare for Employment (COPE) program started in February 1993. It is a collaboration between the New York City Human Resources Administration (HRA) and CUNY to assist students on public assistance in obtaining associate's degrees. With the demographics of its student body, Hostos has a program on site. Sonji Keizs, the director of Hostos's COPE program, described the effort and its context:

> We provide supportive services, including counseling, some help with registration, with academic support, and then with job development–employment toward the end of the students' program. The program started because CUNY and HRA realized that they serve a common clientele, especially at Hostos. We have lots of students who receive public assistance. At one time, I think about seventy percent of our students received some form of public assistance. The number is decreasing over the last few years as a result of welfare reform and some other changes, policy changes. But we still have a substantial number of students on public assistance at this college.

Originally, COPE maintained a strong academic focus. While approximately 3,000 students were on public assistance at the program's inception, only 191 were in the COPE programs, which intensely stressed academics and counseling support. Job placement was secondary in COPE's small classroom setting. Students in the program were divided into "blocks" categorized by major. Each of these clusters of students followed a similar curriculum. The academic approach was working well, and the program produced a couple of valedictorians with 4.0 grade point averages.[7]

But with President Clinton's Conciliation Act of 1996, which altered the entire face of welfare, the emphasis of COPE shifted to work before and over academics. The "work first" emphasis, according to Keizs, is strongly shared by New York's Mayor Giuliani and the head of HRA, Jason Turner. Keizs suggests that the initial emphasis on education first was more logical. She posed the question, "Well, how are they going to work if they don't have the skills and education?"

The legislative shift required students on public assistance to work initially twenty hours per week for the city in workfare or "WEP" jobs. Keizs noted:

And we found that is certainly a conflict—between doing WEP and coming to school full time and trying to complete a degree. It's just not really congruent. So the colleges, the university, and other welfare advocates advocated for college students being able to use work study and internships toward meeting their work requirements—it made sense, the work study and the internship, their training, training for work, which is what the work experience program is supposed to be about. So we strongly encouraged for those activities to count toward WEP. And HRA didn't give in at all. It took a court case for them to finally agree that work study and internship is work. So, now I say the emphasis is less, well not less on academics, but more on getting people employed. So HRA has really pushed for CUNY to just get people working, and so that's our emphasis now. It's to really try to balance the academics with getting people working. So the job development aspect of our program has really become the primary focus over the last year and a half or so.

Prior to the legislative changes, the three priorities of the program were retention, graduation, and then job placement. Now that COPE is on a performance-based contract, job placement is the only priority, since the program's funding is conditional upon its ability to place students in jobs. Performance is measured only by that criterion. According to Keizs, "Our program alone has generated something like 20 percent of funds for all of the CUNY campuses." Although COPE is obviously doing well at placing students, which is probably partly due to the sheer volume of workfare-eligible students, WEP jobs do not fit the type of employment opportunities that the program originally wanted to develop. WEP jobs are not jobs of choice, rather they are means by which those on public assistance can collect their benefits. Keizs said of program participants, "They'll have more control of their lives if they're themselves employed, as opposed to being told by the city, 'OK, you must do your workfare and forget about school.'"

Furthermore, workfare has placed a number of students far away from the neighborhood. The COPE program has been trying to develop relationships with local employers. Since many of the students at Hostos major in early childhood development and gerontology, the COPE program has built relationships with child-care providers, schools, and programs targeting the elderly. On the one hand, these students get placements in the neighborhood, and on the other, they help provide services to seniors and children in the area. The university program benefits, at least in terms of its streamlined mission, and the neighborhood benefits. Average salaries for the jobs are $8.96 per hour out of a range of $7.45 per hour to $11.71 per hour.

Hostos's COPE program has been a victim of its own success as HRA has required them to place students in jobs of 25 hours or more per week as opposed to the previous target of 20 hours or more. Jobs under 25 hours no longer count, even though the majority of the program's placements have ranged between 20 and 24 hours. This will render coursework at Hostos "a part-time activity" for full-time students who happen to depend on public assistance. Said Keizs, "We're not here to pull people out of school; that's counterproductive to the college's mission."

Keizs makes an important point about mission. The experiences of the students in the COPE program underscore the need for Hostos to ensure that the provision of extensive supportive services is central to its mission. This scenario is both academic and economic. Hostos depends on the tuition of its students, so it needs them to stay in school. Academically, it needs to do everything possible to graduate its students, and services of this sort will help them do that. On a more general note, it is very difficult to take these students out of the context of their families. Some of these students raise families on these salaries. The well-being of the families of students is inextricable from that of students.

In the program, each student is assigned to a case manager. Those students who express a need for employment are matched with a job developer. Job developers help the students with resume and cover letter writing as well as interview skills. Keizs explained that students come to the program by referral: COPE does not actively recruit because HRA has not been supportive of recruitment. Not only do the circumstances of the students present a challenge, but the external requirements of local government significantly compound the demands of the work. Keizs came to Hostos because of the challenge. She said of the work:

> It's never dull. I'm telling you, every day is a new challenge. It does not get stale. With the city changing, the policies, the regulations, and raising the bar, you know, it's a constant challenge. It's exciting and also we know that we're providing a service to the students. We know that if we're not here, students would be at a disadvantage. If there were no case managers that attend fair hearing, students would just give up. I've, we've seen it often. All it took was for someone to intervene and say, "All you have to do is to do a fair hearing." "Fair hearing? What's a fair hearing?" "You know, do the fair hearing and write it up." The case manager faxes it right up to Albany. The next week, the student gets a response. The case manager and the student go to the fair hearing; it's resolved. The student gets her back pay, her back money, you know. A lot of people would just—the bureaucracy and the paper of it—just get overwhelmed and say, "Forget it. It's not even worth my time." And also encouraging people to stay in school and encouraging them to get jobs. You know, just encourage them to aspire to things that maybe they wouldn't have done. You know, inspire them and encourage them to aspire to whatever their dreams were. And that's the reward there too.

As many of the community residents in the last chapter indicated, dealing with administrators and faculty from an institution of higher education, even if it didn't completely change their life circumstances, helped them question authority and gain greater knowledge about the systems that affect their lives. Keizs refers to situation where the public system dominates residents. Residents have a right to a fair hearing, but it takes someone like Keizs to remind residents of that and underscore to them that they should feel entitled to exercising their rights. Communities that have been pushed around and beat up over the years can sometimes feel worn down, feel that nothing or no one is on their side because few have demonstrated otherwise.

Hostos Women's and Immigrants' Rights Services (HWIRS) is another important tool for student and community development. HWIRS was founded in 1988 by a group of students, faculty, and administrators wishing to create a vehicle to address the particular needs of women and immigrants. It is described as "a student and community oriented project designed to empower individuals through civil and legal rights, advocacy, education, and direct service."[8] Volunteer attorneys, faculty advisors, and students operate the program. This is another example of an initiative that had to be developed to meet the needs of the mostly immigrant, mostly female student body of the campus. This effort is also central to the mission by providing a service that can keep students in school and prevent them from being taken advantage of in a new country.

Given the myriad challenges in the lives of students and their families, counseling services are essential. Counseling at Hostos is designed to address both academic and personal issues facing students. Upon entering the college, the Counseling Unit matches students with counselors, who "provide a supportive environment in which students may work on academic issues, family problems, stress reduction, decision making, conflict resolution, and other personal concerns."[9] Both individual and group counseling are available, as are any necessary referrals to outside agencies. According to the Hostos College catalog, "The Counseling Unit maintains a close and supportive relationship with the institutional faculty, to whom it is available as a resource."

President Fernandez believes the supportive services for students pay off in the end:

> I would like to track some of our students. Because I think that if you track the Hostos students as they move into four-year schools and then watch them as they go through that school, I wouldn't be surprised if our students do better on the state tests than a student that may not have come to a program like ours. Because of the intensity of the program, because of the way the program is designed with intensive counseling . . . I mean that's one thing about this school. The professors here are more than professors, you know. Their doors are open and our students have a multitude of problems because they're older students, they're married, some of them are single mothers, fathers.

Fernandez was speaking particularly of the Elementary Education Program, but the issues in her comments appear to be true for the college as a whole. Carlos Acevedo, a faculty member, discussed his relationships with students. He said:

Let me give you one example, which I have from last semester. A student comes into my office ... a great number of our students are female. As a practice, I always have my door open, but I also have a lot of students coming in. This young woman, probably in her early thirties comes in crying. I said, "What's happening?" From that point she starts sobbing and explaining. I closed the door a little bit. And basically what happened is that this woman is being abused, and had just come from a very violent situation that day.

Hostos's Women's Center provides services for abused women. Through the center, that student was placed in a shelter on that day. A bilingual domestic violence hotline is being added to Hostos's existing services in this area. Hostos is working with the New York State Domestic Violence Task Force on the hotline, which according to Ruiz will become "part and parcel of the Women's Center." Moreover, Fernandez explained that Hostos currently is seeking to identify housing in the neighborhood that could be transformed into a "transitional living space," which could be a "safe haven" for students in "real crisis."

Acevedo continued discussing his experiences as a faculty member dealing with this student body and described some of the personal pressures on students and some of the ways in which the faculty might attempt to compensate:

Where normally you would just be inclined to deal with some of the academic issues, this becomes part of the overall function that you wear that hat in addition to the many others. Sometimes we wonder, car's out there ... you will see them around 2 o'clock, 3 o'clock. [We] used to think in the beginning, "Oh these husbands are very supportive." And it's that sometimes these husbands are very jealous, and they just want to make sure that [their wives] come here, and when they finish, they go right back. And that type of thing. So we have to provide, while here in class, provide those additional support mechanisms in tutoring—build it in as additional compensatory hours of the classes, so that the student can do work here, because sometimes they can only do it after they go home, prepare food, take care of the kids, and then maybe at 11 o'clock start working. So we try to build it in from the curriculum perspective into hours that they spend here.

It is essential that Hostos tailor its services around these student needs. The problems exist on so many levels that the college is continually developing new support mechanisms. Fernandez spoke of homelessness among students, "We have students who are homeless that will not speak up. We have students that, in the middle of the semester, are thrown out. That happened this semester with one of our nursing students, and everybody pitched in and did a collection— enough to stabilize her for two months, so that she could stay in her apartment without being thrown into the streets with her two kids. But that's the kind of problems we have; we don't have just run of the mill problems." She continued:

I was told, I never met the person, but I was told we had a student here living on the subway for a year, you know. And that's not uncommon, you know. That's scary. But I know, I see them in the morning, the same face, and I know they've been here all night. And the security guards are good. They know, and just leave them alone as long as they're not being disruptive or anything. Most of them just want to go in a corner and just do their homework and sleep there. And that's not right. And when I listen sometimes to the discussions that go on down at the board and in the newspapers around kids not going through college in four years. So you have to go to community college within two years. I always stop them when they tell me I'm a two-year school. I say, "No, I'm a community college; I'm not a two-year school." And because of the complexity of the lives of the young people that come to us . . . I don't think people realize. They don't realize.

Allowing homeless students to sleep in the building probably does not qualify as a Hostos-sponsored program, but it represents the flexibility necessary in meeting the needs of its students. Hostos wishes to expand its counseling options. They are budgeting for more counselors and collaborating with Hunter College's Graduate Counseling Program. Fernandez is hoping that Hunter counseling students will work with Hostos students as a part of their internships. Fernandez was previously a faculty member at Hunter, a four-year CUNY institution. She recalls that students at Hunter were from low socioeconomic backgrounds, but she now realizes that they don't face the same crises as typical Hostos students. In terms of counseling, Acevedo recalls a time when there was one counselor for every eight hundred Hostos students. He credits Fernandez's administration with recognizing the enormous need for counseling among the students and taking the appropriate measures toward expanding the college's capacity in this area.

The Women's Center was founded in 1988 as the result of a series of conversations among faculty and staff. They concluded that the college needed to take more responsibility for the surrounding community, particularly in the areas of immigration, domestic violence, and HIV and AIDS. These ideas ultimately were manifested in the Women's Center, which began by focusing on partnerships with schools and expanded into legal services, counseling, and other activities. Mercedes Moscat, the center's director, has, consistent with other Hostos activities, shifted the focus of the Women's Center to bringing the community into Hostos—in other words, student recruitment. Counseling was the primary focus of the center, but limited funding has diminished these services, placing such work in the hands of off-campus nonprofit organizations. Moscat stresses the similarities between the community and the student body. She said, "Students come with the same kind of issues that the community comes with." The center is trying to keep counseling activities afloat through part-time staff and "lobby activities." These activities attempt to provide the same type of information that students once would have gotten more intensively: "Say we are doing domestic violence. I'll get a bunch of agencies to come in where they can give them the same kind of information to students on that.

Or I'll have presenters to have workshops and stuff, rather than a domestic violence counselor."

In terms of "community college" versus "two-year institution," the Dean of Faculty and Academic Affairs, Carole Berotte-Joseph, said, "I don't care how long they take as long as we hold the standards that when they leave, their degree means something. So some of them take four years, some of them seven; they're in and out because of different issues. They take leaves and come back." Hostos has resigned itself to adapting to the students' circumstances.

But it appears that the very problems faced by students are the same reasons why some faculty and administrators want to work at Hostos. Indeed, social work and academia blend in the Hostos environment, and it would take a particular personality to thrive in such an environment. Associate Dean of Academic Affairs David Hadaller said, "If you really want to work in higher education that serves people, this institution is the place to be." He continued, "This is the cutting edge; it's happening right here in front of your eyes." Berotte-Joseph recounted her twenty years at City College. Now that she has been at Hostos, she realizes that "faculty here are more willing to sit and talk and look at themselves, and see what they are doing. In other institutions, they know there are problems but, you know, faculty just want to continue doing the same old things they're doing."

Curriculum at community colleges tends to be geared toward training in a specific area in which one can gain employment, but it also must be designed to prepare students for four-year colleges. One challenge for Hostos is to identify those areas where they can place students in careers, but cater both to employment after graduation or to continuation toward a bachelor's degree. Health is Hostos's strong suit, as previously mentioned. It is planning to expand its training in that area through programs in dietetics and nutrition. The approach is to create two programs in similar areas. One, dietetics, is for those wishing to move on to a bachelor's degree. The other, nutrition, is geared toward those wishing to move into the job market upon graduation.[10] This duality of purpose is a part of Hostos's multilayered mission.

For Hostos alumni entering the job market, the bilingual education to which they have been exposed is an asset. Hostos as an institution has not yet taken full advantage of this reality, but it is in their plans. Given the significant demographic shifts over the last few decades, Spanish effectively has become America's second language. Changes are not immediate, but due to the ripple effects of the demographics, the economy gradually will respond more and more significantly to the growing presence of Spanish-speaking people. Berotte-Joseph discussed areas in which she is beginning to see an increased demand for proficiency in both English and Spanish. She said, "I know in the business program we have a lot of internships now, because companies know of our students and the skills they bring—the fact they are bilingual." She continued, "I was surprised when I accompanied the president to Lincoln Hospital, for example. They're right down the block from us, and we haven't done anything with them—no outreach. And when we went there, they told us, 'Oh, we have doctors who need Spanish because all their patients, you know, are Spanish speakers, and they know very little Spanish. So, can you offer conversational courses for us?'" Not only will Hostos graduates be increasingly marketable, but it appears that the primary added value of Hostos to the community as a whole might be its bilingual education.

Hostos's Office of Academic Affairs is in fact bolstering the college's tradition of dual-language education through the proposed establishment of a new Academic Department of Language and Cognition. Carole Berotte-Joseph wrote in a 1998 position paper, "By the year 2003, Hostos Community College will have established a fully articulated dual-language model in all of its degree programs. The expected outcome will be the preparation of competent, biliterate and fully bilingual graduates in the various programs we offer, ensuring their successful pursuit of higher education and/or access to meaningful and well-paid employment." All departments, as a result of this effort, will teach bilingual education. All graduates of Hostos should, consequently, have some proficiency in both English and Spanish. Berotte-Joseph distinguishes this current approach from the previous form of bilingual education at Hostos, which focused on teaching Spanish-speaking students English. Hostos's new methodology also emphasizes "the reverse, where people of other cultures and languages could learn Spanish." Hostos is also enhancing its bilingual education programs in collaboration with community schools. According to Fernandez, "We're working on a true bilingual program for all kids."

Community Outreach Beyond Hostos's Campus

Although Hostos is an outgrowth of a collective community-based demand, it has not been engaging the neighborhood at the level proposed by the current administration. Berotte-Joseph maintained, "If we're really a community college, then we need to be out there and responding to the needs of the community. In the past, that wasn't really being done. So, for now, I think we're moving in the right direction."

The college does have some existing initiatives, but many activities that engage Hostos's resources beyond its campus and its student body are relatively new. Hostos provides some courses for non-matriculating students from the community through its Office of Community and Continuing Education, which "offers educational, career, and personal development opportunities designed to address the needs of the South Bronx, Bronx, and Upper Manhattan communities."[11] This includes the Adult Basic Education Program (ABE) and the ESL College Preparatory Program. Some, but not all, of the courses in the programs are free. ABE helps students improve reading, writing, and math proficiency, often in preparation for higher education. Pre-GED and GED programs are included in ABE. In the ESL program, free courses are offered to those with little or no English proficiency. This intensive program focuses on critical thinking and writing in Spanish, and verbal and written communication in English. Offered during both the day and evening, this program also stresses computer literacy. Students for these courses often come from referrals by local community-based organizations.[12]

Hostos's central administration does not feel the college does enough in continuing education. Under Fernandez's initiative, they are building a survey instrument that will assess the continuing education desires of the local population, and they will expand the program accordingly. About 1,400 people have responded to the survey, according to Berotte-Joseph, who supports Fernandez's desire to enhance continuing education. She indicated her desire to get the results of the survey to guide her, in her capacity as the Dean of Academic Affairs, in reconstructing the program, which she refers to as "basically dead."

"Continuing Education" now is called "Continuing and Workforce Education" due to some of the same issues around welfare and employment that have affected Hostos's enrollment and programs like COPE. Laurel Higgins is the director of Continuing and Workforce Education. She said of the name change, "Until about a year ago it was Continuing and Community Education. . . . I think it has to do with that whole shift with the welfare-to-work stuff. I think that was the purpose because a lot of the grant monies are coming through to us through HRA and DOL, Department of Labor and Human Resource Administration. So what they're trying to do is train people who are not working or people who are working at low-paying jobs . . . if at all possible, to stay off public assistance." Her feeling is that training people to work may be at the expense of liberal arts. The dilemma is clear; if the funding is available for a particular type of education, an underresourced institution like Hostos must secure those grants. However, the limitations of those grants may not allow for the kind of education that Higgins and others may see as most appropriate for the population. Hostos would have a better chance of truly furthering its mission with more flexible sources of funds. As will be discussed later in this chapter, Hostos has not made any aggressive efforts to raise private dollars, particularly from alumni.

Continuing and Workforce Education is so underfunded in general that it can't meet basic expenses. Higgins notes, "Being tremendously underbudgeted, we don't have the kind of funds to be able to produce brochures or mass mailings. Most of the offices don't do in-house stuff—you ship it out and have it done professionally. We haven't been able to do that so I've been relying on my Vista volunteers. It's a grant we got literally to go out in the community, kind of one-on-one." While many at Hostos agree on the need to increase the scope of continuing education, they don't really have the internal capacity to make that a reality. "Hostos has never really supported continuing education the way it should have from the beginning," says Higgins. Her persistent struggle to keep the program going is a matter of resources. External funds are difficult enough to raise, but the internal support system has been weak as well. Higgins continues, "I'm not on the internet. I can't get email. I can't do research because I don't have access. I don't have a fax. Just so many things wear you out." The nature of working in a community college is often far from the world of many doctoral and masters-level universities. Though community colleges are valuable resources to local residents, they often do not have as much to give as they could. It is worth asking a college like Hostos whether or not it is institutionally committed to community partnerships, but it is important to understand the context. These institutions need their own assistance in building their infrastructure. Despite the difficulties, the Hostos continuing education program is making efforts to improve its curriculum. For example, it is incorporating computer literacy into its courses due to the vast need for computer skills among residents, and it is making sure to ground its curriculum in resident priorities. The Vista volunteers surveyed 1,200 residents. Most wanted courses in English, computers, remedial math, and writing. They wanted GED preparation as well.

Housing a curriculum that is useful to neighborhood residents is a part of what makes community colleges local assets. Hostos must determine how it can be most useful to the community. Some initiatives may require external grants and significant dollars. However, there are probably a host of low-cost ways in which Hostos could be helpful to residents whose needs are so multiple. For example, something as simple as meeting space is often the desire of many community-based organizations according to Hemansu Mangal of a local organization called Agenda for Children Tomorrow. Hostos happens to have an exceptional modern facility. In a city like New York, space is always at a premium. With high real estate values, it is often difficult for community-based organizations to find affordable office space. On Saturdays, Hostos allows neighborhood organizations to meet, and sometimes run programs, at Hostos.[13] This, however, is an area around which community-based organizations think Hostos could improve.[14] Anita Cunningham, chair of Allied Health, has been at Hostos since the very beginning, and she sees a change in community organizations' access to Hostos. She recalls, "There appeared to be a lot of community outreach. The community groups were constantly here. They were constantly supporting us when the college was in jeopardy." Changes in administration, according to Cunningham, have been significant in this regard. Hostos's many different presidents' policies varied with respect to community groups on campus.

Hostos and Public Schools

Building a pipeline between Hostos and local public schools is a critical aspect of Hostos's community partnerships. Recall that Xavier helped build its science-based education through its activities with local elementary schools. Understanding the "k–16" continuum may be the easiest entry point into community partnerships for many institutions of higher education, especially those that draw primarily local students. Hostos is increasingly realizing this potential; therefore, they are housing a few programs that put public school students in direct contact with resources at Hostos.

Projecto Access, sponsored by Hostos's mathematics department, is one example. It is designed to recruit junior high and high school students who are interested in math, science, and engineering. Humberto Canate, the chair of the department, describes the program: "The objective is to develop students' abstract reasoning and problem-solving skills, acquaint students with professional opportunities in engineering, and reinforce students' mathematics preparation at the secondary-school level. So, mainly they come in for eight weeks, start early in the morning until around four, and they take heavy courses: introduction to engineering, computer science, math. And most of the students are at a higher level when they go back to their schools." The ultimate hope is that these students will attend Hostos. In the short term, their facility with technical issues is enhanced. The program has an 88 percent success rate; 118 of the 134 students who started the program successfully completed it.

The Hostos–Lincoln Academy of Science is a college preparatory program sponsored by the New York City Board of Education and CUNY. It, along with the Center for Pre-College Alternatives, is a part of the New York State Department of Education–funded Liberty Partnership Program, which works with local students on a range of educational activities to further and enhance their educational opportunities. The Academy of Science is a four-year program that admits junior high school students who are at or near grade level in reading and math, from the Bronx and upper Manhattan, into a college that serves as a resource for classroom instruction. Admitted students can take college courses free of tuition once they meet certain criteria and later use those credits towards an associate's degree. Students in the Hostos–Lincoln Academy are considered members of the college community, able to make full use of all Hostos facilities. They are tutored year-round, particularly in preparation for New York State Regents examinations on reading and math as well as the SAT and PSAT. All who graduate from the program are guaranteed admission to Hostos.

Ultimately, this initiative is a feeder program for Hostos's enrollment. Overall, the needs of students and potential students are central to Hostos's approach to community partnerships. The Hostos–Lincoln Academy, however, also has a Parent Involvement Program on Saturdays, which enables parents and members of the community to join with students in receiving computer training, ESL, and GED programs, along with, interestingly enough, stained-glass classes. Some parents tutor the students in the program and act as mentors. Child care is provided for the small children of the parents.

The Center for Pre-College Initiatives provides educational opportunities for "historically underserved Latino and African-American students." Established in 1990, the center provides "an integrated academic and cultural arts enrichment program with comprehensive support services for at-risk minority students living in the South Bronx."[15] The center is another partnership with the Lincoln Academy of Science along with other high schools, such as William H. Taft High School and Adlai Stevenson High School. Many of the services are provided on Hostos's campus, especially for students at high schools in the immediate area. The center's activities are sometimes brought directly to schools, particularly those located farther away. For example, the New School for Arts and Sciences, because it is not in walking distance of Hostos, sends its students on Saturdays. "But during the week," said Betsy Hernandez, Director of the Center for Pre-College Alternatives, "we provide services . . . we bring in teachers; we bring in resources."

According to Hernandez, since the local public schools are simply "overwhelmed", the services of the center fill a void, providing the attention necessary for a quality education. The program does tend to approach different schools in the neighborhood, offering its services. Hernandez said of the process of making connections with high schools, "It's not very hard to make the connections because the schools are overwhelmed. As they are, they have a lot of students. The rosters are over 4,000 in some of these schools. And they would welcome as many resources as they can that would help their students become successful." As in other case studies in this book, community-based institutions tend to welcome the overtures of institutions of higher education, largely because the need is so dire. The community institutions do not have the capacity to fully address the myriad challenges that most poor urban neighborhoods bring. They need the assistance of outside entities, especially those with significant resources. Unless representative community-based institutions can initiate the relationships with institutions of higher education, it is difficult to determine if the true priorities of the community are being met or if the most appropriate strategies are being employed.

Over six hundred students have been assisted in graduating from high school as a result of the center's efforts to enhance the academic as well as social skills necessary for success in higher education and life. Veronica Batista, who arrived in the United States from the Dominican Republic at the age of twenty in 1991, was a beneficiary of the center's work. She spoke very little English when she enrolled at Taft High School. With overcrowding in the school, she was unable to receive the necessary individualized attention to get assistance with English and the overall curriculum. Other students referred her to the center, where she received tutoring in math, science, and English. Now a high school graduate, she is pursuing a degree in criminal law at the John Jay College for Criminal Justice. She, like other successful alumni, has returned to the program to serve as a mentor and role model to the center's current students.[16] Most graduates of the program have, in fact, gone on to attend institutions of higher education. Overall, the center's graduates are representative of the development of the local population for local gain, evident in the tendency for alumni to return as mentors.

The program services about three hundred students on a grant of less than $200,000 per year. Hernandez said, "It's very cost effective, and in my life span, we've seen over eight hundred students come through the program and graduate. Our graduation rate is fairly good. It's about 88 percent you know. And, again, we're working with at-risk students, you know, not the upper echelon of students, not the high achievers." She credits the success of the program to "one-on-one attention, counseling, leadership activities, and peer mediation. We're able to reach them, you know, right in the ninth grade. Right when they start, we start recruiting all the kids until we see them graduate." Retention is one of the challenges facing the program. The fact that the office is open six days per week until 6:00 p.m. helps, since the students can go to the office and talk or eat, or do whatever they want. The office serves as a supportive space. Students in the program bring with them a great deal of problems from home, but in Hernandez's words the program offers them "something stable, something quiet." She went on to say, "The goal is to encourage kids to stay in school and provide support services that will help them stay in school and see them through high school or through the work force." Activities in the program are matched with student needs. "We have populations of students that are immigrants that have difficulty with their English. And in those schools we concentrate on ESL courses and activities. We have special programs according to the grades they're in and the different needs of the students. And we've linked up with Cornell Cooperative Extension, which is an extension of Cornell University, and they provide us with some services also." The Cornell Extension actually matches juniors and seniors in the program with a Cornell alumnus who can serve as a mentor.

Students in the center are engaged in specific projects in order to practice what they have learned. The "Rocking the Boat" project, for example, allowed students to use their learning in math and engineering in building an 1890s Whitehall rowboat seating six people. Through the process, students learned woodworking and carpentry skills. Over the course of several months, students met every Saturday and during two afternoons per week in a shop at Hostos under the tutelage of carpenter Adam Green.[17] They launched the boat on the Harlem River amidst a celebration.

Students are given access to the range of facilities at Hostos. Hernandez said, "You know, we're housed on campus, so therefore we have the advantage that we can use libraries . . . we can use facilities, kids use the gyms, the swimming pools, the basketball courts. And we're right here. They are able to get exposed to some of the cultural activities, you know, that we have on campus, and the theaters, the gallery, special performances here. And it's right here in their community." Exposure to college life broadens students' horizons, opening their eyes to a world that they may never have imagined. According to Hernandez, students in the program "feel like they can be a part of an institution, that they belong there, that the faces they see are the same faces they see in their neighborhoods." With a local student body enrolled at Hostos, it is easier for local secondary school students to visualize themselves in college. The fact that Hostos is located in the center of the community only enhances this fact.

Hostos and the Arts

As an institution and in its community partnerships, Hostos stresses the importance of the arts. The Hostos Center for the Arts and Culture exhibits nationally and internationally renowned artists, as well as established and emerging local artists. Its stated mission is as follows: "Located in the South Bronx and pledged to address the cultural needs of that and similar inner-city communities, the Hostos Center for the Arts and Culture presents artists of national and local renown to audiences who do not have the means or the inclination to attend arts events in midtown Manhattan."[18] More than 150 events per year are produced by the center, which emerged from a long history of Latino "multi-arts." Its precursor, The Hostos Cultural Program, founded in 1982, had exhibited numerous well-known Latino artists.

The center sponsors an individual artists program, including commissions and residencies. Through the center's children's series, concerts are performed for over 15,000 children from local schools. The series also includes a new gallery education program, which will present the visual arts. A long list of artists representing various arts media have performed through the center, including Ruben Blades, Dizzy Gillespie, Marc Anthony, Faith Ringold, and others. Additionally, the Hostos Repertory Company stages three major productions per year.

While most of the community partnership activity in this book focuses on education, economic development, environmental concerns, housing, and other critical social issues, Hostos's approach to the arts is also a form of community development. The mostly Latino South Bronx community, as well as the predominantly African-American and Latino upper Manhattan and central and northern Bronx communities, can have access to nearby high-quality arts performances. These performances and exhibits also speak directly to the experience of local communities, as Latino and African-descended artists are showcased. Moreover, Hostos provides exposure and training for local artists who otherwise may not have had access to such opportunities.

The arts appear to pervade Hostos's overall approach to community partnership. In the Liberty Partnerships Program, which serves more than two hundred educationally disadvantaged Latino and African-American students per year, for example, "culture-arts enrichment" is incorporated into the overall educational process.[19] It is through arts and culture that the significance of the relationship between Hostos and the community becomes most evident. As a primarily Latino-serving institution in a predominantly Latino area, Hostos communicates with the neighborhood through the arts. It is a clear area in which the college and the community have a common ground. Consequently, the arts become a gateway to relating to local residents in other areas, such as education and economic development. Language, which is of great significance to the Latino population in the South Bronx, is intertwined within arts and culture. On the one hand, proficiency in English for the heavily immigrant local population is required for professional success. However, maintenance of Spanish is a means of remaining connected to various Latino cultural traditions and communities.

Hostos and Health

Anita Cunningham founded and designed Hostos's Allied Health Program, which is a part of the Dental Hygiene Unit. Close to 5,000 patients from the community per year visit the program's dental hygiene clinic next to the campus. Cunningham explained, "It is open to the public and it's free. We provide preventive dental care and then make the referrals when we need to."

One of Hostos's prized possessions is its Nursing Program, which has a 100 percent passing rate. Elizabeth Errico, the coordinator of the program, is determined to preserve its integrity and the reputation of their ability to take, for example, poor single mothers and train them to be health care professionals. This program demonstrates one of the ways in which students can apply their training in their community after graduation. Graduates tend to work in local hospitals, which serve people like themselves and their families. Errico says, "We have a lot of graduates working at Lincoln Hospital; we have a lot of graduates working in Harlem; we have a lot of graduates working at Bronx Lebanon, Jacobie." This trend is an important advantage to local residents because trained members of their community stay and use their knowledge to address local problems. Students in the program are trained to think about serving their communities. When students work with communities, they focus on "screenings and assessments," often at residents' homes. Errico notes, "When you go into someone's home or into their community, you're on their terms, and so you have to adjust what you do for them. And it's why people feel better getting care at home; they maintain a little control over themselves." Students have conducted screenings and assessments at local churches and hospitals, as well.

But the concept of working with community in the Nursing Program is not just service-oriented. They developed a "legislative component." "You shouldn't just be satisfied to go and do your job, but you should be trying to make policy," Errico said.

> How do we make health care better? Do we need to do something about licensure? Do we need to do something about the ratio of licensed to unlicensed professionals in an agency or a clinic or a nursing home and whatever? And how do you do that? So [for] anyone who could vote . . . see we have a lot of students here who can't vote, so we'd arrange the package so that we find out who was who's legislator, and we'd make appointments to see them so that they'd have to go and argue whatever, whether it was education or health care. It helps them to know you're not just punching a time card.

They are trying to build a better relationship with Lincoln Hospital, directly across from campus. Errico is encouraging joint activities between the program and the hospital. A part of what she would like to do is further let residents know their health care rights. She maintains, "My responsibility as a health care professional in this area is to try and get some information out. Maybe somebody's got a cough and they're worried about it, but they're afraid maybe it's going to cost too much, whatever. Maybe they don't know that by law you must be seen for certain problems, and even if you don't have two shekels to your name, somebody has to take care of you. But people are afraid if [they] don't know the language." Errico speaks to a role that all health-related departments in higher education could play. None of what Errico discusses is exceptionally expensive, it just takes extra time, attention, and commitment. This same approach is needed with this particular student body.

Hostos and Economic Development
The Business School is another department with a burgeoning community partnership in the form of the Hunts Point Initiative. The Initiative is a partnership between Hostos and the Hunts Point Economic Development Corporation, which houses more than twenty-seven vendors in the Hunts Point community. Hunts Point is an industrial waterfront section of the South Bronx, which, Business School dean Bibiano Rosa explained, is the largest wholesale food distribution center in the world. The market is a significant local asset, as food landing on shelves across the nation passes through Hunts Point. Rosa said of the market, "Hunt's Point is a little peninsula out there. Those companies do their thing. It's a twenty-four-hour operation. Trucks come in, leave, and they go all over the United States. Food comes in from all over the world into Hunts Point, and it is shipped out to all of the United States. And lord knows where it all ends up. Little do you know that it came out of Hunts Point Market."

However, access to the market is very difficult. The Economic Development

Corporation manages the shipping of produce for the vendors every day. The Economic Development Corporation, as a result, is one of the few institutions connected to the various participating for-profit entities. The initiative is equipped with a project coordinator, a job developer, and an administrative assistant. Much of the infrastructure of the initiative is funded by Hostos. But, for the most part, implementation of this effort depends upon pro bono assistance, according to Rosa. Helping the community fits with the college mission; however, it still takes a great deal of commitment beyond self-interest to successfully implement an effort like the Hunts Point Initiative. This Hostos effort engages the resources of one of Hostos's departments on behalf of local economic development. This effort is closer to the kinds of partnerships discussed in previous chapters. Rosa's use of the term "pro bono" suggests that in his view this kind of a partnership is something that should or could be paid work. It almost suggests that the partnership work is extra. At a national level, the thrust of the higher education/community partnership movement seems to be looking for ways to naturally incorporate community partnerships into the expectation of departmental responsibilities. Therefore, by this logic partnerships would not be considered pro bono, rather they would be treated as a part of one's responsibilities.

In the initiative, Hostos is helping the corporation develop a business plan. Assistant to the President Sandra Ruiz notes, "The business plan talks about basic training in computer science and computer skills for all of their employees. So we're going to start with that phase. And the second phase is to develop courses based on a survey that was conducted, [for] a certificate in food management, and an associate degree in food management and distribution. So it would be two degrees eventually. And this is long term. So right now we're in phase one, the development of the plan and the basic skills program with the office personnel." Ruiz's comments reveal that this work is not really "pro bono" in the end because it is the testing ground for the development of a new degree program. Therefore, as in most of the examples in the book, the institution of higher education is furthering its own mission through community partnerships. Hostos is going to gain, and it appears that the development corporation and its employees will also.

This initiative grew out of community demand; it was created in response to a survey of the 10,000 employees in the market. The employees particularly indicated their desire to learn computer skills.[20] Courses in the initiative will be held, instead of on the campus, at the Economic Development Corporation. This effort is one means by which Hostos is beginning its improvement of continuing education. As with its other non-degree coursework for local residents, Hostos's potential long-term gain lies in the possibility of non-degree students entering the core curriculum. Again, since Hostos's core student body is drawn from the proximal population, community partnerships can lead to increased enrollment and thus more tuition dollars as well. Partnership activities build relationships between Hostos and residents, exposing the college to new prospective students, and exposing residents to the resources that Hostos can offer. Because Hostos's prospective student body includes local residents of all age groups, the institution, like most community colleges, is really designed for community partnerships. If any group of institutions of higher education stands to gain from perfecting community partnerships, it is that of community colleges. Hostos depends on the local population and must to respond to its needs for its survival. In surveying the various local people, Hostos is taking the logical steps toward ensuring its compatibility with local priorities.

Hostos's long-term approach in the Hunts Point Initiative is based on mutual gain between the college and the vendors. Vendors will have the immediate gain of an increased technological capacity in the Economic Development Corporation, while Hostos will build a new degree program based on the relationship with the Hunts Point Market. Existing and prospective vendors could become students within the program. Graduates could apply their skills in the local market, and students of the degree programs could be exposed to experiential learning in Hunts Point. Due to its relationship with the Hunt's Point Initiative, Hostos is expanding its food service curriculum and adding a new certificate.

According to Rosa, many opportunities spring from building relationships with the various companies working with the market. He speculates, "Can we reach out to these companies, so that we can develop internships for our students? Is it possible that we can develop work sites for our students? Places where our graduates can go? This is absolutely ripe. And then to be looking at our mission . . . our mission is clear. We are here to train students for entry-level jobs, number one. Number two, for those who are so qualified, to transfer to a senior college. That's why we exist." Rosa's approach is compelling given the proliferation of higher education/community partnerships. For him, as well as others at Hostos, it is important to be constantly aware of emerging opportunities both to further the mission of the institution and to provide some form of assistance to community-based initiatives. Rosa's ideas about mutual benefit in community partnerships stem from the business school's 90 percent placement rate. In order to build upon and extend such successes, he sees the Hunt's Point Initiative as an opportunity: "That was what prompted us to consider Hunt's Point; it was the idea that here is a place that is tied in with our mission." He continued, "It's an opportunity for us to practice what we preach."

In many ways, the community outreach dimension of Hostos's community partnerships fills gaps in services that likely would exist in other communities. For example, Fernandez mentioned that Hostos is using its site for a YMCA summer camp. There is no YMCA in close proximity to the South Bronx, so Hostos will be taking in more than one hundred children, the offspring of students and otherwise, every summer. The program is available to any child residing within the Empowerment Zone,[21] since the federal initiative is providing partial funding.

Hostos is making a greater effort to draw upon the resources of its strongest programs for use in the broader community. This is particularly true with respect to health care. For example, the dental clinic is being moved out of its fourth floor location in the dental hygiene program to a position more accessible to the broader neighborhood. President Fernandez said of this move, "It's free to the community, but what we find is that people from the community feel a little inhibited coming into a building, getting into an elevator, going up four floors, you know, and all that kind of stuff. So, we're putting it at street level, and really, you know, really opening up to them. But I also want to get some nursing skills in there as well, because our nursing program [can provide other services]." Greater efforts to involve the nursing and dental programs in community partnerships are a product of a longstanding collaboration between Hostos and Bronx Lebanon Hospital. Of Bronx Lebanon, Fernandez said, "They really have reached out to us and really want to work with us around our nursing program and our dental hygiene program and our radiology program."

Finally, like many urban areas, the South Bronx lacks greenery. Hostos's biology program collaborated with community residents in creating a garden, which is across the street from the institution. This "community garden" is open to the public every afternoon. As Fernandez described it, "People come, they sit down, there are tables, you know, it's nice. And we're hoping to have some music in there, so people will feel comfortable."

Hostos is still a relatively young institution, trying to find its role in the community and simultaneously uphold high academic standards. It is increasingly realizing its interdependency with the community. The losses in enrollment, for example, have been a true wake-up call. The community has changed, and Hostos must make sure that it is in touch with the current realities of the South Bronx and northern Manhattan, from where it increasingly is drawing students. While many of the original community residents who pushed for Hostos's founding remain on the advisory board, new local realities have emerged. The complexities of the lives of students seem to keep Hostos most in touch with the circumstances in the community. While the institution is responding accordingly, the magnitude of the issues far exceeds what most universities see. A community college such as Hostos really must have a dual approach to community partnerships—supportive services for students and community-building initiatives (including the arts) with non-student local residents. But, as will be discussed further, the challenge is resources. Community colleges may be better matched for mutually beneficial community partnerships than other institutions of higher education, but they don't have endowments and other resources to support the enhancement and expansion of these efforts. In the case of Hostos, which is still fighting for its survival, infrastructure is often lacking.

The Impact of Community Partnerships on Campus and Community

In the other case studies, the universities clearly benefited from engaging in community partnerships. Experiential learning opportunities for students were one of the goals in the cases of Penn, SFSU, and Xavier. Hostos does not have an established service learning structure. The thinking is different. Many of the activities are targeted toward solving the problems that face students rather than creating curriculum that places students in partnerships with community organizations. However, at Hostos, the principle of encouraging students to be socially responsible is the same, and maybe surpasses that of any institution profiled in this book. Hansy Perguero, a student from the South Bronx, said of Hostos, "They teach you that you should give back to your community, because without giving back, you're nothing." As previously discussed, students at Hostos gain the training that allows them ultimately to work in their communities. Perguero also pointed to Hostos's attention to the immigrant aspect of the student body: "I believe Hostos is a real community college. It serves two communities. Lately, you know, native countries would have disasters, like hurricanes and all that, and Hostos has been the first reaching out to help [by having] toy drives and food drives, all sorts of things." Perguero is from the Dominican Republic—a first-generation immigrant like much of the student body. Not only is Hostos expected to address its students and its neighbors, but their home countries as well. Perguero sees Hostos constantly working in the community, "Now the college is going to work with the Census Bureau and the students are going to be counters, which means we are very involved in what's going on. It's not like we come to school and we go to classes to learn the academic stuff. We come to school and we also learn to interact with our communities."

Students at Hostos want to learn how to be helpful to their communities. Hostos seems to provide an appropriate atmosphere, but community partnerships don't appear to be an explicit part of the curriculum. The institution has not taken the same approach toward institutionalization as the four-year institutions. It may be that socially responsible tendencies already are institutionalized. Students have taken it upon themselves to be very involved. Hostos is more than a school to them. Even though it is a commuter school, many of the students are involved in clubs. Nathanial Cruz, Assistant Dean of Students, mentioned that 3,000 students attended an event to encourage students to form clubs. They were expecting 1,000. Students refer to the atmosphere on campus as a "participatory democracy," a "community on campus."[22] Sheyla Amador, also a student from the Dominican Republic, said of the students' sense of community, "I think lots of all kinds come from the same background. We all may not be the same, but we have the same problems, the same concerns, and we try to support each other. When you are in a situation, I can understand what you're going through because we are the same. We live the same. That sense of community of being not just friends, but like brothers and sisters." The common circumstances of the lives of the students has created a collective identity and sense of solidarity that institutionalizes Hostos's connection to the community.

As previously discussed, a clear benefit to Hostos by way of community partnerships is enrollment. Hostos's partnerships with local schools produce future Hostos students. Students confirm that word of mouth is how most of them learned of Hostos. Therefore, the more Hostos is present in the community, the more prospective students will know of the college. The more Hostos is making a positive impact on the community, the more of those prospective students will actually attend. Donna Williams-Savuer of Harlem and of Jamaican and Haitian descent says that many students actively recruit on behalf of Hostos. The various student clubs "all set up strategic plans to actually pick certain parts of the community to give information on access to education. Getting to Hostos through word of mouth is typical here. People have family ties, friends, neighbors, and generations. Ten years later, someone's son or daughter or nephew is coming to Hostos." Again, the line between Hostos and the community is so blurred that it is difficult to make a distinction. But Hostos students become ambassadors to their neighborhoods. If they do well by way of a Hostos education, they encourage family and friends to attend.

Jesse Hamilton represents Hostos's first generation. He was among the original activists who pushed for the creation of the college. He has been able to see the evolution of Hostos's relationship to the community. He was the chairman of the board of Lincoln Hospital (across the street from Hostos) and sometimes teaches courses at Hostos. He thinks that Hostos's community partnerships should be tied to its core curriculum. He thinks they have begun to do this through their Allied Health Program and its tie to Lincoln Hospital, but he particularly thinks, "the core curriculum should have some relationships with the business community." Hamilton, who is African American, spent all of his adult life in the Bronx and has lived only blocks from the college for many years. During the '60s, the South Bronx was Puerto Rican and African American, and "the community wanted to have a community college focused on providing education for Hispanics and blacks. I think the focus of the college has shifted. Originally, this was a predominantly Puerto Rican area. That's not so anymore. Dominicans are now coming in." According to Anita Cunningham, Hostos's community partnerships have shifted away from any focus on African Americans. Although the community is predominantly Latino, about 30 percent remains African American.[23]

Along with demographic changes come shifts in local leadership. Hostos does not have the same established relationships with community-based organizations that it once had. The relationships, according to Hamilton, are less organized. He maintains that Hostos previously partnered with a more cohesive collaboration of community-based organizations. As in many of the poor neighborhoods discussed in the book, businesses in the South Bronx left or closed. According to Hamilton, banks in particular left the neighborhood. As previously discussed, Hostos was once so tied to the community that massive prostests kept it open. Residents fought to keep Hostos around. I asked Hamilton if today's community would do the same. He answered, "I think they would do it for the mere fact that this is one of the few institutions that we have here. The only people that have an interest in Hostos are the people that are right here" Hostos is a community institution. There is a local stake in keeping it around. But Hamilton does not speak to more than that. He does not say that people would fight for Hostos because it has been so good to the community. Despite the commitment demonstrated by students, Hamilton suggests that Hostos has fallen victim to complacency. He encourages Hostos to look back to its history to rejuvenate its sense of purpose. He thinks "the history of Hostos should be shared with the students more. This is where it came from, understand how we got here, and understand why we are here." He sees alumni straying from the original mission of the institution. Those who have gone on to successful careers have not connected back to Hostos. Hamilton thinks this cycle needs to be halted. He wants this generation of students to understand the college's purpose and keep it with them forever.

He also suggests that curriculum was once more securely tied to community partnerships. Usually Hamilton teaches a course in the business department, but enrollment is so low this year that he didn't get a course. He recalls when his courses were very community oriented. In one of his classes, he challenged his students on the issue of empowerment:

> I asked them a question, "You live in the Bronx?" "Yeah, I live in the Bronx." "Do you have a tenant's association? Do you participate in your community?" "No, no, no . . . " And so that told me something about how students perceive their own world, you know. So I gave them a challenge, "I want you to organize the tenants in your building, and I'll show you how to do it." And we had meetings and we had flyers, and they called the meeting in their building, and I would go and visit them in the evening and sit in on the meeting and tell them, you know, "If you have problems with the landlord . . . " You know, really giving them something that they can hold on to, and the people started realizing, "Yeah, we don't have to take this, you know, if we stick together."

As the students mentioned, they all have similar life circumstances. This example by Hamilton used that fact to simultaneously educate and empower students, their families, and their neighbors. This is the potential that Hostos presents. Professor Meyer also thinks the curriculum should be more explicitly linked to the community. In his vision, the "core curriculum would be to educate students for citizenship, that they become active in their communities. The community should be seen as a resource in terms of the syllabi of courses."

While Penn, SFSU, and Xavier all seem to be improving their relations with the community, Hostos appears to be trying to return to a level of synergy with its neighbors that has been assumed since its founding. In the case of SFSU, there was also a strong sense of public responsibility to the city. Hostos faces the same sort of expectation as a public institution, but it is much more targeted to specific populations and specific communities.

Incorporation of Community Partnership into Long-Term Mission and Operations

Incorporating community partnerships into the curriculum is one area in which Hostos has not been able to demonstrate a consistent institutional commitment. But it is important to keep this in context, since the expectations are much higher for a community institution like Hostos. As discussed previously, the nature of the student body seems to be one of the main ways in which a sense of social responsibility, particularly to the surrounding community, has persisted over the years. As in previous chapters, much of this still comes down to committed people. While the centralization of community partnerships at Hostos might not be what it is in other places, many faculty and administrators want to be at Hostos because of the mission, the activist history, and the composition of the student body. As indicated in the last two chapters, this is also the case at San Francisco State and Xavier. It makes a difference when the college or university-based participants have activist backgrounds. Their personal commitment at least helps to stimulate an institutional commitment.

Hostos does have a community advisory board, but according to Anita Cunningham, "The only board that holds the college accountable is the Board of Trustees for all of the City University of New York." It does not appear that the advisory board has been a significant force in shaping the college's community partnerships, even though many of the original activists are on it. As with all of the institutions in this book, a community advisory board will be only that—advisory—unless specific steps are taken to give that body power, for example, the veto power of the community advisors working with SFSU or the board of the Xavier Triangle. Especially with the persistent turnover among presidents, an institutional commitment at Hostos would require some community-based decision-making body that could build and enhance a system for community partnerships.

One of the more obvious infrastructural differences between Hostos and institutions such as the University of Pennsylvania and San Francisco State is coordination. At these universities, an office has been designated to monitor, coordinate, and promote community partnerships. Anita Cunningham notes, "As long as I've been here, we have not had anyone who was assigned to community relations." Hostos has many activities internally and externally targeted toward the community, but they do not appear to intersect or to be coordinated in any centralized fashion. Berotte-Joseph said, "We've been very aggressive in meeting with different components of the community—the hospitals, the community centers. We have several grant-funded programs reaching out to the different components." The challenge according to Berotte-Joseph is "how to bring all of those under one umbrella, to have one person coordinate it."

As in all of the other case studies, senior administrative support appears to be essential to the development and survival of community partnership activities at Hostos. Obviously, Fernandez is committed to engaging the local community, but she has envisioned the Renaissance in a manner that clearly benefits the institution. In other words, involvement in the community is essential to the long-term mission of the institution. This could be the beginning of a stronger commitment, but those who have witnessed the evolution of the central administration's commitment to community suggest that the desire has always wavered. Bibiano Rosa said of senior administration, "Their attitude toward some of this fluctuates. And it probably fluctuates or varies depending on the budget or their emphasis or where they want to put their money." Nevertheless, Rosa believes that the institution has been good with outreach overall. He does, however, make an important point, which may be due to the turnover at the presidential level. Hostos has had approximately ten presidents in its thirty-year history. How can any large institution develop any consistency with such shifting leadership? Jesse Hamilton believes that Hostos's commitment to the community has shifted with these presidential changes: "The change of presidents in the college brought different perspectives as to where the college should be going."

Faculty at Hostos generally are encouraged to be involved in community partnerships, but to a large degree, their involvement does not exceed assistance to students. It may be that faculty in an institution such as Hostos are so busy with teaching, advising, counseling, and tutoring students that they are given little room to venture into other activities. Rosa said of faculty and community outreach, "There's no incentive to do it. I mean, why do it? It's the same problem in the law firms. You do it because it's nice to do pro bono work. It's part of your overall assessment of an associate on his way up to be partner. So there's really no benefit to engaging in it. Although in evaluations of instructors who apply for promotion, one of the things we take into account is community involvement." While Hostos does have a reward system tied to community outreach, Rosa said that publication is the most significantly weighted factor in faculty review. This is ironic given that the mission of most community colleges is not primarily to produce research. The essence of Hostos's core mission appears to focus on the training of students either for direct placement in employment in a particular trade or for acceptance into a senior college/university. Student-related activities do play an important role in faculty review, certainly more so than community outreach, according to Rosa, but even at a community college, publication commands the most attention.

Laurel Higgins has been a resident of the South Bronx for many years. She was a single parent and Hostos student years before becoming the director of Continuing and Workforce Education. She sees a noticeable change in the nature of Hostos faculty. When she was a student, faculty did not mind the extra work to be involved with the community because they were so committed to the idea of Hostos: "Teachers were teaching at Hostos back then because they really wanted to be here. They knew what Hostos was about, and they knew it was a revolutionary idea." Her sentiments seem to resemble those of others who have been associated with the college for many years. The idea of a college emerging directly out of social protest is probably not familiar to many current academic administrators and faculty. As new people enter the institution, it is difficult to orient people to the original mission. Moreover, the mission will change with the times. Higgins also believes that the "shift to conservatism nationally has had a tremendous effect on us here." Getting by as a community college is difficult in itself, but trying to maintain a tradition as a revolutionary community college is even more daunting. Hostos never developed the consistency to preserve the intensity of its mission, and in the face of broader political shifts, it never raised the necessary funding from sources who are supportive of their original activist, community-oriented tradition.

One Hostos tradition that Humberto Canate is trying to resurrect is their "Learning Centers": "We used to have that years ago, where teachers would go to a certain community center and teach mathematics, biology, psychology, and the people in the community would have that access." According to Anita Cunningham, Hostos once held courses in prisons as well. It seems that the will still exists at Hostos to be deeply involved in the community, but there is less consistency across the college community. Cunningham suggests that the size of the institution is significant. "When we were smaller, and our position in the community was not as stable, we may have been more connected. Then, as we became a little more comfortable with where we are, then we may have forgotten about it."

Challenges Confronting Partnership

Given that Hostos's student body heavily overlaps with the local population, expectations for community involvement are high. While other institutions in this book stressed funding as a major issue, Hostos is in a more dire situation.

Having lost so much in tuition due to decreased enrollment was a major blow to the institution. However, infrastructure is again the critical factor. Many community colleges do not have the expansive and sophisticated resource development offices present in many universities. As a public institution, Hostos does receive significant government funding; however, as is the case with San Francisco State, the needs of the institution far outpace public support. Hostos is beginning to think more seriously about diversifying its sources of income. Berotte-Joseph pointed out some interesting resource development opportunities. She said, "We don't have an alumni association. And the college is almost thirty years old. It was only after the incident two years ago that we started thinking maybe we should bring our graduates back. And then we're finding out that we have graduates who are now vice-presidents in universities, who have gone on to Ph.D.s and have done great work." Fernandez does intend to create an alumni office. That effort in itself will, of course, require funding.

As had surfaced in the other case studies, the level of preparedness of the community to partner with an institution of higher education has arisen in Hostos's partnerships. Rosa notes, "The problem, as we have found in these programs where we have tried to do some kind of social work, is that the organization is usually not strong enough, or it doesn't have the credibility or stability in the neighborhood." In Hostos's partnership with Lincoln Hospital, for example, the hospital was too dependent upon federal funding. In another effort, a small community group partnering with Hostos also did not have significant infrastructural capacity, and expected Hostos to put up 100 percent of the funding.

Conclusion

One of the great ironies of the burgeoning national movement around higher education/community partnerships or civic engagement is the limited involvement of community colleges. Indeed, one might say that community colleges don't need a movement in this area because they already have inherent ties to proximal neighborhoods. However, that is precisely why community colleges should be involved alongside doctoral, masters, and baccalaureate institutions. Because deep knowledge of local communities is required of community colleges, senior colleges and universities may stand to learn a great deal from their junior counterparts. Berotte-Joseph advocates for partnerships between community colleges and senior colleges/universities for the purpose of community outreach. She said, "Just as we're partnering with community-based organizations in schools, I think the senior colleges and research institutions can also partner with community colleges and with schools." For those community college students who go on to attend four-year colleges or universities, community colleges essentially play an intermediary role on the "k–16" continuum. More broadly, community colleges are a step closer to the kind of poor and disenfranchised urban communities with which the University of Pennsylvania, San Francisco State, and Xavier wish to partner.

Community colleges such as Hostos are also accustomed to responding directly to the needs of employers along with the immediate needs of local residents (that is, jobs and directly marketable skills). According to Berotte-Joseph, senior colleges and universities are beginning to encounter competition from corporate universities. She indicated, "Senior colleges are beginning to face competition because a lot of companies are beginning to set up their own universities. I mean, there's Toyota University and all of these private businesses setting up their places. So if you can't respond to my needs, what I need from my company for my staff, then I'll create my own university. And I think that's what's shaking up the traditional colleges for them to now say, 'Well if we don't open up and serve the needs of our partners in addition to the traditional degree kind of thing that we do, then we're not going to survive.'" Community partnerships are linked to the future survival of higher education.

Chapter 6

Comparisons and Conclusions

From community colleges to major research universities, relations to surrounding communities are central to the higher educational agenda. The institutions of higher education profiled in this book are using various strategies to revitalize local neighborhoods while concurrently fulfilling some aspect of their institutional mission. The original aim of this research was to determine whether or not community partnerships could be compatible with the missions of institutions of higher education. At all levels of higher education, I would have to conclude that community partnerships make sense to varying degrees for colleges and universities, in both academic and economic dimensions of their missions. Mutual interests between local communities and institutions of higher education do exist, and they seem to become more apparent through lengthy relationship-building processes. Colleges and universities seem to face the greatest challenges when they attempt to institutionalize these efforts. So we know that community partnerships make sense for institutions of higher education, but how can they, for example, become more compatible with the institutional culture and raise long-term external funds?

Another important aim of this research was to determine the factors that influence the nature of higher education/community partnerships. They are numerous. To restate, those factors that I found presented themselves most prominently include: the type of institution of higher education, the historical relationship between the partners, power relationships between the institution and the community, the availability of external funding, the relative support of the public sector, the capacity of community-based institutions and governing structures, the institutional culture of the college or university, the historical mission of the college or university, the backgrounds of the higher educational representatives, and demographics (in both community and institution). But the factor on which this book places the most emphasis is the type of institution.

Comparisons and Institutional Commitment

The type of institution is clearly a central factor shaping the nature of these partnerships, although every institution has a particular tradition, which may or may not be related to its institutional type. Although it is a major research university, for example, the University of Pennsylvania historically has been cast as a democratic institution. While its relationship with West Philadelphia has been mixed, Penn has been one of the premier institutions for service learning. Upon its founding by Benjamin Franklin, Penn was conceived to serve Philadelphia. Xavier University follows the path of many historically black colleges, which were founded as tools for developing African Americans' potential. But as a private, Catholic institution, Xavier has another set of historical factors that guide its commitment. A commitment to social justice has been explicit in its mission since its founding. This was seen as an extension of the religious beliefs of the Sisters of the Blessed Sacrament.

Many faculty and administrators I met at San Francisco State stressed the significance of the institution's public responsibility. As public employees, they feel responsible to the city. In the case of a public urban university, a sense of social responsibility to the hosting city is assumed. At community colleges, the degree of expected responsibility to the local area is even stronger. Most community colleges are established to train a local population. Many of their graduates subsequently remain in the neighborhood, effectively developing the local area. Of the four institutions of higher education addressed here, Hostos has been least able to sustain its academic mission, not to mention its community partnerships. However, its historical mission guides its desired commitment to the community.

Both the academic and economic aspects of a college or university's mission can be served through partnerships. Through community partnerships, institutions of higher education may gain more than they actually give. New methods of experiential learning and knowledge creation, not to mention opportunities for public relations, emerge in all of the case studies. Hostos is a bit of an exception as its approach to service may be more "inreach" than "outreach" due to the demographics of its students.

All of these institutions of higher education have mission statements that prioritize service. However, institutionally, there is less consistency. They are all searching for the win/win situation, in which the mission of their institution is being met through the process of partnering with local communities. For a community college, this may be relatively automatic, but the other institutions grapple with greater complexity. The institutional commitment to and sustainability of partnerships can be, particularly in the case of major research universities, limited by the institutional culture.

As complex organizations, colleges and universities are communities in themselves. Departments are practically independent entities. Faculty and administrators do not always collaborate. In all of the case studies, there are some community partnership activities that are not collaborating with others. Xavier and Hostos are both small enough so that different faculty and administrators can coordinate their efforts, so size is a factor in this regard.

While an excellent example of community partnership initiative, the University of Pennsylvania does not have explicit reward systems for faculty engaged in service. As a major research university, the research aspect of the mission far outweighs service or teaching. Some very committed faculty members have found ways to incorporate their community outreach into their research. Only tenured faculty, in many cases, are officially encouraged to be involved in community service for fear that junior faculty would be sidetracked from the traditional research activity that will lead to tenure. Ira Harkavy, the head of Penn's community outreach office, is a fervent supporter of outreach. He encourages multiple departmental involvement in service, and has been a longtime partner with most local community-based organizations. However, many in the community suspect that he may be the essence of Penn's commitment. Were he to leave, some suggest, outreach initiatives would fold.

Once the territory only of students and certain progressive faculty at San Francisco State, community partnerships more recently have been embraced by the central administration. Nonetheless, many SFSU faculty also struggle to stay afloat because their community work is not sufficiently rewarded. The Urban Institute is the administration's attempt to centralize community partnerships, yet other unrelated efforts persist in other departments.

Many of the faculty involved in community partnerships at Xavier contend with teaching four courses per term and few opportunities for release time. The importance of community service is quite explicit in Xavier's mission and history, but implementing community partnerships is challenging. Getting overwhelmed faculty involved in some of the administration's efforts has been difficult.

Hostos has been shut down and has had a few other close calls. Its academic programs have come under significant scrutiny. But it has to expend as much energy on supportive services for its students as on academics. Even with the internal services, local residents and activists who are not students expect Hostos to be more involved in the community. While the expectations for Hostos are high, the institution has limited capacity. To a lesser degree, Xavier and San Francisco State also face high external expectations that they will be involved in local community-building efforts. In these cases, local residents see some compatibility between mission and a commitment to the local area because local people can attend those institutions. In the case of the University of Pennsylvania, and many other institutions of its type, urban residents appear to expect less, although many demand greater social responsibility. But Penn's student body generally is not reflective of the local population. Although San Francisco State is not located in or near a distressed area, its *students* tend to come from some of the poor neighborhoods throughout the city. The students inform the faculty and administrators of the conditions in their neighborhoods. Service learning courses give those students the opportunity to go back home and do something for their families and neighbors. Student recruitment and retention in such cases is interdependent with the conditions of poor urban neighborhoods.

When students are drawn from local neighborhoods, mission and community partnerships in those areas are very compatible academically and economically. The development of those areas, particularly their school systems, ultimately keeps tuition flowing and enhances the academic ability of students. For those institutions located in distressed areas, the development of the neighborhood impacts the livability of the area for faculty, students, and administrators. This facilitates recruitment and enrollment. These are win/win situations as long as community residents do not get displaced by economic development, or find their access to the university limited when it decides that it can raise tuition and standards because the quality of its students has improved. Service learning can be more mutually beneficial to institutions of higher education and communities when the improvement of conditions in local neighborhoods is treated with the same importance as learning opportunities for students.

Unless community partnerships affect the core academic missions, particularly regarding research, they are not easily justifiable for the long term, barring any radical shifts in internal reward systems. Faculty need publishing opportunities emerging from partnership efforts. At Penn, for example, a number of faculty in various disciplines have bolstered their careers based on locally gathered data. However, it is not a win/win relationship until the results of such research projects are made useful for local residents.

The central faculty or administrators involved in community partnerships in each case tend to have activist backgrounds. Brian Murphy at San Francisco State and the majority of faculty working with him, including President Bob Corrigan, have been activists since the 1960s. This is not necessarily the case at the University of Pennsylvania, but Ira Harkavy was a student activist over thirty years ago at Penn. His influence on other Penn faculty and administrators has been tremendous. Many of the Xavier administrators and faculty were involved in the civil rights movement. So, one might say that these current partnership efforts are at least influenced by, if not extensions of, social movements dating back to the civil rights movement.

Other important factors include the type of neighborhood and historical relations between the institution and the neighborhood. Partnerships take a long time to develop. A number of discussions and trust-building activities are necessary. If the historical relationship has been contentious, it takes even more time.

Institutional Commitment

Institutional commitment can be assessed through indicators of institutional priority. Do community outreach efforts transcend one person or a very small handful of people? Are faculty who are engaged in community partnerships rewarded by their institutions? Is the central administration placing a high priority on community outreach? Is service incorporated into both the core academic mission and the economic mission of the institution? Are service learning courses as concerned about community interests as experiential learning opportunities for students? Are various campus-based community outreach efforts coordinated? Without such elements of institutional commitment, community partnerships run the risk of being marginalized. Without institutional commitment, community partnerships could end when the external grant goes away or the principal investigator[1] leaves town. For most projects in the academy, this would not pose a problem, but with community partnerships, the well-being of local residents may be at stake, not to mention their perception of institutions of higher education.

Challenges to Partnerships

Two of the most significant challenges within the organizational culture of institutions of higher education are: 1) the extent of faculty and administrative involvement in developing and agreeing upon central institutional goals, and 2) institutionalized practices that may be inconsistent with the rhetoric of the mission statement.

Faculty reward systems, for example, do not tend to significantly incorporate outreach activities, especially at major research universities. In such situations, outreach is effectively extracurricular, regardless of a written or spoken institutional commitment to the local neighborhood. Those individual faculty or administrators who carry the banner of community outreach tend to stress the value of community partnerships to not only the community, but the institution of higher education as well. Value to the institution tends to be articulated as either academic or organizational. *Organizational* value focuses on the survival of the institution in terms of public image and economics. *Academic* value focuses on student learning and faculty/student applied research.

The mission of higher education flows first from the academic side, supported by the organizational one. However, since colleges and universities have grown into significant institutions, transcending a solely academic role, organizational issues are equally important. Therefore, if community partnerships are going to become incorporated into the overall role of institutions of higher education in this new millenium, then they should be justifiable academically and organizationally. They should be rewarded accordingly, making logical use of higher educational resources, and enhancing both the organizational and academic aspects of the mission. Additionally, internal coordination among faculty, students, administrators, and departments engaged in community partnerships should be a priority.

As community-based stakeholders are challenged to identify who exactly represents the collective interest of the university or college, it is probably equally difficult to identify who represents the community's. Institutions of higher education are often clear about the geographical boundaries of community in their community partnerships. However, the composition of the actual target population is harder to decipher. For example, many institutions of higher education often are partnered with a community advisory board to monitor and shape various outreach activities. Advisory boards frequently do not represent the primary recipients of outreach initiatives. In other words, the populations that stand to gain the most from community partnerships sometimes have limited say in the initiatives. Their ideas may be represented by "community leaders," but grassroots constituents are often left out of the process. When an institution of higher education declares its partnership intentions, those who have designated leadership positions and a certain degree of organizational and political savvy are most likely to come to the table. And institutions of higher education are more likely to seek out those who are readily identified as community leaders.

Traditional discussions in the academy have focused more on studying rather than working with poor and working-class communities. The current movement in higher education may be the beginning of a significant shift toward partnership with these populations. When this particular population has achieved a certain level of knowledge about higher education and the infrastructure of community-based organizations, they will be more likely to approach colleges and universities, speaking for themselves about their priorities and the potential uses of higher educational resources on their behalf. If institutions of higher education have the capacity to provide assistance to local residents while remaining relatively distant to those most in need, then those local constituents who are tied to the college or university should serve as bridges between the institution and the grassroots.

It is important to ensure that knowledge is being transferred from higher education into local communities, promoting self-sufficiency rather than fostering dependency among local constituents. The distinctions between self-sufficiency and dependency are at the heart of the difference between the traditional notion of service and the concept of capacity building. Capacity building involves residents in decision making and stresses the need for local in-house skills, while service does not automatically suggest such nuances. Service can merely involve assistance, stressing a dichotomy between service provider and recipient. The traditional notion of service has tended to presuppose that one party has power and maintains it while the other receives it. Capacity building would suggest the transference of power from one party to the other. Furthermore, when both parties are treated as if each has something to offer, the opinion of the traditional "recipient" influences the nature of the relationship. Ultimately, the "recipient" is more likely to buy into the partnership when engaged as a contributor throughout the process. Indeed, when grassroots constituents are brought to the table, unique details about their needs and circumstances surface, often altering the tide of conversation and action.

Conclusions and Recommendations

Average citizens in this country are thinking about life within a new economy, where the gap between the wealthy and the poor is expanding. Universities are being asked to address enormous challenges in neighborhoods with which they coexist. Campuses contain a wealth of human and capital resources as well as endless access to information. Indeed, the informed tend to have the greatest access to employment, benefits, housing, and other resources. The potential is extensive and our society must think of innovative and productive ways to make the wealth of higher educational resources more useful to the broader society.

All of the cases suggest the need for additional attention to community partnerships. The good news is that each of the profiled institutions of higher education has experienced some degree of increased internal commitment to outreach, particularly the major research university and the public urban university—both of which have sought to transcend historical tensions with local constituents. My travels to various institutions of higher education over the last couple of years and my conversations with funders, consultants, and other interested parties suggest progress in the field in particular areas. Indeed, the verbal commitment to outreach and the recognition of mutual interest between institutions of higher education and their neighbors have increased. Specific attention to involvement in local school systems, employment and workforce development, and housing and urban planning is included among recent advances.

Relevance to Scholarly Research

The communitarian literature is right to focus on the common ground that can be found between even the most unlikely parties. Mutual interest can be reached. However, it is critical to take account of uneven power relationships, that often can place a greater onus on a particular party. Given the relative power of institutions of higher education in many urban communities, it is critical not only that they find some institutional benefit to engaging in local initiatives, but also that they should be willing to extend beyond mere structural interests.

The engagement of complex organizations in external partnerships raises important questions regarding institutional mission. While various activities within complex organizations have survived and sometimes thrived without being challenged to reflect broader institutional goals, relations with external partners may depend upon consistency within the mission. In the case of partnerships between institutions of higher education and local (particularly impoverished) neighborhoods, residents need assurances. Additionally, mass involvement of internal stakeholders also depends in part upon the degree of importance assigned to external community partnerships.

While focusing on the specific subject of higher education/community partnerships, this research raises a number of broader theoretical issues, applicable to various situations. The notion of external partnership, for example, is central not only to higher education, but to the private and public sectors as well. What are the institutional factors that should be taken into account when any major institution engages external partners? The idea of social responsibility also transcends higher education. Corporate social responsibility, for example, has been in focus for some time. In general, there is a need for research that identifies strategies for using effectively the resources of major institutions and industries on behalf of disenfranchised populations. As the expanding gap between rich and poor continues to hold the spotlight, we must grapple with better ways to enable those who are left behind to share in both the knowledge and wealth that continue to be produced in this economy.

I am in the process of creating the Center for Innovation in Social Responsibility, which will be based at Columbia University and designed to improve the effectiveness of partnerships between major institutions or industries and poor and disenfranchised communities. It will continue some of my research on higher education/community partnerships but expand the conversation to include corporate social responsibility relations between the philanthropic industry and communities as well as the investment and technology industries and communities. It will also help students grapple with how to incorporate social responsibility into their career goals. The center's methodology will mirror the research in this book—finding examples and searching for best practices as well as weaknesses to influence greater effectiveness in the field.

The center ultimately will provide a forum for greater discussion around these issues through workshops, seminars, meetings, and conversations over the internet. It will continue the spirit of my work at the Rockefeller Foundation. For example, in May of 2000, The University of California at Santa Barbara, along with Rockefeller, and PolicyLink hosted a monumental strategy conference on the higher education/community partnerships in California. It took a regional approach to the issue, enabling a significant community presence alongside college and university representatives, foundations, and public officials. The conference led to concrete efforts to affect local policy in this area. The center intends to convene similar critical meetings in other parts of the country in the future in collaboration with any number of important institutions in the field. The research and dialogue emanating from the center will serve as a resource for community residents and organizations wishing to know how they can benefit from partnerships with major institutions and industries. It also will help major institutions and industries gain insight into how to work with communities, particularly in a manner where communities can accrue long-term benefits toward their self-sufficiency rather than dependency.

In addition to the idea of bringing communities in closer contact with resources and information, this book also continues to grapple with the centuries-old question about the purpose of higher education. Since teaching, research, and service have been the stated priorities of so many colleges and universities, we need more research that addresses the numerous dimensions of service and critically analyzes the impact of partnerships on the community. Although partnerships ideally find mutual benefit between both parties, it is important to ensure that communities truly benefit, especially since they fall on the short end of the power dynamic. Further critical analysis of the relative preparedness of higher education to genuinely incorporate service into both theory and practice is needed.

Policy Recommendations

Overall, this research suggests that the relationship between higher education and communities is progressing, but a number of factors must be addressed if higher education/community partnerships are going to become an essential engine of community development and community building.

Identifying who actually serves a community's interest is critical to understanding the future implications of higher education/community partnerships. Most of these partnerships emerge out of some desire to serve the needs of underprivileged populations; however, many higher educational institutions find themselves working with those who do not always reflect the interests of poor and disenfranchised residents. For example, a university could partner primarily with local business people without consulting less-advantaged residents and still say it is working in a community partnership.

We must figure out more effective means to enable grassroots community-based constituents to initiate partnerships with higher education. If it is true that higher education is becoming more receptive to the notion of community partnerships, then how do communities proactively take advantage of this opportunity? If community-based organizations and individuals do not have a certain level of capacity, they may be engulfed by powerful institutions with all the answers. It is important to find ways to ensure that higher educational institutions are passing knowledge to communities in a way that fosters self-sufficiency over dependency. Intermediary organizations might also play the role of bridging institutions of higher education and grassroots residents. As previously stated, many community residents do not know where to begin communicating with institutions of higher education, especially major research universities. Who can fill this void? Who is connected to both grassroots residents and institutions of higher education? In some cases, it might be particular students and faculty, but an intermediary organization designated to broker such relationships could be extremely beneficial to the future effectiveness of these partnerships.

Since different types of institutions of higher education have very different sets of resources to offer and varying institutional cultures, we should work to establish more effective ways for creating diverse intercollegiate partnerships. If, for example, an Ivy League university and a community college each adds a particular value, they should work together on issues facing a common area. How do we leverage the unique advantages of each different type of institution of higher education on behalf of communities?

Not all academic disciplines are practically applicable in an obvious way. Indeed, professional schools, social work, urban planning, and a few others tend to be more readily engaged in partnerships among these case studies. However, a greater effort is needed in bringing in the humanities and the social and natural sciences. Problems facing communities are, by nature, multidisciplinary. All aspects of higher education bring something useful to the challenges facing urban neighborhoods. In fact, faculty members who have been engaged in solving problems in communities comment that they have been forced to reflect upon the limitations of their particular disciplines. The various disciplines need incentives to be engaged, and maybe more appropriately, they need to be shown how together their disciplines can be made useful to communities.

We need better ways of coordinating the various community partnership activities taking place on particular campuses. Internal communication within higher educational institutions facilitates more effective institution-wide partnerships with external partners. Persons like Harkavy are well-positioned to provide the glue on campus at the University of Pennsylvania, but a number of colleges and universities do not have specific point people to galvanize internally various individuals and departments and centers. Having such a central convening entity appears to be one of the critical best practices in the field.

It is important to assume that higher education has something to learn in partnerships. In their daily lives, academics usually are not expected to know how to build relationships in communities. Despite their particular expertise, they may know very little about working at the community level. Many higher educational institutions need to develop training programs if they are going to venture out into communities. Again, a brokering intermediary institution could help an institution of higher education understand the dynamics of working in communities. Absent of a history of deep community relationships, an institution of higher education is not automatically going to know with whom it should be communicating in the community. Given that many community folks don't necessarily know with whom they should be speaking at institutions of higher education either, more frank conversations about the realities and limitations of colleges and universities are needed. Greater understanding about the true picture can help ground expectations.

Finally, the sustainability of these partnerships certainly is dependent upon the availability of resources internal and external to higher education. Funding from HUD and an increasing interest among private foundations may carry partnerships for a few more years. However, true institutionalization into the higher educational mission will not take place unless institutions of higher education are willing to significantly commit their own resources toward these efforts. Private institutions might consider drawing from their endowments or developing targeted alumni-giving campaigns. Public institutions may have fewer funds at their disposal, but San Francisco State is one example of a public university that has drawn from its central budget in support of community partnerships. Higher education also must be willing to expand its criteria for faculty rewards to open up opportunities, particularly for junior faculty, to use their expertise in service of the community.

The national conversation about higher education/community partnerships has been taking place largely among higher educational stakeholders. Indeed, community-based organizations, too, are wondering about the potential for greater partnership with higher education, but there do not appear to be enough opportunities for the two to come together and discuss the big picture issues related to community partnerships. Given the broader implications of these initiatives, it is important to bring community-based organizations, public officials, foundations, and others into the broader conversation. The May 2000 Santa Barbara conference "A Dialogue on Partnerships" began to move in this direction. As a regional event, focusing specifically on the state of California, it was easier to convene diverse groups with common interests. With common interests comes potential to impact policy. The outcomes of the conference are geared toward influencing California's approach to these issues. The critical issues raised by conference participants were as follows:

- There is a need to address frankly the power dynamics between institutions of higher education and communities, and to forge more effective ways to enable the voices and interests of community residents to drive partnerships.

- Consistency and longevity are critical to the success of partnerships, and better efforts to institutionalize community partnerships into institutions of higher education are needed.

- Effective communication is essential. It is important to build healthy relationships and trust between communities and institutions of higher education.

- Greater capacity in communities and in institutions of higher education is necessary for more effective partnerships. Community-based organizations are better able to stand their own ground in partnerships when they have greater internal capacity and knowledge of the inner workings of higher education, and institutions of higher education are better partners when they have the capacity to understand the nuances of communities and the internal systems to support partnerships.

- Institutions of higher education need a greater number of clear and institutionalized incentives and reward systems for faculty and others on campus who engage in community partnerships.

- Institutions of higher education need widespread buy-in from multiple departments around community partnerships.

- Top-level officials in colleges and universities should provide support and leadership for community partnerships.

- More external funding from private and public sources should be targeted toward partnerships.

- Good public relations can enhance the profile and growth of higher education/community partnerships.

- The full range of higher educational resources should be leveraged in partnerships, from faculty to students to jobs and contracts.

This last point addresses the need for communities to expect institutions of higher education to be both resources and local economic engines. This book discusses both the academic and economic missions of institutions of higher education. Early on, I mentioned how institutions of higher education increasingly are the largest local employers. In the case of Penn, both the academic and economic missions are being addressed. On the economic side, they are creating local jobs and enhancing the access of local businesses to university contracts. I have been more directly involved with the efforts of UCSF (University of California at San Francisco) to do something similar in San Francisco. What is interesting about this effort is its approach to long-term economic development. The university has been working closely with the Southeast Neighborhood Jobs Initiative, a Rockefeller Foundation grantee, to stimulate job opportunities for local residents in UCSF's various campuses around the city. Since so many of the university's jobs are outsourced, we had to revise our strategy to include contracts to local small businesses, which in turn could hire residents from various disadvantaged neighborhoods like Bayview–Hunter's Point and Visitacion Valley.

While UCSF historically has had tension with residents in these communities, the economic development strategy is generating trust. All of the critical issues raised in the Santa Barbara conference are interrelated. As UCSF builds trust, it provides income-generating opportunities for local residents. Those jobs and contracts are filled for the university. Yes, the university invests in their training, but with the hope that they will stick around. In a tight labor market like the one in which we are now living, longevity among employees is critical, so this is a win/win situation. If trust is generated because the university is a good local employer, then opportunities for other partnerships arise, and other departments in the university get involved. Trust is attained partly because community residents have been at the table from early in the process. Funding is partly in place, but success will attract other funders.[2] Of course, success can drive public relations. How can any partnership clearly demonstrate what success looks like? What kind of strategies exhibit mutual gain? In the UCSF partnership, both parties are learning how they each operate through constant dialogue. A senior-level administrator is involved and the president of UCSF is very supportive. This partnership helps the image of the university overall, and it has the potential to be useful to the community in the most basic way—economics.

The ideas of the crowd of about one hundred in the recent Santa Barbara conference are in line with issues raised in this book. More are coming to common agreement as to what constitutes best practices for partnerships, from this diverse crowd in Santa Barbara, to the various HUD grantees, to the many community-based organizations doing their best to navigate the often confusing world of higher education. The HUD COPC grantees and various community-based organizations are in fact creating an independent consortium.[3] David Cox of the University of Memphis, the former director of HUD's Office of Community Partnerships, is spearheading the effort along with Cynthia Farrar of Yale's Office of New Haven Affairs and others. It has the potential to become the nucleus of a burgeoning movement. It will be the vehicle by which partnerships nationwide can share ideas and strengthen their effectiveness. The combination of this sort of institutionalized network, foundations feeling more confident in investing in partnerships, research on the various dynamics and potential of partnerships, greater publicity and widespread dialogue on the issue, and policymakers verbally and financially supporting partnerships can move the idea of higher education/community partnerships to another level.

In conclusion, the ideal win/win situation can take partnerships only so far given vast power differentials between institutions of higher education and community partners. The case studies in this book tell us that there is room in the higher educational mission for engaging in local economic development, taking responsibility for the quality of public schooling, enhancing experiential learning, and improving public health. However, higher education must be willing to allow itself to change its internal way of doing business in order to support such an expanding reason for being. Particularly in major research universities, a shift in vested interests is required, so that service becomes a higher priority in the actual core mission.

Colleges and universities must have the will to engage communities at this level, and as this book discusses, it is in their interest to do so. But ensuring community benefit requires a greater sense of social responsibility. Community partnerships make sense for higher education at all levels. I focused less on the moral dimensions of these efforts, but if I must in closing: taking responsibility for improving the conditions of local neighborhoods and the life circumstances of local residents is the right thing for higher education to do. Higher education/ community partnerships are extensions of the social conscience of colleges and universities. Colleges and universities are institutional citizens, which should feel responsible for those around them, especially when they are in need. Yet, simultaneously, these partnerships make sense in relation to the mission of higher education. Mission and social responsibility converge. Colleges and universities should not be concerned solely with their self-interest, but if their missions are furthered by partnerships with local communities, all the better, as long as communities are not harmed in the process. As this movement continues, it likely will usher in a new era of higher education. We should have high expectations for innovative and responsible uses of higher educational resources because it is logical and right for higher education and communities alike.

Appendix

The following is a list of those people interviewed over the course of this research who are cited in the book*:

Acevedo, Carlos, Professor, Hostos Community College, Bronx, NY 1999
Alunan, Susan, San Francisco State Urban Institute 1999
Amador, Sheyla, student, Hostos Community College, Bronx, NY 2000
Barlare, Anne, Professor of Pharmacy Administration, Xavier University, New Orleans 2000
Barnes, Mark, Center for Community Partnerships, University of Pennsylvania 1999
Bechet, Ron, Chair, Art Department, Xavier University, New Orleans 2000
Bell, Larry, Philadelphia 1999
Bensen, Lee, Professor, University of Pennsylvania 1999
Berotte-Joseph, Carol, Dean of Academic Affairs, Hostos Community College, Bronx, NY 1999/2000
Bordenave, Diane, Center for the Urban Community, Tulane and Xavier, New Orleans 2000
Bowman, Cory, Center for Community Partnerships, University of Pennsylvania 1999
Buckner, Omar, CAP Program, CJ Peete Housing Complex, New Orleans 2000
Canate, Humberto, Chair, Department of Mathematics, Hostos Community College, Bronx, NY 2000
Cazenave, Rene, CAREERPRO, San Francisco State University Urban Institute 1999
Clark, Della, Philadelphia 1999
Corrigan, Bob, President, SFSU, San Francisco interview 1999
Cruz, Nathaniel, Assistant Dean of Students, Hostos Community College, Bronx, NY 2000
Cunningham, Anita, Chair, Allied Health, Hostos Community College, Bronx, NY 2000
Davallier, Brenda, Director, Xavier Triangle, New Orleans 1999
Eisman, Jerry, Professor, San Francisco State University 1999
Errico, Elizabeth, Coordinator, Nursing Program, Hostos Community College, Bronx, NY 2000
Fernandez, Delores, President, Hostos Community College, Bronx, NY 1999
Fleming, Larry, activist, San Francisco 1999
Francis, Norman, President, Xavier University, New Orleans 2000
Givens, Joe, Director, All Congregations Together, New Orleans 2000
Goslin, Neil, CAP program, CJ Peete Housing Complex, New Orleans 2000
Hadaller, David, Associate Dean of Academic Affairs, Hostos Community College, Bronx, NY 1999
Hale, Rosalind, Chair, Division of Education, Xavier University, New Orleans 2000
Hamilton, Jesse, resident and Hostos Advisory Council member, Bronx, NY 2000
Hannah, Celeste, CAP Program, CJ Peete Housing Complex, New Orleans 2000

Harkavy, Ira, Director, Center for Community Partnerships, University of Pennsylvania 1999
Hernandez, Betsy, Director, Center for Pre-College Initiatives, Hostos Community College 1999
Higgins, Laurel, Director, Continuing and Workforce Education, Hostos Community College 2000
Hurst, Larry, resident, CJ Peete Housing Complex, New Orleans 2000
Jasper Alcorn, Nedra, Associate VP for Student Services, Xavier University, New Orleans 1999
Keizs, Sonji, Director, COPE Program, Hostos Community College, Bronx, NY 1999
Kury, Felix, Professor, San Francisco State University 1999
Labov, Bill, Professor, Linguistics, University of Pennsylvania 1999
Long, Vernon, Visitacion Valley Jobs, Education and Training Project (VVJET), San Francisco 1999
Mangal, Hemansu, Planner, Agenda for Children Tomorrow, Bronx, NY 1999
Marshall, Jocqueline, resident, CJ Peete Housing Complex 2000
Marshall, Rona, Board Chair, Xavier Triangle, New Orleans 1999
Mason, Ron, President, Jackson State University (formerly of Tulane/Xavier partnership) 1999
Meyer, Gerald, Professor, Department of Sociology, Hostos Community College, Bronx, NY 2000
Morial, Sybil, Associate VP, Public Affairs and Communications, Xavier University, New Orleans 1999
Moscat, Mercedes, Director, Women's Center, Hostos Community College, Bronx, NY 1999
Murphy, Brian, Director, San Francisco State University Urban Institute 1999
Nass, Karl, Director, PHENND, Philadelphia 1999
Pecoul, John, Office of Development, Xavier University, New Orleans 1999
Perguero, Hansy, student, Hostos Community College, Bronx, NY 2000
Poole, Darlene, resident CJ Peete Housing Complex, New Orleans 2000
Powell, Larry, Director Center for the Urban Community, Tulane and Xavier, New Orleans 2000
Robinson, Gib, Professor, San Francisco State University 1999
Robles, Josephine, Center for Community Partnerships, University of Pennsylvania 1999
Rosa, Bibiano, Dean, School of Business, Hostos Community College, Bronx, NY 1999
Rubin, Victor, Director, Office of University Partnerships, HUD 1999
Ruiz, Sandra, Assistant to the President, Hostos Community College, Bronx, NY 1999
Sampson, Isabel, Director of Penn VIPS, University of Pennsylvania 1999
Sandoval, Judith, Director, Geneva Valley Development Corporation, San Francisco 1999
Scheman, Carol, Vice President of Government and Community Affairs, University of Pennsylvania 1999
Scott, John, Professor, Art Department, Xavier University, New Orleans 2000
Shannon, Jack, Managing Director of Economic Development, University of Pennsylvania, 1999
Siegal, Lenny, Director, CAREERPRO, San Francisco State University Urban Institute 1999
Spirn, Ann, Professor, Fine Arts and Urban Studies, University of Pennsylvania 1999
Taku, Michael, Associate Professor, School of Business, Xavier University, New Orleans 2000
Weeks, Joann, Center for Community Partnerships, University of Pennsylvania 1999
Williams-Savuer, Donna, student, Hostos Community College, Bronx, NY 2000

*Several people were interviewed, but not quoted or cited in this book. The many others who I interviewed, while not indicated, helped shape the thinking in the book.

Notes

Introduction

1. "Community partnership," for the purposes of this work, refers to any of a range of initiatives based at an institution of higher education, designed to enhance local neighborhoods through some working relationship with residents and institutions in those areas.
2. See Bowen and Bok, 1998.
3. See Lucas, 1996.
4. See Nelson and Watt, 1999.
5. See Lucas, 1996; Karabell, 1998.
6. See Johnson and Bell, 1995.
7. What has become known as "service learning" often prioritizes experiential learning opportunities for students through projects with organizations in local communities.
8. "Participatory" or "applied" research implies that faculty or student research focuses either on active participation with the subjects during the course of studies or on research that is explicitly geared toward solving particular problems external to academia.
9. Partnerships working with administrations could, for example, focus on employment or vending opportunities at the university or college for local residents.
10. My methodology was qualitative; I formally interviewed approximately ninety faculty, administrators, and community partners in a combination of one-on-one and group interviews. I examined numerous documents from each site, as well as literature from various important institutions in the field. The results of this research were also significantly influenced by my work at the Rockefeller Foundation. My site selection was heavily influenced by referrals from sources whom I had contacted over the course of my Rockefeller Foundation field assessment. I intentionally searched for a private major research university, a historically black private college, a public urban university, and a community college. Furthermore, I intentionally looked for different types of cities in diverse geographical settings.
11. Recent changes in the socioeconomic environment in the urban core have been well documented by William Julius Wilson (1996) and many other scholars of urban affairs. These discussions have included capital flows from the urban core, leading to unemployment, deterioration, and social isolation.
12. The idea of universities and colleges as institutional assets to poor urban neighborhoods only recently is being addressed in the context of contemporary urban changes. Kretzman and McKnight (1993), in *Building Communities from the Inside Out*, have stressed an asset-based approach to community development, but not specifically focusing on institutions of higher education. While practitioners have been testing the boundaries of the capacity of universities and colleges to impact communities in recent years, ironically, scholarly analyses, which address a variety of case studies representing different types of

universities have not been fully developed. This book is a logical extension of the proliferation of higher education/community partnerships in combination with the current
prominence of asset-based approaches to community development.

13. During the course of my work at the Rockefeller Foundation, a number of sources in the
field cited this statistic.

14. As I discuss in the next chapter, community partnerships are not foreign to the historical
mission of higher education in the United States, which has held teaching, research, *and*
service as its mantra. This makes higher education ideologically suitable for engaging in
community partnerships, maybe more so than some other major institutions and industries. Today, public relations, profit, knowledge, and experiential learning opportunities for
students all are specific ways in which colleges and universities benefit from partnerships
beyond a historical commitment to service. It should be noted that no benefit in higher
education automatically ensures benefit for communities.

15. Partnerships make sense when both institutions of higher education and local communities gain. The level of institutional commitment among colleges and universities is essential, largely due to their power relative to local communities. Institutions of higher
education are more likely to be committed to partnerships when they recognize their self-
interest. Nevertheless, an actual partnership can be attained only when the interests of the
community also are being addressed. Common interests may not be readily apparent, but
they may emerge through a lengthy process of building trusting relationships between
partners. Even if the college or university historically has not demonstrated a commitment
to partnerships, the process of local engagement can influence institutional commitment.
    The notion that ideas and actions are primarily driven by self-interest recently has been
criticized in various circles. Literature on communitarianism, democratic participation,
and the common good addresses some civic responsibility, collaboration, and consensus as
a function of human beings' search for a common good rather than individual gain. Social
science studies on ideology or identity have been grappling with questions related to self-
or group-interest in relation to altruism or social responsibility. It would be too cynical to
suggest that all actions are driven by self-interest. Nevertheless, the institutions of higher
education that creatively have found compatibility between their overall missions and the
needs of local communities have put the pieces in place toward the development of an
institutional commitment. If partnerships are treated as extra—ancillary to the overall mission—then they are not institutionalized. Commitment or interest in complex organizations like institutions of higher education is difficult to determine.

16. See Albrow, 1997.

17. See Covey, 1989.

18. See Perrow, 1986.

19. A nonprofit organization called Campus Compact has been organizing college and university presidents around the civic responsibilities of higher education.

Chapter 1: The Mission of Higher Education

1. Higher education is probably one of the slower industries to change. Many argue that
higher education is still caught in a medieval organizational culture, trying continually to
maintain tradition in the face of a society that demands something different. Nevertheless
some institutions of higher education are so dependent upon external realities that they
must change accordingly.

2. The process by which various job responsibilities once taken on by college or university
employees are shifted to the employees of independent contractors.

3. See Etzioni, 1995, 1996; Mansbridge, 1990; Schorr, 1997.

4. See Etzioni, 1995, 1996.

5. See Karabell, 1998.
6. Ibid.
7. Rosenzweig, 1998, p. xiv.
8. Newman, 1996, p. xv.
9. Campbell, 1995, p. 20.
10. Graham and Diamond, 1997, p. 3.
11. Ibid.
12. See Rosenzweig, 1998.
13. The impact of community voices on academia likely would vary by discipline, but the pipeline of community input into the academy would significantly alter the nature of research and teaching.
14. See Campbell, 1995.
15. Ibid., 19.
16. Morris et al., 1996.
17. Campbell, 1995, 24.
18. Ibid., 23.
19. Povlacs Lunde et al., 1995.
20. Between 1986 and 1991, for example, the W. K. Kellogg Foundation funded three projects designed to increase the relevance of curricula in Land Grant institutions through partnerships with businesses and community organizations. The funding supported projects at the University of Wisconsin–Madison, the University of Minnesota, and the University of Nebraska–Lincoln. The Kellogg program, called New Partnerships in Agriculture and Education encouraged more of a problem solving–based education at the three universities. For example, the University of Nebraska–Lincoln developed a new curriculum emphasizing "lifelong learning skills, problem solving, and adaptation, in contrast to time limited knowledge" (Johnson, Bargen, and Schinstock in Povlacs Lunde 1995, 61). After a long process of achieving consensus among various stakeholders, successful implementation remains to be seen. During the process, various indications of resistance to change surfaced, especially by way of the faculty.
21. Benson, Harkavy, Puckett, 2000.
22. See Wilson, 1996.
23. Gurwitt, May 1999, p. 33.
24. I define a social movement as sustained collective action, involving the mobilization of a broad constituency around a common goal.
25. Barbara Holland is the new director of HUD's Office of University Partnerships. Victor Rubin is now the Director of Research at PolicyLink.
26. The Declaration on the Civic Responsibility of Higher Education was developed by the director of Campus Compact, Elizabeth Hollander, and president emeritus of Indiana University, Thomas Ehrlich. Several current and former university presidents gave input. The date of the cited draft is May 13, 1999.
27. Two specific goals indicated in the declaration are as follows: to raise the average number of students involved in public and community service from the current 10 percent to 30 percent by the year 2004, and, by the same year, to have 20 percent of faculty in teaching courses that engage students in community-based learning and problem solving (generally known as "service learning").

Chapter 2: Have Ivory Tower, Will Travel

1. As the community partnerships discussed in this book demonstrate, institutions of higher education learn through connecting with local communities. Students gain experiential learning, while faculty produce knowledge through participatory or applied research.

Even in the administrative and economic dimensions of institutions of higher education can learn about how to navigate local communities. They can learn about civics, relationship building, and listening.

2. In the university's strategic plan, Agenda for Excellence, June 1997, s-2.
3. The University historically has been at the forefront in service learning.
4. Judith Rodin in the *Pennsylvania Gazette*, November 1997, 10.
5. Ibid., 10.
6. Ibid.
7. University of Pennsylvania internal document, 1998.
8. Agenda for Excellence, June 1997, s-7.
9. *University City Review*, July 2, 1998.
10. Carrie Rickey, *Philadelphia Inquirer*, October 3, 1998.
11. *University City Review*, October 8, 1998.
12. *Philadelphia Inquirer*, April 3, 1998.
13. Ibid., April 1, 1998.
14. Ibid., June 22, 1998.
15. Ibid., June 18 1998.
16. Mensah Dean, *Philadelphia Daily News*, June 19, 1998.
17. Ibid.
18. *Philadelphia Inquirer*, June 18, 1998.
19. Public schooling in Philadelphia is divided into twenty-two districts, each of which is managed by a "cluster resource board," a collaborative group of local organizations, residents, school staff, and businesses. These boards were developed by the school superintendent, David Hornbeck.
20. Center for Community Partnerships, March 1999, 2.
21. Ibid.
22. The ground underneath buildings literally was giving way, causing homes gradually to sink into the ground.
23. Carol Scheman interview.
24. *Ebonics* is the term used in reference to a distinctly African-American dialect. It was controversial because some believed that Ebonics should be taught in school. They suggested that cultural and linguistic patterns prominent among African Americans were being ignored in school, and that African-American students ultimately were being shamed for expressing their own cultural heritage. Opponents suggested that the mere recognition of Ebonics as a language and field of study was an excuse to prevent African-American students from learning standard English.
25. Center for Community Partnerships, March 1999, 2.
26. *Philadelphia Inquirer*, April 1, 1998.
27. Recall that Sansom Commons is directly on campus. The location of the supermarket project is a few blocks off of campus.

Chapter 3: Living Up to a People's University

1. Lynton, Ernest, in *Metropolitan Universities: An Emerging Model in American Higher Education* (University of North Texas Press, 1995), xi.
2. Robinson interview 1999.
3. The California State University system actually has been encouraging its universities to be more involved in community partnerships.
4. An institution of higher education designed to train and prepare teachers.
5. *SFSU 1998–1999 Facts.*

6. The McCormick Institute was created in Boston by Jóhn McCormick to use higher educational resources to address a number of issues.
7. San Francisco State Urban Institute position paper.
8. The City of Service Higher Education Consortium pamphlet.
9. Ibid.
10. San Francisco State Urban Institute pamphlet.
11. Office of Community Service Learning pamphlet.
12. Murphy, *SFUI Quarterly*, Spring 1996, 3.
13. *San Francisco Policy Center Position Paper*, 1–2.
14. Community Development Block Grants are funds from the federal government given to localities to be spent on local matters related to community development.
15. The SFPC is managed by an executive committee, which meets twice monthly, evaluating all of the center's activities. The committee is composed of two representatives from the SFUI and the SFIC (San Francisco Information Clearinghouse).
16. Gib Robinson and Jerry Eisman, October 1998, 5.
17. Robinson and Eisman, 1998, 3.
18. Jim Wood, "Uplifting Neighborhoods: Visitacion Valley, San Francisco," 1998, 1.
19. Amy Hittner, "The San Francisco Urban Institute and Visitacion Valley Jobs, Education, and Training" in *SFUI Quarterly*, Spring 1996, 14.
20. Susan Alunan, "A Conversation with Vernon Long" in *SFUI Quarterly*, Spring 1996, 17.
21. Wood 1998, 31.
22. *San Francisco Urban Institute* pamphlet.
23. Paul Liotsakis, "The San Francisco League of Urban Gardeners" in *SFUI Quarterly*, Spring 1998, 24.
24. Lenny Siegal, "Brownfields in Brown's City" in *SFUI Quarterly*, Spring 1998, 34.
25. CAREERPRO expanded upon its original focus on military bases to include brownfields. It also currently cleans up brownfields in a similar manner.
26. Essentially the same as what I have been referring to as "major research universities." "Research one" was the old Carnegie classification for institutions of this sort, which are now technically classified as "doctoral universities."

Chapter 4: Community in the Roots

1. Sybil Morial interview 1999.
2. *Xavier Fact Sheet* 1999.
3. *Xavier Gold*, Winter 1999, 8.
4. *Xavier Fact Sheet* 1999.
5. Ibid.
6. John Pecoul interview 1999.
7. Ibid.
8. A university once known for training students in education and the social sciences, Xavier emerged into a premier university in the sciences. Not only have the sciences moved to the core of the institution's overall mission, they have become a salient income-generating force.
9. *Comprehensive Community Plan*, 1997, 28.
10. *Community Outreach Programs: Xavier University* pamphlet, 9.
11. GIS technology allows one to develop a computerized map of a community, indicating all of its commercial and residential addresses as well as resources and services.
12. *Community Outreach Programs* pamphlet, 2.
13. *Xavier Gold*, Winter 1999, 8.

14. Ibid., 9.
15. *Comprehensive Community Plan*, 1997, 11.
16. Unfortunately, Davallier has passed on since the writing of this book.
17. *Xavier Gold*, Winter 1999, 13. Cooperative housing is a more affordable and easier path to home ownership. Residents collectively own shares in a larger property, but maintain most benefits of being a home owner, i.e. tax breaks.
18. Morial interview 1999.
19. *Comprehensive Revitalization Plan*, 1997, 36.
20. *Comprehensive Community Plan*, 1997, 14.
21. Ibid., 15.
22. Ibid., 34.
23. Mason is currently the president of Jackson State University.
24. *Crescent City* position paper, 1999, 2.
25. Ibid.
26. Individual Development Accounts help low-income residents save for a particular major purchase (often a house) with their own funds, matched by funding from a specific bank.
27. The reference in the introduction to this book was to the effort at C. J. Peete, where the Campus Affiliates Program is based. It is helping residents cope with their relocation. Over three hundred families have been relocated. The relocation process was supposed to have been faster, but there are so few places for poor people to go, residents are being forced to double-up with other families. Simultaneously, New Orleans has about 30,000 unoccupied housing units according to staff members at CAP.
28. *Crescent City* position paper, 1999, 3.
29. Ibid., 3.
30. Larry Powell interview 2000.
31. Nedra Jasper Alcorn interview 1999.

Chapter 5: Just Getting By

1. *Hostos Community College Catalog 1999–2000*, 8.
2. Karen Arenson, "Last Minute Requirement Stuns Students at Hostos" in *The New York Times*, May 29, 1997.
3. *Hostos Community College Catalog 1999–2000*, 10.
4. Ibid.
5. *Hostos Community College Catalog 1999–2000*, 43.
6. Ibid., 44.
7. Sonji Keizs interview 1999.
8. *Hostos Community College Catalog 1999–2000*, 44.
9. Ibid., 44.
10. Carlos Acevedo interview 1999.
11. *Hostos Community College Catalog 1999–2000*, 49.
12. Carol Berotte-Joseph interview 1999.
13. Ibid.
14. Hemansu Mangal interview 1999.
15. Division Newsletter, 6.
16. Division Newsletter, 6.
17. Kilgannon, Corey, "Staying Afloat: Building a Boat Helps Keep Students Anchored" in *The New York Times*, April 6, 1997, section 13, 3.
18. Hostos Center for the Arts and Culture fact sheet.
19. Liberty Partnerships Executive Summary.
20. David Hadaller interview 1999.

21. Significant parts of the South Bronx and Harlem are within the boundaries of the federally funded Empowerment Zone, which is designed to revitalize distressed urban communities.
22. Hansey Perguero, Sheyla Amador, Donna Williams-Savuer group interview 2000.
23. Jesse Hamilton interview 2000.

Chapter 6: Comparisons and Conclusions

1. The investigator is someone, usually an academic, given the primary responsibility for a project (usually a research project).
2. While some external support among foundations exists for higher education/community partnerships, many foundations are waiting to see greater effectiveness. They are waiting to see partnerships that legitimately are engaging the interests of community residents.
3. This organization, the Association for Community and Higher Education Partnerships (ACHEP), has been formed, and will seek to enhance, promote, and sustain higher education/community partnerships.

Selected Bibliography

Books

Albrow, Martin, 1997. *Do Organizations Have Feelings?* Routledge, New York.

Alperson, Myra. 1996. *Measuring Corporate Community Involvement.* Conference Board Report number 1169-96-RR, New York.

Bowen, William G., and Derek Bok. 1998. *The Shape of the River: Long-Term Consequences of Considering Race in College and University Admissions.* Princeton University Press, Princeton, NJ.

Bowen, William G., and Harold T. Shapiro, eds. 1998. *Universities and Their Leadership.* Princeton University Press, Princeton, NJ.

Boyer, Ernest. 1990. *Scholarship Reconsidered: Priorities of the Professorate.* The Carnegie Foundation for the Advancement of Teaching, Princeton, NJ.

Brinckerhoff, Peter C. 1994. *Mission-Based Management: Leading Your Nonprofit into the 21st Century.* Alpine Guild, Inc., Dillon, CO.

Campbell, John R. 1995. *Reclaiming a Lost Heritage: Land Grant and Other Higher Education Initiatives for the Twenty-First Century.* Ames: Iowa State University Press.

Coleman, James S., and David Court. 1993. *University Development in the Third World: The Rockefeller Foundation Experience.* Pergamon Press, Oxford, UK.

Covey, Stephen R. 1989. *The Seven Habits of Highly Effective People: Restoring the Character Ethic.* Simon and Schuster, New York.

Elliott, Jane, Hywel Francis, Rob Humphreys, and David Istance, eds. 1996. *Communities and Their Universities: The Challenge of Lifelong Learning.* Lawrence and Wishart, London.

Escobar, Miguel, Alfredo L. Fernandez, Gilberto Guevera-Niebla, and Paulo Freire. 1994. *Paulo Freire on Higher Education.* State University of New York Press, Albany, NY.

Etzioni, Amitai, ed. 1995. *Rights and the Common Good: The Communitarian Perspective.* St. Martin's Press, New York.

Etzioni, Amitai. 1996. *The New Golden Rule: Community and Morality in a Democratic Society.* Basic Books, New York.

Graham, Hugh Davis, and Nancy Diamond. 1997. *The Rise of American Research Universities: Elites and Challengers in the Postwar Era.* The Johns Hopkins University Press, Baltimore.

Himmelstein, Jerome L. 1997. *Looking Good and Doing Good: Corporate Philanthropy and Corporate Power.* Bloomington, IN: Indiana University Press.

Johnson, Daniel M. and David A. Bell, eds., 1995. *Metropolitan Universities: An Emerging Model in American Higher Education.* University of North Texas Press, North Denton, TX.

Karabell, Zachary. 1998. *What's College For? The Struggle to Define American Higher Education.* Basic Books, New York.

Kretzman, John P. and John L. McKnight. 1993. *Building Communities From the Inside Out:*

A Path Toward Finding and Mobilizing a Community's Assets. ACTA Publications, Chicago.

Lucas, Christopher. 1996. *Crisis in the Academy: Rethinking American Higher Education.* St. Martin's Press, New York.

Mansbridge, Jane, ed. 1990. *Beyond Self Interest.* University of Chicago Press, Chicago.

Muller, Stephen, ed. 1996. *Universities in the Twenty First Century.* Berghahn Books, Princeton, NJ.

Nelson, Cary and Stephen Watt. 1999. *Academic Keywords: A Devil's Dictionary for Higher Education.* Routledge, New York.

Newman, John Henry. 1996. *The Idea of a University.* Yale University Press, New Haven, CT.

Perrow, Charles. 1986. *Complex Organizations: A Critical Essay.* Random House, New York.

Povlacs Lunde, Joyce, with Maurice Baker, Frederick Buelow, and Laurie Schultz Hayes. 1995. *Reshaping Curricula: Revitalization Programs at Three Land Grant Universities.* Anker Publishing Company, Boston.

Powell, Walter W., and Elisabeth Clemens, eds. 1998. *Private Action and the Public Good.* Yale University Press, New Haven, CT.

Reeves-Ellington, Richard H. 1997. *Business, Commerce and Social Responsibility: Beyond Agenda.* Lewinston, NY: The Edwin Mellen Press.

Rosenzweig, Robert, 1998. *The Political University: Policy, Politics, and Presidential Leadership in the American Research University.* Johns Hopkins University Press, Baltimore.

Schorr, Lisbeth B. 1997. *Common Purpose: Strengthening Families and Neighborhoods to Rebuild America.* Anchor Books (Doubleday), New York.

Senge, Peter M. 1990. *The Fifth Discipline: The Art and Practice of the Learning Organization.* Doubleday, New York.

Wilson, William Julius. 1996. *When Work Disappears: The World of Work of the New Urban Poor.* Vintage Books (Random House), New York.

Articles

Alunan, Susan. "A Conversation with Vernon Long" in *San Francisco Urban Institute Quarterly,* Spring 1996.

Arenson, Karen. "Last Minute Requirement Stuns Students at Hostos" in *The New York Times,* May 29, 1997.

Bensen, Lee and Ira Harkavy. "Effectively Integrating the American System of Higher, Secondary, and Primary Education to Develop Civic Responsibility and Help Realize the Promise of American Democracy for All Americans," April 30, 1999 (unpublished as of this date).

Bensen, Lee, Ira Harkavy, and John Puckett. "An Implementation Revolution as a Strategy for Fulfilling the Democratic Promise of University-Community Partnerships: Penn–West Philadelphia as an Experiment in Progress" in *Nonprofit and Voluntary Sector Quarterly,* March 2000, pp. 24–45.

Dean, Mensah M. "Penn Hails a 'Great Moment': Joins City in New Schools" in the *Philadelphia Daily News,* June 19, 1998.

Editorial. "Penn's Pal: School District Gets Major Boost from the University" in the *Philadelphia Inquirer,* June 22, 1998.

Editorial. "All the Original Woodwork, Too" in the *Philadelphia Inquirer,* April 1, 1998.

Editorial. "Homesteaders: Penn Helps Renew Penn's Stake in the Community" in the *Philadelphia Inquirer,* April 3, 1998.

Gurwitt, Bob. "Town, Gown, and Survival" in *Governing,* May 1999.

Hittner, Amy. "The San Francisco Urban Institute and Visitacion Valley Jobs, Education and Training" in the *San Francisco Urban Institute Quarterly,* Spring 1996.

Kilgannon, Corey. "Staying Afloat: Building a Boat Helps Keep Students Anchored" in the *New York Times*, April 6, 1997.

Liotsakis, Paul. "The San Francisco League of Urban Gardeners" in *San Francisco Urban Institute Quarterly*, Spring 1998.

Morris, Aldon with Walter Allen, David Maurrasse, and Derrick Gilbert. 1996. "White Supremacy in Higher Education: The Alabama Higher Education Desegregation Case" in the *Black Law Journal of the University of California at Los Angeles*.

Rickey, Carrie. "Redford and Penn Officially Leap into Project" in the *Philadelphia Inquirer*, October 3, 1998.

Robinson, Gilbert, and Gerald S. Eisman. "Partnerships for a Technology Campus in Hayes Valley" October 1998 (unpublished working paper).

Rodin, Judith. "Penn and West Philadelphia: A New Model for Progress in the Community" in the *Pennsylvania Gazette*, November 1997, p. 10.

Siegal, Lenny. "Brownfields in Brown's City" in the *San Francisco Urban Institute Quarterly*, Spring 1998.

Wood, Jim. "Uplifting Neighborhoods: Visitacion Valley, San Francisco," a publication of the United States Department of Housing and Urban Development, 1998.

Index

CPSIA information can be obtained at www.ICGtesting.com
Printed in the USA
BVOW08s1547250816

460135BV00001B/11/P